Changing Law

Arthur T. Vanderbilt by James McBey *(courtesy of New York University School of Law Collection)*

Changing Law

A Biography of Arthur T. Vanderbilt

Arthur T. Vanderbilt II

Rutgers University Press
New Brunswick, New Jersey

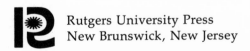

Library of Congress Cataloging in Publication Data

Vanderbilt, Arthur T   1950–
    Changing law.
    Includes bibliographical references and index.

    1. Vanderbilt, Arthur T., 1888–1957.   I. Title.

KF373.V3V3   347′.73′3634 [B]   76-24917
ISBN 0-8135-0811-8

Contents

Illustrations

i

Preface

I

For lack of a speaker of national renown, the American Bar Association in 1906 invited Roscoe Pound, a young law professor from Nebraska, to address its annual meeting. On August 29, in a talk entitled "The Causes of Popular Dissatisfaction with the Administration of Justice,"[1] he carefully diagnosed the deficiencies in the way the law was being administered in American courts. Today his factual and analytical presentation seems anything but revolutionary. Yet before Pound, no one had studied or publicly exposed the weaknesses of the administration of justice in the United States.

The audience that evening in Saint Paul, Minnesota, listened courteously to Pound's indictment of its legal system and might have said nothing to express its displeasure; but before the next speaker could be introduced, a lawyer rose and moved that copies of the address be printed and sent to every member of the American Bar Association and to the judiciary committees of Congress. This "outrageous motion"[2] released the astonishment and anger of the audience. The veteran leaders of the profession took the floor. "A more drastic attack upon the system of procedure could scarcely be devised," one declared; he would undertake "to show the contrary of every one of the material positions taken in the paper."[3] Another lawyer, believing that the American system of justice was "the most refined and scientific system ever devised by the wit of man," denounced Pound's assessment of the judiciary as an attempt "to destroy that which the wisdom of the centuries has built up."[4] With the floor claimed by indignant representatives of the bar decrying the paper as "intolerable" and "impossible,"[5] the motion to print it never received a seconding vote.

Pound had ventured before a hostile audience: at that time it was deemed almost sacrilegious to challenge the effectiveness of the courts, to question the conduct of judges, or to doubt that the law was the perfection of reason. Successive generations of the legal profession had recognized stability and predictability as the characteristics of a reliable system of jurisprudence. But as fundamental as were those characteristics of constancy, an equally important quality of the law was its flexibility, its capacity to change.

The law and methods of administering the law could not be static without working injustice—whether through judicial opinions based on outworn principles or through the delay, obfuscation, and expense that could result from the use of inadequate judicial machinery. From ancient trial by combat, to trials by ordeal with appeals to the supernatural, to trials based on rational methods of proof conducted by judges and assisted by lawyers, the laws of a society and the manner in which they were administered had long provided a means of measuring the civilization of a people, for the law, though often imperceptibly, was always in a state of flux and change. Through court decisions, legislative acts, executive policies, administrative rulings, and constitutional amendments; through the courses of law professors, the legal classics of scholars, the work of bar associations, the platforms of politicians, the votes of the populace, the problems of litigants, the causes of special interest groups, and the skills of lawyers—the law was molded piecemeal to do justice in the present. The law, however, did not respond quickly to new conditions. A legal system functioning with doctrines and tribunals of earlier periods stood until the ill effects of attempting to settle contemporary controversies with outmoded laws, obsolete procedures, or archaic courts were so acutely felt that necessary alterations began to emerge through the endless process of legal change.

As fervently as Pound's paper had been rejected by the audience at the American Bar Association meeting and as completely as it seemed buried that night, it was, in the words of Dean John H. Wigmore, "the spark that kindled the white flame of progress."[6] Thereafter, individual members of the legal profession gradually began to perceive that the velocity of social, technological, and economic change in the twentieth century was without precedent, as was the consequent strain on the law. But for many years the flame of reform merely smouldered as the bench and bar failed to adopt measures to remedy the problems in the courts that Pound had delineated.

As the early decades of the century passed and the gap between the speed of social change and the creeping pace of legal change widened—intensifying the crisis in the courts in many jurisdictions—one New Jersey lawyer began to take action to improve the administration of justice. Trial and appellate lawyer, professor of law, leader of an insurgent political reform movement, Arthur T. Vanderbilt recognized from his varied perspectives that the technicalities of procedure, the inefficient use of cumbersome judicial machinery, and the interminable delays of the courts were making the administration of the law increasingly tortuous and were threatening to make substantive law and legal rights ineffective. By seeking solutions, through legal change, to the limitations of justice he encountered, he began to give substance to Pound's call for judicial modernization.

While he was president of the American Bar Association, Vanderbilt's warnings brought to the attention of the profession and public the massive problems impeding the administration of justice in the nation's courts. He was a member of committees that drafted legislation establishing the Administrative Office of the United States Courts, the Administrative Procedure Act, the Federal Rules of Criminal Procedure, and amendments to the Articles of War. As dean of the New York University School of Law, he started courses and programs to instill in law students and lawyers an understanding of the problems that confronted the law, and he founded the Institute of Judicial Administration and the Law Center at New York University—institutions created to contribute to the continual task of modernizing the law. He spearheaded a seventeen-year drive to reorganize the antiquated New Jersey court system which culminated in the adoption of a new state constitution. And as chief justice of New Jersey, he made his state's judicial system a model for other states and nations by showing how the mounting problems of administering the law could be met.

His careers merged and placed him at the front of the struggle to simplify and adapt the law to the changing conditions of the complex society of the twentieth century. "His work for law reform, organization of courts, organization of the administrative work of the courts and for legal education," wrote Roscoe Pound in 1957, "make a consistent whole and mark him as entitled to a high place among those who have raised our institutions of justice to their highest possibilities."[7]

II

Reasons for the dearth of biographies of persons prominent in the legal profession readily become apparent to anyone who writes one. Whether to emphasize close analysis of cases and legal theories and thereby risk leaving the nonlawyer or nonspecialist behind, or to write for the layman and risk superficiality; whether to explore only the legal career, or to examine the whole life when often those traits which make a lawyer or judge successful are the same traits which make their lives outside of the law scholarly or prosaic; and whether to concentrate on a person's unique contribution to legal history, or to deal completely with his life in the law when the bulk of any lawyer's practice consists of ordinary cases just as the grist of any court's docket contains few cases that raise outstanding legal questions—these are some of the dilemmas which confront any biographer. Yet that such obstacles, or others, have so restricted the number of legal and judicial biographies is unfortunate because of the importance of the role of lawyers and the law in any era and because of the need to dispel the unnecessary aura of the unknown that surrounds the work of the legal profession. Truly it might be said as did Professor Charles Fairman, a leading legal historian, that "[n]o biography of a judge is so poor that there is no one to speak well of it and none is so good that there is no one to find it disappointing."[8]

The particular course of a subject's life coupled with the nature of available source materials will ultimately determine the form a biography will take. Given the preservation of much of Vanderbilt's thinking about the law in his own writings, including ninety-eight volumes of briefs, twenty-four volumes of the New Jersey Reports, several books, and scores of articles, and given the inherent action in his crowded years at the bar, in the political arena, in the classroom, and on the bench, which has never been fully chronicled, it seemed natural to write a biography that focused on the historical course of his life. "Arthur T. Vanderbilt was a robust, hardy, vigorous man who was not just a scholar, or just a teacher or just a reformer," wrote former Governor Thomas E. Dewey; "he was a man with a twinkle in his eye—a man with two tough fists and a sharp tongue who could go in and fight harder and better than anybody else around him when it was necessary for a client or for a cause. He was a man who selected his causes with wisdom and then gave them a degree of vigor and imagination which has been rarely equaled in our history."[9] In the final analysis, perhaps as important as what Vanderbilt accomplished in the law was his sense of the special responsibility of the lawyer as citizen to take action to help maintain and advance the great ideals and institutions of a democratic society. "These promptings of the spirit are strong upon some men: in the shaping of large plans and in lending to them a compulsiveness," one of his closest colleagues, Judge Alfred C. Clapp, reflected. "Arthur Vanderbilt might have said that for him it was a matter of citizenship—not only a citizenship rebelling against refractory forces in government, but a citizenship in all things undertaken, and particularly in the law. . . ."[10] His papers, which in 1971 became part of the Collection on Legal Change at Wesleyan University, afford considerable insight into this spirit of action and sense of responsibility, and so made such a focus possible.

Rather, therefore, than run the substantial risk of losing in a maze of material of solely parochial interest what was most significant in his work, I have attempted in untangling the threads of his life to extract the important currents and themes and to spin together the portrait of a man.

This, then, is the story of the life of Arthur T. Vanderbilt, of his efforts through politics, legal education, and the law to change the methods of administering justice and thus to improve the quality of justice rendered in the nation's courts. As his work touched many of the initial battles for judicial reform, it is a history of the origins of the movement for the modernization of the American judiciary. And as his ideas often had their clearest immediate impact in his own state, it affords a perspective of New Jersey's political and legal history. But more, it is a study of a man who believed in the efficacy of individual action even in an increasingly complex and impersonal age. It is a study of a man who recognized from a lifetime of experience that changing the law was "no sport for the short-winded or for lawyers who are afraid of temporary defeat,"[11] and yet who was certain that "individual men have the capacity to stake out the course of the future rather than merely to observe social forces, powerless to change them."[12] It might therefore be that as significant as are the changes he brought about in the law is the story of how he attained them.

III

The help and interest of many people—some of them contemporaries of my grandfather who searched their files and memories for information and recollections, others who assisted in the multitude of tasks of preparing a book—provided much of the momentum and enthusiasm that was necessary to sustain this project during the five years it took to complete it. To them, and to the librarians who offered their assistance—in the Library of Congress, the New Jersey Room of the Newark Library, the New Jersey State Archives in Trenton, the New York University School of Law Library, the Princeton University Library, the Special Collections Division of the Rutgers University Library, the Summit (New Jersey) Public

Library, the University of Virginia School of Law Library, and the Collection on Legal Change, Olin Memorial Library, and the Wesleyan Room at Wesleyan University—I am indebted more than this listing can acknowledge: Miss Evelyn M. Adams; Judge Peter Artaserse; former Chief Justice Raymond E. Baldwin; Professor Edward J. Bander; Professor Robert L. Benson; Mrs. Eva Bibber; Professor Ralph F. Bischoff; Mr. Justice William J. Brennan, Jr.; Professor Samuel H. Brockunier; Hon. Herbert Brownell; Michael J. Busman; Mrs. Katherine G. Butterfield; Dr. Victor L. Butterfield; Dr. Colin G. Campbell; Judge Alfred C. Clapp; Dr. Robert C. Clothier; Professor Richard J. Connors; Mrs. Raymond N. Crane; former Governor Alfred E. Driscoll; Professor Shelden D. Elliott; Hon. Morris L. Ernst; Hon. James A. Farley; Lloyd M. Felmly; Mrs. Eleanor P. Finlayson; Professor Clyde O. Fisher; Judge Edward Gaulkin; Professor Walter Gellhorn; Mrs. Doris P. Gerard; Professor Eugene O. Golob; Justice Frederick W. Hall; Judge Joseph Harrison; Professor Willard Heckel; Isidore Hornstein, Edward F. Johnson; Elwood C. Kastner; Hon. Robert Winthrop Kean; James Kerney, Jr.; Professor Fannie J. Klein; Professor James Kraft; Mrs. Elinor V. Krier, former Governor Alf M. Landon; Professor W. Barton Leach; Richard Lum; Edward B. McConnell; Judge Philbrick McCoy; Professor Carl McFarland; Professor Dayton D. McKean; Mrs. Abbie W. Magee; Ross L. Malone; Eric P. Marcus; Mrs. John J. Marcus; Orison S. Marden; Mrs. Elaine Marinaro; Miss Ann K. Marshall; Carlile B. Marshall; Milward W. Martin; Judge Harold R. Medina; Anthony P. Miele; Miss Ellen A. Miyasato; Joseph Morningstar; Senator Edmund S. Muskie; Mrs. Donna Mutch; Dean Russell D. Niles; Mrs. Jean Parrish; Dr. Lawrence L. Pelletier; Mrs. Mildred T. Pugh; Professor Paul A. Reynolds; Philip L. Rockwell; Newton M. Roemer; Mrs. Rosalind K. Roth; Mr. and Mrs. James V. Ryan; Miss Margaret T. Ryan; Mrs. Doris L. Sassower; Professor Bernard Schwartz; Carrol M. Shanks; Judge Arthur L. Simpson, Jr.; Judge Julius Sklar; Charles Skrief; J. T. Small, Jr.; Professor Wilbert Snow; Dean John W. Spaeth; Dean E. Blythe Stason; W. Paul Stillman; Joseph T. Sullivan; Miss Patrica Ann Sullivan; James R. Sutphen; Miss Sue Taishoff; H. Edward Toner; Miss Edith Topping; Miss Elsie Topping; Judge Walter Van Riper; Mrs. Arthur T. Vanderbilt; Leslie L. Vanderbilt; Miss Marjorie W. Vanderbilt; William R. Vanderbilt; Mrs. William R. Vanderbilt; Professor Clement E. Vose; Miss Agnes Wahlgren; Professor Willard M. Wallace; Judge Alexander P. Waugh; Miss Edith W. White; Miss Margaret White; Mr. Ralph P. White; Dr. George H. Williams; Dr. Henry M. Wriston; Thomas Wu; Henry Young, Jr.

Changing Law

I A Morning in Connecticut, 1909

THE INSTALLATION

November 12, 1909. Middletown, Connecticut. A sleepy town whose wharves on the Connecticut River and mansions on the hill were all that remained of a once-thriving seaport; a quiet town passed by the new growth of commerce and industry: Middletown had never entertained such an assembly of distinguished educators, churchmen, and politicians, nor had Wesleyan University ever been honored by such a memorable ceremony.

Promptly at ten o'clock that Friday morning in the Middlesex Theater on Main Street, the alumni and friends of Wesleyan gathered on the main floor of the house and the undergraduates crowded in the upper gallery rose and watched as the academic procession filed in and filled the stage. The exercises of installation of the ninth president of Wesleyan University, Dr. William Arnold Shanklin, had begun. The faculty, the board of trustees, a delegation from the Methodist church, presidents or professors from seventy-eight universities, state assemblymen, and the congressmen and governor of Connecticut walked briskly down the aisle to their seats. Senator Elihu Root of New York and Vice-President James S. Sherman, Dr. Shanklin and the president of the United States, William Howard Taft, brought up the rear of the procession.[1] Having made their way past the throngs of cheering sightseers lining the streets, shouting from balconies, and waving from open windows, past the parades of school children, government employees, and civic groups, and past the formations of the Grand Army and the Governor's Foot Guards, they were greeted with prolonged applause as they entered the only building in Middletown large enough to accommodate the crowd and took their seats at the front of the stage.

After the singing of a hymn and an invocation by the bishop of Connecticut, Dr. Shanklin was inducted into office in a short ceremony that was followed by a long series of addresses of congratulation. Without doubt, the second speaker, the president of the Wesleyan student body, had anticipated this occasion with the same dread that would persist throughout his life before he made any address so that even at the age of sixty-six, after years of public speaking, he would admit that his commitment to deliver a lecture had for weeks hung over him "like a black cloud."[2] It therefore would have been surprising if twenty-one-year-old Arthur T. Vanderbilt had felt any surge of confidence as he rose that morning before the imposing gathering to read the three paragraphs he had prepared, pledging to Dr. Shanklin on behalf of the undergraduates "our loyalty, our enthusiasm, our devotion," and the support of the "growing classes, who will in the future be led to Wesleyan by your guidance."[3]

The other addresses continued for well over an hour: Stephen Henry Olin speaking for the alumni; Dr. Bradford P. Raymond, the former president of Wesleyan; President Abram W. Harris of Northwestern University representing the colleges of the West and the Methodist colleges; President Melancthon W. Stryker of Hamilton College, Shanklin's alma mater; President Arthur T. Hadley of Yale University appearing for the New England colleges; Senator Root, who spoke briefly about the importance of a college education in developing the character of the men who would be the nation's leaders; and President Taft, who expanded Root's theme to emphasize the duty of the college graduate to take an interest in public affairs and to be active in politics—all preceded Dr. Shanklin's inaugural address. Finally, after the conferring of nineteen honorary degrees and the benediction, the academic procession, followed by the audience and scores of Connecticut citizens, proceeded up the hill from Main Street to the Wesleyan campus for a day of oratory and celebration.

It was an interesting coincidence of legal history that Taft, Root, and Vanderbilt shared the stage that autumn morning for ahead of the three lay similar roles in improving the American judiciary. As president of the American Bar Association in 1913, Taft would help bring about the acceptance of minimum standards of qualification for admission to the bar. As chief justice of the United States from 1921 to 1930, he would focus national attention on the morass of litigation which had arisen in the postwar years, advocate a simplification of procedure and a reorganization of the federal court system to expedite the trial of cases, organize a conference of senior circuit judges, thereby introducing the first element of coordination to the federal judicial system, and prove himself a strong administrator of the Supreme Court, bringing its dockets almost to date before his retirement. Senator Root, who would be appointed president of the American Bar Association in 1915, would join Taft in his campaign to improve legal education and to warn of the swelling mass of statutes and opinions continuously being added to the body of the law. It would be through his influence that the Carnegie Corporation would finance the founding in 1923 of the American Law Institute, an organization for the clarification and simplification of the common law through the work of leading law professors, judges, and practitioners in drafting Restatements of the Law. Elected president of the American Bar Association in 1937, Vanderbilt would spend his year in office bringing to the attention of the profession and public the growing problems in the administration of justice in the state and federal courts. As a lawyer, law school dean, and chief justice, he would put into practice methods for improving legal education and for modernizing court administration, organization, and procedure, constructing at New York University a law center where lawyers and laymen could collaborate on the tasks of simplifying the law and its administration.

The work of the three men to improve the quality of justice administered in the nation's courts lay in the future. But a brief conversation Root had with Vanderbilt that morning in Connecticut touched another topic of mutual concern, a topic that both Root and Taft had developed in their addresses.

At his new home on High Street less than an hour after the benediction, President Shanklin was surprised to see his undergraduate speaker serving at the luncheon for several of the distinguished guests. It was there that Senator Root spoke to Arthur, remarking with an obvious sigh of relief that their congratulatory addresses had shared a rare virtue: "they were the shortest speeches in a very long program."[4] Continuing, the renowned lawyer, who had been the leader of a Republican reform movement in New York City, secretary of war under President McKinley, secretary of state to President Roosevelt, and now was a senator from New York, asked what Arthur planned to do after graduating from Wesleyan in June. When told he was considering a legal education, the senator expressed hope that as a lawyer Arthur would also become involved in politics, that "one should begin to perform his civic duties early."[5] President Shanklin, who overheard the conversation, foresaw a promising future for Arthur whatever field he pursued—law, politics, or education. He stated later that "Arthur T. Vanderbilt was the most unusual and gifted undergraduate I have known in all my college experience."[6]

"ONE STUDENT GOING PLACES"

In this short exchange, Senator Root might well not have perceived anything unusual or gifted about the morning's undergraduate speaker or the afternoon's waiter. Five feet ten, of medium build, reserved, and soft spoken, his only significant physical characteristics were three facial features which in combination gave him a somewhat serious appearance for a college senior: blue-gray eyes set deep under his eyebrows, a prominent nose, and what later in his life mystified politicians would call a "Mona Lisa smile."[7] Together, these features made it difficult to discern his emotions and, when coupled with his quiet nature, made him seem austere to all except his intimates, who knew the mischievous twinkle that could appear in his eyes at the least provocation.

His personality mirrored this same combination of austerity and prankishness. Those who could penetrate the serious student and perpetual worker discovered a friend with a quick wit and playful sense of humor.

One cold winter night in 1908 when the heating system had broken down at Wesleyan's Delta Kappa Epsilon house, one of the brothers, Fred Gilman, was growing increasingly annoyed as he shivered in his drafty room. Unable to study or to stand the cold any longer, he announced that he was going to find "Art Van," the steward of the house responsible for such matters, and give him a piece of his mind. Overhearing this proclamation, Art's roommate raced up the backstairs to warn him. When Gilman opened the door, there sat the steward at his desk, deep into his studies, his coat and collar on a chair, his shirt sleeves rolled over his elbows, with every window wide open and the winter winds tearing through the room. After staring at the scene for several minutes, Gilman quietly closed the door and returned to his room. He shook his head hopelessly as the other brothers gathered to hear of the encounter and its outcome. "It's no use," he sighed. "You can't do a damn thing about it when you have an Eskimo for a steward."[8]

Of Dutch and English ancestry, Arthur's forbears had been "honest farmers in Hunterdon County, N.J., for the past three or four generations."[9] The elder of two sons of Lewis Vanderbilt, a Western Union telegraph operator of Newark, New Jersey, and Alice Leach Vanderbilt, an energetic, self-educated woman who for many years was a trustee of the Roseville Methodist Church of Newark, Arthur was born on July 7, 1888, and had grown up in a small two-story house at 14 North Ninth Street between the railroad station and the church.[10] Among his earliest recollections of boyhood activities was the time when he and his brother Leslie "stood on a bridge and tried to throw rocks down the stacks of locomotives passing underneath. . . ."[11] Much later he concluded that in those days he had been a "dangerous character" and quite lucky "to be out of jail."[12] By his own account, he was a listless student "until I hit the fourth grade where they had a brand new teacher who really wanted to teach and knew how and I skipped a half year. I had the same teacher again in the sixth grade and again skipped a half year. By that time I was started . . ."[13]

It was in high school that a familiar life pattern first became evident. A top student, editor of the school's paper, *The Acropolis*, and president of his class for four years, Arthur was remembered by the principal of Newark Public High School as "a natural leader who was president of everything in school."[14] Despite his devotion to his studies, he was a favorite of his classmates, who predicted in their yearbook:

> Our long suffering President Arthur:
> A brilliant, brilliant prophecy!!!
> No actor, pastor or
> well "fusser" he
> But—lawyer, senator
> U.S. Pres.—*May-be!*[15]

When Arthur graduated from high school in 1905, he questioned whether he should attend college or begin working. "In my last year of school I rather doubted whether it was worthwhile for a chap in my circumstance to go to college."[16] Encouraged to continue his education by several of his teachers, his mother, and his maiden aunt Sarah Leach, who lived with the Vanderbilts and was an artist who decorated fine china, Arthur selected Wesleyan University as his goal, both because its Methodist background appealed to his family's strong religious convictions and because of its inexpensive tuition, and set out to earn his first year's expenses. Working throughout 1905

on a surveying crew that was laying a line of the Lackawanna
Railroad through the hills of northern New Jersey, by the end of the
following summer, when his earnings were supplemented by a gift
from his Aunt Sarah, he had accumulated $400—enough to pay for
the first year of college.

Only a longer acquaintance with the college senior would have
revealed those traits which President Shanklin found so unusual—
an intense energy and drive, a capacity for work, and an enjoyment of
working—traits which combined successfully both in his scholastic
and extracurricular activities. Having "arrived in Middletown, green
and hopeful"[17] in September of 1906 along with seventy-eight other
freshmen, Art Van within four years won many positions of leadership at Wesleyan: manager of the football team; secretary-treasurer
of the debating society; manager of the debate council he had
organized; joint editor-in-chief of the college paper, *The Argus*,
which he had transformed from a weekly magazine into a paper
published twice a week; member of Phi Beta Kappa; a leader of his
fraternity Delta Kappa Epsilon; president of his senior class; and
president of the college body. At the same time as he pursued a
course of studies to earn a bachelor of arts degree, he started in his
senior year to take extra courses toward a master of arts degree in
history and government. He also worked as a night telephone operator, playground instructor, construction timekeeper, bookkeeper and
bill collector for the Forest City Laundry, campus reporter for the
Middletown Sun, eating club manager and steward of his fraternity,
and a waiter at college functions like Shanklin's luncheon to pay his
expenses, learning to plan his time skilfully and to work rapidly and
well.

What convinced President Shanklin that his undergraduate
speaker was gifted was the seemingly effortless way in which he
accomplished so much. Though modest, Arthur was not unaware of
his ability. When asked by younger fraternity brothers how he managed to stay on top of his studies and also participate in so many other
activities, he replied, "Self-discipline; a man can do half a dozen jobs
at once if he has proper control of his time."[18]

Thirty years later in a letter to his son, who was then a freshman at
Wesleyan, he offered a more revealing answer: "The best suggestion
that I can make is to get yourself into the habit of working steadily
when you work and relaxing and enjoying yourself when you don't
work. . . . The thing to do is to do the work and get it behind you. Try
starting off and seeing that you utilize every moment of your morn-

ings. If you get up at 6, by 12:30 (allowing for the interruptions of breakfast and chapel) you have got two-thirds of your work behind you." An equally important word of advice that perhaps was the secret of his own "effortless" work followed: "On the other hand, let me caution you not to tell anybody that you are resolved to squeeze out every moment of the morning in the library or wherever else you may want to hide yourself. It is one of the immemorial traditions of college life that there must be a certain amount of bluffing about not doing too much work. It is the bunk, of course, but there is no use making yourself obnoxious."[19]

Although during his years at Wesleyan he was "spread out so thin" that if he had attempted anything more "the elastic band would surely have burst,"[20] the challenge of attempting to do all that he wanted and the joy of sometimes succeeding were real pleasures and would be throughout his life. "Those were great years, happy years."[21]

. Certainly other aspects of his Wesleyan experience were a part of these sentiments: knowing some of the outstanding professors on the faculty, a time when "life really began";[22] the beauty of the Middletown countryside and especially High Street, a street Charles Dickens had called "the most beautiful I have seen in America,"[23] with its ivy-covered walls of the brownstones of college row, the broad campus green, the stately old homes built from rum-trading fortunes, and the vistas of the river winding into the green hills of Cobalt and Haddam; making in his fraternity and with the students of the college the "abiding friendships of a lifetime";[24] and being in love and engaged in his senior year to his high school sweetheart, Florence Althen. For amid the continual effort poured into courses and campus activities and part-time jobs, he had found early a pleasing balance in his life.

In reflecting on my college days, I am constantly reminded of lines [by Wordsworth] that Professor [Caleb] Winchester was fond of quoting:

> Bliss was it in that dawn to be alive,
> But to be young was very heaven.[25]

He had discovered at Wesleyan the secret of finding enjoyment in work and the recognition that often more could be accomplished than ever anticipated. "Here," realized his history professor George M. Dutcher, "was one student going places."[26]

AN EXAMPLE TO EMULATE

The chance words Senator Elihu Root spoke to Arthur about the importance of citizen participation in politics had fallen on fertile ground. Throughout his boyhood, "dinner table discussion of local politics as gleaned from newspapers was the order of the day."[27] In 1903 when he was a junior in high school, these discussions unquestionably turned to the actions of a Newark neighbor, actions prompted by a tragic accident.

Early one morning at the Clifton Avenue railroad crossing in the Roseville district of the city, nine of Arthur's high school classmates on their way to school were killed by a train. Outraged by this accident, one citizen took measures to ensure it could never happen again. Frank H. Sommer, a young Newark lawyer and a professor at the New York University School of Law, stirred the Newark community to action with speeches and public meetings, and initiated a resolution to eliminate all railroad grade crossings throughout the state, later defending the resulting legislation before the New Jersey courts and the Supreme Court of the United States.

Born in the poor Roseville section of Newark, leaving school at the age of twelve to help support his younger brothers and sisters, Sommer had by his energy and integrity become one of the most prominent lawyers in New Jersey and a respected legal scholar. His concern with the welfare of his community and state and his willing involvement in public affairs made an indelible impression on Arthur. A lifelong admiration of Sommer began. A desire to become a lawyer was kindled.

"Next I remember seeing him [Sommer] portrayed in the many cartoons in the *Newark Evening News* during his campaign for Sheriff."[28] With the community cohesion engendered by the Roseville tragedy, Sommer in 1905 organized a reform group, the New Idea movement, within the county Republican party. Its purpose was, not only to eliminate the growing laxity and corruption which was beginning to characterize government affairs in the city of Newark and in all of Essex County, but also to introduce a spirit of change by pledging to exact a fair share of taxation from railroads and utilities, to institute direct primaries to reduce boss rule, and to endorse a civil service plan and an employee liability program.

"Though but a lad in high school," Vanderbilt later wrote, "I attended many of the political meetings at which he and the robust group of individualists with whom he was associated aroused the public from their lethargy and led the people to victory over a decadent political machine."[29] During his one term in office as sheriff of Essex County, Sommer helped bring about many progressive community reforms: from the passage of an act to control the sale of narcotics for medicinal purposes, to the creation of the first municipal playgrounds in New Jersey, to the erection of a house of detention for juvenile offenders to separate them from convicted prisoners. Although the New Idea movement failed to win control of the county Republican machinery, much of its platform was later incorporated into that of Woodrow Wilson's successful gubernatorial candidacy of 1910.[30]

This was how political and social change was brought about: by active men like Sommer, who, seeing a problem, would take steps to meet it, who would fight for what they felt. "The man of consequence," Vanderbilt would often repeat later, "is the man who not only knows what to do, but acts when action is indicated."[31] And so when Senator Root spoke to the Wesleyan senior about civic duty, the example of Sommer's actions—his use of the law and public involvement to help solve the myriad problems of a city and state— was sharp in the undergraduate's mind. The authority of Root's words perhaps even helped to crystallize Arthur's thinking about the subject. Seven months later, when he competed for the Rich Debate Prize on the day of his graduation in June of 1910, he spoke on "The College Man in Municipal Government," emphasizing that municipal government was a level of government that needed to be "cleaned and redeemed,"[32] a task that could be begun if more citizens took an interest in local political affairs.

II The Germinal Years, 1910–1920

THE CLERK

"The day after I left college I entered Sommer's office as a law clerk and the inspiration I gained then from contact with him has continued to this day. He has influenced my life more than any man I have ever known."[1]

A lawyer and professor of law since 1893, thirty-eight-year-old Frank Sommer was also actively engaged in New Jersey politics and serving in various elective and appointive capacities. He was president of the Newark board of education, chairman of the New Jersey board of bar examiners, and special counsel to the chancellor on the question of the court of chancery's jurisdiction to disbar. He was, at the call of Governor J. Franklin Fort, a member of the state railroad commission, and, at the appointment of Governor Woodrow Wilson, the draftsman of the New Jersey public utility act, workman's compensation act, civil service act, zoning code, and commercial arbitration statute. For Sommer, working with the law was more than a profession; it was both his vocation and avocation.

It was in the summer of 1910 in the firm of Sommer, Colby and Whiting at 738 Broad Street, Newark, that even before beginning law school Arthur first entered the lawyer's world, running errands and filing papers for the partners for ten dollars a week. Sommer took a personal interest in his new clerk because of the similarity of their Newark boyhoods and perhaps because of his recognition of a kindred spirit. He introduced Arthur to legal classics like Pollock and Maitland's *History of English Law* and took him to the court of chancery and the court of errors and appeals at the old State House in Trenton, where "many of the greatest cases in this State in corporate matters were being heard."[2] There Sommer pointed out that the day was not won by the eloquence of a courtroom argument, the aspect of the trials that had at first captivated his young clerk, but rather by the ability of a lawyer to be the master of the facts and the law of his case. Each day of those summer months, Sommer's own "extraordinary legal mind" and his standards of "common honesty and simple decency"[3] continued to impress the clerk and develop within him a high conception of the purpose and possibilities of lawyers and the law.

In September, Arthur enrolled as a first-year student at Columbia University School of Law. He left his home in Newark at 7:40 each morning, crossed the Hudson River to New York City, and took a subway train uptown, reaching the law school two hours later. After a day of classes, in order to earn enough money to continue his legal education and to try to save money to be able to marry his fiancée Florence Althen, he taught four half-hour classes from seven to nine o'clock each evening at Newark's Central Evening High School, for which he was paid four dollars a night. After classes, late into the night, he prepared his high school lessons for the next day, studied law, on Sommer's advice became familiar with the leading New Jersey cases covering the legal principles he was learning, and worked on his thesis, "The Origin and Establishment of the Supreme Court of the United States," to complete the degree requirements so he would receive his master's at the Wesleyan commencement of 1912.

"How are you, my dear 'boy'?" wrote President Shanklin in the summer of 1911. "I hope you are not killing yourself by overwork."[4] And a fraternity brother concluded, "Art, you are verily the personification of Industry. If you live through all that you are doing now I will know that you have a constitution of the best carbon steel."[5]

While Arthur was struggling at Columbia to master the formalities of common law pleading in his procedure courses, feeling as if he had been left to himself "without a map or compass or means of communication with the strange forms around me,"[6] Sommer was taking steps to eliminate from practice similar encrustations of procedure that had been recognized for years as a serious impediment to New Jersey justice. Although common law pleading based on the English system of procedure had long been prevalent in the United States, it had been discarded in England in 1875 with the passage of the English Judicature Acts and, with the persistent agitation of law reformer David Dudley Field, replaced by forms of code procedure in most of the United States by the beginning of the twentieth century, but not in New Jersey. Addressing the New York State Bar Association in 1890, Lord Chief Justice Coleridge of England had delighted in deriding the complexities of these ancient procedures which often resulted in the merits of the cases never reaching trial. "Special pleading [common law pleading] finds no refuge upon the habitable globe except, as I believe, in the State of New Jersey in America."[7] Looking toward New Jersey he asked:

Could it not be arranged that, with the sanction of the State itself, some one State should be preserved as a kind of pleading park, in which the glories of the *negative pregnant, pleas giving express color, absque hoc, the replication de injuria, rebutter* and *surrebutter,* and all the other weird and fanciful creations of the pleader's brain might be preserved for future ages to gratify the respectful curiosity of your descendants? And that our good old English judges, if ever they revisit the glimpses of the moon might have some place where their weary souls might rest—some place where they might still find the form preferred to the substance, the statement to the thing stated.[8]

With his encyclopedic mind, Sommer had been able to master all the intricacies of common law pleading early in his career, all the while having fun in demonstrating the absurdity of this overgrown branch of jurisprudence. Once a fellow attorney came to him with the complaint that a district court judge had interrupted him in oral argument and dismissed his case. The attorney wondered what could be done about it. Without hesitation Sommer responded that what was needed was a Writ of Pluckitendo. The attorney confessed that he had never heard of this type of writ and so asked Sommer to prepare one for him, a task that Sommer was only too happy to accept and complete at elaborate length.

The object of this apocryphal pleading was to "pluck" the proceedings from the district court and transfer them to the court of common pleas. When the attorney presented his writ to the common pleas judge, the judge seemed rather skeptical until he learned that Sommer had prepared it. With confidence in Sommer's mastery of pleading, he signed it and sent it to the county clerk who, though he too had never heard of a Writ of Pluckitendo, assumed that the judge knew more about special pleading than he and so attached the seal. The district court judge, upon receiving the bogus writ, was furious, but according to its terms literally tore out the pages of the district court proceedings and sent them to the common pleas judge. (Sommer was later summoned before the common pleas judge and informed that if the story ever got out in the judge's lifetime, he would hold Sommer in contempt of court.)[9]

Goaded by the obvious deficiencies of common law pleading and the resulting backwardness of the administration of justice in the state courts, a group of New Jersey lawyers drew up the 1903 Practice Act, which helped abolish some of these useless procedural barnacles embalmed in the statutes. Though a step forward, this act barely scraped the surface of the debris that had been impeding the flow of the law for decades, but it did inspire the attempts in 1903 and 1909 to amend the entire judicial article of the New Jersey Constitution. These amendments were defeated at the polls, but they prepared the way for one progressive offshoot: the Practice Act of 1912 drafted by three members of the New Jersey bar—Charles H. Hartshorne, Judge Alfred S. Skinner, and Frank H. Sommer—an act that did much to modernize New Jersey's system of pleading and procedure.

The Practice Act provided for the transfer of causes between a court of law and a court of chancery in cases in which there had been a mistake in choosing the forum; for a court of law to determine equitable [specific performance] questions incidentally involved in a law case and for a court of chancery to determine legal [money damages] questions incidentally involved in equity cases, thus alleviating the delay and expense of multiple suits to settle a single controversy; and for the transfer from the legislature to the judiciary of much of the power to make the specific rules governing court procedures, a change which would simplify procedure and make it more responsive to the realities of litigation.[10]

Although litigants were enthusiastic about the Practice Act, although similar measures had already been passed in England and Connecticut and had proved successful in facilitating the trial of cases, and although the act would be cited for years as a model law that worked notable reforms, it was perhaps inevitable that a substantial group of members of the state bench and bar would be adamantly opposed to it. Daily after the act was promulgated, Arthur watched as "ancient practitioners" stormed the doors of Sommer, Colby and Whiting, threatening to quit their practice or resign their commissions. Some were bitter, others fearful or almost frantic that, with the changes of judicial procedure that made obsolete much of what they had learned through years of study and practice, their livelihoods would be lost, their careers ended. The new Practice Act brought tears to the eyes of some of the older lawyers who had carefully learned the subtleties of special pleading and mastered the volumes of procedure that had been adapted, amended, and expanded by the legislature until they had become an almost impenetrable mass of bewildering detail. The thought of learning a new system, though known to be simpler, more flexible, and more effective, was understandably not a happy one. The members of the bar had no desire to disturb the familiar routine of their work even when it was widely recognized that a proposed change would be to their long-run advantage and to the immediate advantage of their clients.

It was with some relief and a great deal of interest that Vanderbilt observed, as Sommer had predicted, that after a period of several months the benefits of the Practice Act became obvious. Most of the bar had become equally adept if not more so in working with the new system, no one had quit his commission, and no one had found himself out of work.

The importance of beginning his legal career in one of the few jurisdictions where the law was still hopelessly enmeshed in the formalities of common law pleading, of having a preceptor who poked fun at this maze of technicalities and called it all "intricate nonsense,"[11] and of learning that the law need not be rigid and immutable cannot be overemphasized in understanding Vanderbilt's early awareness of problems in the administration of justice and of the possibilities of law reform.

THE LAWYER

Shortly before graduating from Columbia in 1913, Vanderbilt was told by Dean Harlan Fiske Stone—later attorney general, associate justice, and chief justice of the United States—that, while he was well qualified to be a teacher and student of the law, he lacked the drive and toughness prerequisite for a practitioner.[12] Either disregarding this pronouncement or resolving to acquire such attributes, on September 15, 1913, he sent out cards announcing the start of his own practice:

> ARTHUR T. VANDERBILT ANNOUNCES THAT HE
> HAS OPENED AN OFFICE FOR THE GENERAL
> PRACTICE OF LAW IN THE NATIONAL STATE
> BANK BUILDING, 810 BROAD STREET, NEWARK
> NEW JERSEY[13]

The office was actually desk space in an outer office of the law firm of Jerome T. Congleton, one of the men who had helped Sommer organize the New Idea movement. Vanderbilt shared with Congleton's stenographer an office that was so small that "if two clients were to come in at once, someone had to stand out in the hall."[14] In the spring of 1914, after several months of helping the clients and handling the small cases referred to him by Sommer and Congleton, Arthur Vanderbilt and Chester Wilson Fairlie, a Wesleyan graduate and Newark lawyer three years his senior, rented an office at 790 Broad Street and established the firm of Fairlie and Vanderbilt.

The year 1914 was one of beginnings, not only of a partnership, but also of a new profession, marriage, and a major case. Early in June, Sommer took Vanderbilt into New York City to introduce him to Dean Clarence D. Ashley of the New York University School of Law, who was looking for a replacement for two of his professors who had recently left the night school. Anxious to find an instructor before the new school year began and satisfied with Professor Sommer's recommendation of the twenty-six-year-old lawyer, Dean Ashley hired Vanderbilt to teach common law pleading, wills, quasi contracts, corporations, and bills and notes two evenings a week for a total of seven hours a week.

The "munificent stipend of $1,400"[15] that he would receive as an instructor made it possible for him to marry Florence Josephine Althen on September 12, 1914, "the luckiest thing"[16] he ever did. In love since their high school days in Newark when Arthur had been president of the senior class and "Floss" had been secretary, engaged since Arthur's senior year at Wesleyan, they had a rare marriage of happiness during the next forty-three years. Beautiful, light-hearted, a graduate of the Institute of Musical Art of New York City and a piano teacher, Floss would be always the "indulgent wife, tolerant toward the demands of the jealous mistress, the law,"[17] appreciative of her husband's capacities, unmindful of his excesses, devoted to him completely.

Fortunately so, for Arthur's dedication to the law sometimes seemed to exceed reasonable bounds. Fairlie liked to recall a certain Saturday when he left the office at noon. Passing Vanderbilt's room on the way out, he saw him surrounded by stacks of law books, busily writing at his desk.

"Arthur," said Chester, "it's 12:30."

"I know, but I can't leave now because I have to finish this brief."

"But Arthur," his partner persisted, "you have to be at the church at two o'clock for your wedding."[18]

After buying his bride a baby grand piano, the young lawyer was left with only $100 in cash. But opportunities abounded then for the many lawyers practicing in Newark.

Between 1900 and 1910, the population of the city had grown from 246,000 to 347,469, and by 1920 it would increase by another 67,000. Business boomed with the influx of immigrant labor and the growing national demand for manufactured goods. Factories smoked and steamed. Trucks, gas buggies, and as many as 532 electric trolley cars each hour clattered across Broad Street and Market Street blocking the way of a horse-drawn grocery wagon or a private carriage waiting at a cobblestone intersection. Crews of hundreds of men dredged thirty-five-foot channels into the acres of meadowlands around Newark Bay, constructing modern storage facilities, laying twenty-seven miles of tracks, and building the docking space for deep-sea vessels that would make Port Newark one of the major seaports of the East Coast. By the beginning of the twentieth century, Newark—by virtue of its geographical position between New York City and Philadelphia, its deepwater port, its railroads at the start of the western trunk line, and its supply of diversified labor—was the manufacturing and financial hub of New Jersey, ranking high among the nation's important industrial cities, second only to New York City as the insurance and banking center of the United States.

Vanderbilt's first major case came to him by luck. One of the casualties of the nationwide recession of 1913 was the Roseville Trust Company of Newark, which, reorganized as the Mutual Bank of Roseville, was faced with the job of collecting the former bank's debts and mortgages in arrears. Every lawyer President Clifford McEvoy asked to undertake the job told him either that the debts were uncollectible or that he did not have the time to spend on the tedious job. Not quite able to accept this conclusion and loss, McEvoy asked Fairlie if he knew of a young lawyer with a good deal of energy and without much work to undertake a long and complicated job. Fairlie recommended his partner, who went to see McEvoy the next day. After an hour's conference, they negotiated a contract to collect the money for a fee of 5 percent, a contract that could be terminated by either party.

Starting the collecting and court actions, Vanderbilt soon discovered that, while time-consuming, the job was not as hopeless as the other lawyers or McEvoy had anticipated. Yet McEvoy's reputation for driving a shrewd deal led him to reason that if the Scotsman realized this, he would try to negotiate a new contract with a less favorable compensation. To circumvent the possibility, Vanderbilt decided that if he did not send periodic bills for his services, if he could refrain from sending any bill until his work was near completion, there would be a good chance that McEvoy would not notice how much money his young attorney was collecting and would let the contract run. Sommer was pleased with this perceptive insight into his character. "Don't send him a bill until you've collected all you can," he counseled his former clerk.[19]

Working full time at the collecting job throughout 1914 and into the winter of 1915, Vanderbilt gained his first courtroom experience and his first exposure to the difficult art of advocacy. "After I got to be quite an expert at entering judgment by default in the grand manner, which, after all, is quite an art, I began to get cases which were actually contested. The very first thing I discovered was that it was much more difficult to try a contested case than it was to try an uncontested case. . . . There were certain judges who even when I had the facts and the law with me did not seem to be at all impressed with my case." One day Sommer told him that there were some judges a lawyer just had to "holler" at in order to get what he was entitled to. Several weeks later, Sommer took him aside and said, "You are doing very well at hollering and you are winning individual cases, but you are making some of the judges very sore at you. You have to learn to holler without raising your voice."[20]

By the following spring after many court appearances, Vanderbilt had gathered and turned in to McEvoy receipts for $700,000. In addition, with a great deal of outward assurance but inward anticipation, he included the first bill for his services: $35,000. Within a week he received a certified check for that amount.

A year later, equal good fortune directed another important client his way. One of the leading citizens of New Jersey had fallen into bankruptcy, leaving a maze of debts and obligations that embarrassed his associates. Learning of Vanderbilt's success with the Roseville Trust Company work, they engaged him to set the estate in order. Later, pleased with his management of what had seemed to them a hopeless job, they fixed his fee at 10 percent of the $300,000 he had recovered.

As Vanderbilt's reputation as a capable lawyer spread in the city, more people came to him with their problems.

One afternoon as I was returning from an argument in our Supreme Court, I found a client waiting for me at the railroad station. He was the head of a large tool manufacturing concern and at the time we were in the midst of World War I. He told me that one of his most important foremen had been

arrested the day before, charged with driving his automobile while intoxicated and that he was going on trial before a local justice of the peace that
evening. I suggested that we interview the foreman, but my friend said that
would be useless, that he not only had been happily drunk but he had driven
his car several times up over the sidewalk for the sheer joy of frightening
people, though he had not injured anyone. I inquired about the judge and
my client told me that he was a retired school teacher, a man of probity, very
strict and fond of reading "The Lives of the Chief Justices," to whom, it was
suspected, he saw some slight resemblance in himself. The offense carried
with it a minimum mandatory jail sentence of thirty days. The prospect was
not alluring, especially as the foreman had picked out a Sunday morning
right after the close of church services when people were on their way home
from divine worship to try his sidewalk jumping. And the foreman had a
name that was decidedly Teutonic.

The justice of the peace usually held court in his kitchen, but in this
instance the audience was so large that he had a table brought into his
garden and set up there. I shall not attempt to tell you how many witnesses
testified to the foreman's antics. Fortunately, none of them seemed to bear
him any ill will. His previous conduct had been exemplary. They all commented on his character and his good nature. There was little evidence I
could offer beyond his record of hard work for long hours seven days a week
for many months in the war effort and the fact that he had three sons at the
front. With the evidence all in, the justice asked me if I had anything to say,
with the accent significantly on the word "anything." Without stressing my
words too much I said that I had no intention of attempting a jury speech
which I knew in the circumstances and with his reputation would be
unavailing, but I did want to point out some significant facts. First of all, the
charge was driving an automobile while intoxicated. True, several witnesses
had testified that the defendant was drunk, very drunk in fact, but not
disagreeable and malicious, just happy and carefree, but he had been a good
family man with a fine record up to the time of the present charge and his
services were much more needed in the factory superintending the production of war tools than they were in the county jail repenting his folly. Once
more I managed to bring in the word "intoxication" in the complaint in
contrast with the word "drunk" in the testimony, but I made no effort to
press the distinction. I noticed however, a glint in the judge's eye, whether
friendly or not I could not fathom, as I continued with my general remarks on
the state of affairs in the factory, in the world at large and with families
divided, the flower of youth doing their duty all over the globe. The foreman's two daughters fell to weeping silently and before long most of the
women in the audience were teary eyed and more than one grown man was
busy blowing his nose. I reminded the judge of his hard responsibility and
wished that I could suggest some way out of the dilemma, but I realized that
he was sworn to do his duty and I was no man to dissuade him, but where
there's a will there's a way and the world was tumbling all about us. When I
concluded the judge went into his kitchen and came out with a copy of the

Revised Statutes, which he opened ostentatiously. He read the section that the defendant had offended. He reviewed the evidence, I must say, with great effect to the accompaniment of tears from the feminine part of his audience. He commented on the danger of the public resulting from the defendant's conduct. He spoke too, of the great strain that the defendant had been under and the service that he had been rendering his country as well as of the courage of his sons. He then referred again to the statute book and called attention to the fact that the charge was driving while intoxicated and he then laid great stress on the fact that while the many witnesses had testified that the defendant was drunk, not a single one had testified that he was intoxicated. Therefore he had no choice but to acquit the defendant, but in doing so he warned him that the next time he was drunk someone would possibly be found who would testify that he was intoxicated. I bowed in due respect to the judge's wisdom as he received the thanks of the defendant, his wife, his daughters and his friends, who seemed all of a sudden to make up the entire audience. Nobody doubted that in the circumstances justice had been done, whatever might be said of the judge's canons of statutory construction.[21]

These first cases stimulated Vanderbilt's ambition to become a successful lawyer, a goal to which he was committing himself in accordance with Lord Eldon's proverbial advice to young barristers that the only way to become great lawyers was to "make up their minds to live like hermits and work like horses." One of Vanderbilt's first law clerks knew that he never smoked and never drank anything as strong as coffee in an effort to keep his health, nervous reserve, and self-control at their peak to devote to his work as an advocate. But the clerk was surprised one day to notice on his desk a large pad on which he had written thirteen "Rules of Conduct" that had been prescribed by Benjamin Franklin, including such rules as the following:

Silence: Speak not but what may benefit others or yourself; avoid trifling conversation;

Order: Let all things have their place; let each part of your business have its time;

Resolution: Resolve to perform what you ought; perform without fail what you resolve;

Industry: Lose no time; be always employ'd in something useful; cut off all unnecessary actions.[22]

The clerk learned that it was Vanderbilt's practice to be guided by one rule of conduct each week and daily on his pad, as Franklin had recommended, to mark the faults he found that he had committed concerning a particular rule.

Such ascetic practices made Vanderbilt conscious of his goal of attaining prominence in the legal profession and perhaps increased his awareness of ways to move toward it. One day in 1916 while eating lunch with a group of insurance agents in Newark's Down Town Club, Vanderbilt listened closely as one agent posed a problem to the others. Although Vanderbilt made no comment and offered no opinion, once back in his office he began to explore the law and develop a solution, later that afternoon mailing each of the agents a copy of the memorandum of law he had prepared. Impressed both by his industry and his grasp of the law, they began to send him their routine cases.

As larger insurance companies brought him their work, he began to specialize in fire insurance cases. He learned the importance of being able to become an expert in unfamiliar areas, to absorb all the facts of a case, to anticipate the diversity of views as to the facts that would comprise the story of each witness, to develop the ability of repeating the testimony of witnesses in their own words, and to come up as the respondent rather than as the appellant, which could usually be accomplished by devoting as much time to the trial brief as would be given to an appellate brief.

In one of his early cases he was called upon to defend several insurance companies that were being sued for the destruction of paintings which the plaintiff described as old Italian and Dutch masters. Vanderbilt's defense was that the paintings were not by old masters but were reproductions, a position which called for a knowledge of the artists, their techniques and styles, the kinds of canvas on which they worked, and the chemistry of the pigments of their paints in comparison with the composition of the charred remains of the insured paintings.

One of his regular opponents in these cases shook his head in disbelief: "That man," he said, "has memorized every word of the standard fire policy, even to the small type."[23]

Vanderbilt's success in his work was winning him local recognition as was his occasional wit in court. After listening to too many plaintiffs come into court with stories of how their books and inventory lists were destroyed in the fire but their insurance policies, fortunately, had been saved, he put a damper on such tales by dryly telling juries that those "fire insurance policies must be made out of asbestos."[24]

Sitting in the court of chancery in Paterson when Vanderbilt walked in, a lawyer nudged a friend and said, "See that fellow over there? He looks like a farmer, but don't let it fool you. He's one of the shrewdest lawyers in the state."[25]

While certainly opening some doors, a total effort to achieve a goal inevitably closed others. So immersed was he in the practice of law and so great was his need to be in complete control of his practice that he was never successful in a partnership. In 1918 the firm of Fairlie and Vanderbilt dissolved. He later experimented with partnerships with Charles L. Hedden and his younger brother Leslie L. Vanderbilt, but neither succeeded. His life had taken on a singleness of purpose that led him to depend on his own resources, a trait that the future course of his life would repeatedly confirm; he was a good team man as long as he was captain and had full authority and responsibility for the outcome of the work. "Confidentially I must tell you that there are great advantages in working alone whether it be in a law office or in a political organization or in a law school," he wrote to a friend later in his life. "Divided authority does not make for efficiency."[26]

Though he soon became so overwhelmed with litigation and professional responsibilities that he had to take on as many as seventeen younger lawyers as associates and an equal number as law clerks to assist him, the name on the door of his offices on the twenty-third floor of the National Newark and Essex Building remained: ARTHUR T. VANDERBILT: COUNSELLOR AT LAW.

THE PROFESSOR

While his teaching position at the New York University night school had enabled him to marry and to begin an independent law practice, he continued to teach at the School of Law even after his earnings as a lawyer dwarfed his academic salary. He was beginning to perceive that there was no better way of learning something than by teaching it, and in his own practice he daily was aware of the areas of the law he had yet to master. "You can never be sure you know a subject until you can teach it, and in those early days I learned to teach a good many subjects. It was there that my own legal education really commenced."[27]

Commenced and continued. "Evidently I made good, for in the spring [of 1915] Dean Ashley asked me to teach the evening course in Contracts the next year. I do not think I ever felt prouder in my life, because I knew that Dean Ashley regarded Contracts as the most important subject in the curriculum."[28] On the death of Ashley in 1916, Frank Sommer, who had been a member of the faculty and night school professor for twenty-three years, succeeded him as dean. In 1917 Sommer promoted Vanderbilt to the rank of assistant professor and in 1919 appointed him professor of law. From eight o'clock to ten o'clock two nights each week of every school year for thirty-four years, Vanderbilt marched through the curriculum, teaching at one time or another many of the courses, including the administration of justice, administrative law, contracts, corporations, equity, insurance, legislation, municipal corporations, New Jersey practice, procedure, taxation, trusts, and wills.

As he found his teaching benefited his law practice so as a lawyer he brought practical insights to his teaching. To a practicing lawyer, much of the law school curriculum seemed academic or bookish. Vanderbilt had little respect for those professors who were continually quoting cases in conversation and dubbed them "the versus lawyers"—A v. B, C v. D *ad nauseam.* He often told the story of one professor who, when asked by a student "who owned the apples on A's side of the fence when the trunk of the tree was on B's land," replied that he had "no case of an apple tree in New York," but "did have one of a pear tree in Ohio."[29] Vanderbilt brought the world of the courtroom into the classroom. To the discussion of cases and law, he added the experiences and understanding gained from his own work, often illustrating a point with a case then pending or just decided. "Moreover, on those infrequent but unhappy occasions when I found the juries here in New Jersey stupid or the judges a bit opaque, it was a great relief to be able to cross the River and cast my pearls before bright young minds that could appreciate them."[30]

To the classroom also he brought his developing skills of interrogation to draw out, not only the holdings of the cases, but also their importance in terms of history, logic, and contemporary social needs. He found that "the give and take of the classroom and free discussion under the case method of teaching is the best possible training . . . for the trial of cases or the argument of appeals. If one can take with a reasonably intelligent class catch as catch can the discussion of the classroom, he can take what any judge or any appellate tribunal hands out to him anywhere, even including the Supreme Court of the United States."[31]

It was in the teaching itself, however, that he found a special exhilaration, both in the diversion from his workaday activities and in the interaction with new classes of law students. "I doubt . . . if mere zeal for legal learning and for training in the arts of advocacy would have kept me teaching for over a third of a century. Of much greater drawing power was the satisfaction of seeing young men come to life intellectually and learn to use their God-given faculties effectively."[32]

After classes had ended at ten, many of the students continued to pursue discussions around his desk as he put on his overcoat and familiar crushed old hat. Some walked with him the four blocks through the dirty snow and windy nights of the city to the subway entrance, a hearty little band at eleven o'clock still holding a rump class session on the steps of the Hudson and Manhattan tubes at Sixth Avenue and Ninth Street. More than once the heartiest rode the train with him to Jersey City, where Vanderbilt changed for Newark and home and they turned around to return to the law school at Washington Square.

Not the least of the pleasures of teaching were the friendships he made with his students, some of whom served clerkships in his office, several of whom entered his growing law office as associates, others who as young attorneys referred to him cases they were not able to handle, many of whom remained personal friends. In the years that followed, as trips took him to meetings and conferences across the nation as an advocate of judicial reform, Vanderbilt found that he seldom entered a strange city without meeting former students.

With his daily contact with his law associates who came to him while they were still in law school or immediately after graduation, and with his weekly classes with law students at New York University, he began to understand the significance of the favorite toast of Lord Mansfield, one of the greatest of the English justices: "Old books and young friends."[33]

THE POLITICIAN

Vanderbilt's fascination with the New Idea movement of 1905 was such that later whenever he talked to Sommer he invariably turned the conversation to politics. One day at lunch Sommer asked him, "Arthur, do you know how many people there are in Newark?"

"Three hundred fifty thousand," he answered, quoting the 1910 census.

"No," said Sommer. "There are just 300 people in Newark and 400 more in the suburbs of Essex. If you're going into politics your job is to know them well. I don't know them all. They're from different walks of life and different social groups. One is the president of an insurance company. One keeps a grocery store. One edits a newspaper. Another collects half dollars at the entrance of the Holland Tunnel. But these few people are the ones who mold public opinion in this city. Find those people and know them."[34]

Correspondence from the years between 1913 and 1919 suggests that Vanderbilt did just that, slowly beginning to explore the political structure of his county.

In its 127 square miles of hills and ridges in northern New Jersey, Essex County contained both the city of Newark and the fashionable commuter suburbs of New York. Although not large in size, by the time of the First World War the county had a population of over 600,000, a population greater than that of fourteen states. In population, wealth, property valuation, expenditures for governmental purposes, retail sales, wholesale sales, and the value of manufactured products, Essex was one of the six major counties in the United States. Thus many of the decisions of the county's governing body— the Board of Chosen Freeholders, consisting of nine members at large elected for three-year overlapping terms—had significant ramifications throughout the county and the state.

Between 1917 and 1919 the state newspapers, led by the *Newark Evening News*, began to expose the Board of Freeholders' mismanagement of the affairs of the county. In 1914 county engineers had warned the board that the six boilers of Overbrook Hospital, the Essex County Hospital for the Insane, were insufficient to provide the minimum power and heat for the institution. Three years later, the board had not yet taken action to remedy this problem. On December 17, 1917, all the boilers at Overbrook broke down. For three days during one of the harshest winters New Jersey had experienced, the hospital was without heat and light. The *Newark Evening News* asked on the front page in boldface type on December 29, 1917:

Have you a relative who is a patient at Overbrook? Then, for the love you bear your afflicted one, take him or her to your home for a few days at least, no matter what the inconvenience. The temperature in many wards of the hospital was only a few degrees above zero today.

This appeal is authentic. Dr. Guy Paine, Medical Superintendent, told the *News* today that patients taken to their homes now will escape suffering. There is no red tape. Simply apply.[35]

Though the board finally issued a $75,000 emergency appropriation to meet the crisis, it was more than a month before conditions at

Overbrook were corrected. That December, forty-three patients died of exposure. A grand jury charged the members of the Board of Chosen Freeholders with criminal negligence, but each was later acquitted through legal technicalities.

Public disgust with the Republican Old Guard that controlled both the board and the entire Essex political arena found an outlet in the election of 1918 when three Democrats were elected to the board, the first Democratic candidates to win an election in the county in over a decade. These new freeholders immediately established an independent commission to investigate the financial affairs of the county.

The report the commission issued on June 14, 1919, contained little new information about the Overbrook scandal, but it did elucidate the questionable, if not corrupt, nature of the role of political influence in the administration of the county. The report afforded evidence that Essex politicians were benefiting from their office at the expense of the taxpayer, especially through their complicity with contractors. There was blatant circumvention of the law in letting contracts. There was obvious favoritism in assigning contracts. There was failure to enforce contracts, leading to excessive delays in completion and unreasonable additional expenses. County public works were often undertaken without contracts, and the board often passed motions for work to be begun without any estimate of final costs. County engineers and architects evaded the requirements of competitive bidding either by making no estimate of the cost of a county project, by dividing the project into fictitious divisions, or by presenting an unrealistically low bid, confident that they would later be allowed to charge enough "extras" to earn a handsome profit. In addition to these practices, the county freeholders were giving large parties for their friends at the county institutions, the insane asylum and penitentiaries, parties paid for out of the funds appropriated for the care of the inmates. Concluded the report: "The facts disclosed tend to show gross incompetence on the part of the governing authorities and great laxity in the administration of the affairs of Essex County resulting in needless waste and extravagance and loss to the taxpayer." Such practices had already cost the county "untold sums of money, the extent of which it is almost impossible to ascertain."[36]

The report uncovered additional dubious practices that finally converted public indignation to action. When the chairman of the Republican county committee, John B. Woolston, learned through the vantage of his position that the county planned to purchase over one hundred acres of land in North Caldwell and Verona to join the property occupied by the penitentiary, the insane hospital, and the tuberculosis sanitarium, he had bought the land for $95,737. A month later, on December 9, 1915, the board passed its motion to acquire the land and issued bonds for $127,000 to pay Woolston for the acreage, netting Woolston a quick profit of $31,263, a deal that was allowed to come to pass because of his political association and friendship with the members of the board.

At that time, there was in Essex County, in the minds of many, a strong connection between prohibition, law enforcement, and clean government. It was therefore not surprising that James K. Shields, the state superintendent of the Anti-Saloon League, called a meeting for February 20, 1919, to which he summoned those deeply interested in the political problems of the county, "among whom I am sure you are one," he wrote to Vanderbilt.

There probably never was a time when the Republicans of the Party were more thoroughly disgusted with their Republican organization than now; never a time when it would be easier to build a successful machine for accomplishing results at the coming election this fall, when so much depends upon the selection of Governor, who will appoint the judges and prosecuting attorneys for the next three years.

Will you not try and be present if at all possible, coming at five o'clock if you can't possibly come earlier?[37]

At that meeting late Thursday afternoon attended by members of the county Republican party known to be dissatisfied with the administration of county affairs, the Essex County Republican League was born. Thirty-year-old Arthur T. Vanderbilt, who proposed the formation of the League, was elected its first president. The purpose of the League, as with Sommer's New Idea movement fourteen years earlier, was to build an independent reform faction of Republicans, to present a slate of carefully selected candidates under the slogan "Republican League: Clean County Government," and to focus the widespread but heretofore unorganized public discontent in an attempt to elect candidates who would reestablish a conscientious county government. The first goal of the Essex Republican League was to elect as governor Acting Governor William N. Runyon, a man who had long participated in New Jersey affairs. It was decided that, to prevent the Democrats from repeating their success of 1918 and winning majority control of the nine-member board, three freeholder candidates as well as a full assembly ticket would be backed by the League. To Vanderbilt fell the responsibility of finding three citizens to run for the office of freeholder.

He first approached Henry C. Hines, who was favorably known in the Newark community from having served three terms in the assembly as a New Idea Republican. After considerable persuasion, Hines agreed to run if two other acceptable candidates could be found.

Edwin Ball, a former partner of the stone-cutting firm of Car and Ball, seemed to Vanderbilt just the man to fill another spot. Concerned with the welfare of the community and neighborhood, Ball had long been president of the Eighth Ward Improvement Association and a member and former president of the Newark Board of Education. Having retired in 1918 at the age of sixty-seven, he had become one of the regular members of the group of citizens who gathered in Billy Mungle's grocery store at Belleville Avenue and Clark Street to help settle each day, to the satisfaction of the group, the affairs of the city and state.

When Vanderbilt went to see him, Ball readily admitted the need for a general reform of the party but argued that the fate of a number of independent political movements over the past forty years made him doubt any chance for success. What the president of the League lacked in political experience he compensated for in enthusiasm, and Vanderbilt finally convinced Ball at least to consider the offer. "I suspected he desired a little time to discuss the proposition with the Sage of the Corner Grocery Store [Billy Mungle]."[38]

Having given Ball this opportunity, Vanderbilt returned the next morning.

"I will take a chance if Mr. Hines will," Ball said, "but my good friend, Billy Mungle, tells me that you are a clever young man and that this is probably a dodge to get me to put up a big campaign contribution."

"Mr. Ball," Vanderbilt answered, "not only will we not take any of your money, but we will not even ask you to raise any money."[39]

Ball agreed to run on the condition that a third man, satisfactory to them both, could be found. Wilbur N. Driver, a well-known citizen of East Orange, was similarly induced to run.

In the vigorous primary campaign that followed, leading state newspapers that had advocated reform for several years supported the Essex Republican League candidates.

The regular Republican organization, less confident than usual both because of the Democratic victory the previous year and because of the prospective competition from the insurgent Republican League, took special care in its choice of candidates. It renominated only one of the three freeholders whose term was expiring—C. Raymond Swain, who, having been appointed to fill a vacancy, had not been involved in the recent Essex County scandals.

The regular Republicans also made every effort to make it appear that their notorious chairman, John B. Woolston, was in no way connected with their candidates, a fiction that burst shortly before the primary when Vanderbilt stated in a letter to the *Newark Sunday Call* the obvious facts: that the signature of John B. Woolston headed their nominating petition and that Woolston had presided over the meeting that chose their candidates. "It is the violent efforts which are now being made to avoid all connection with Mr. Woolston which aroused my suspicion and which, I believe, must arouse the suspicion of every thinking citizen in our county."[40]

The campaign was hard fought. The regular Republicans reportedly spent between $60,000 and $70,000 on their primary battle. The Essex Republican League was only able to raise $5,358 and spent $4,442.50. "It was to be claimed that we held our meetings in a telephone booth," Vanderbilt joked many years later. "That was not literally true. But it was, in fact, a day of small beginnings."[41] Out of necessity, the League put its hope in the quality of its candidates, the support of the newspapers, and the weight of the aroused commuter vote.

On primary day, September 23, 1919, Runyon did not win the nomination for governor and the League assembly slate lost, but League candidates Hines and Ball were nominated Republican candidates to run for the Board of Chosen Freeholders in November. "[T]he voters of the Republican Party of Essex registered their rejection of their party machine and its discredited leadership," hailed the *Newark Evening News* with a certain amount of prevision.

The machine has been badly crippled, perhaps "smashed" and the reorganization of the County Committee attended by the casting out of the dubious methods which had been permitted to control the workings of the Organization too long for the party's good, may now be looked for. The people of Essex have been sorely tried for the last few years by the low spirit of service which has dominated the County Board. They now eagerly hail the prospect of better things.[42]

Perhaps the enthusiasm was a little too hearty, for the majority by which Hines and Ball had won hardly exceeded a hundred votes. However, at the election in November, the traditional Republican strength of Essex reasserted itself. Ball, Hines, and regular Republican candidate Frederick O. Lindsley were elected over the three Democratic contenders.

With Woolston forced out of the county Republican chairmanship by the campaign and the results of the election, there was no reason to believe that the Essex Republican League would not soon wither away as had innumerable previous local political factions once an immediate goal had been achieved. An unexpected development soon made the victory of the League even more complete.

The new Board of Chosen Freeholders was composed of four regular Republicans, three Democrats, and the two League Republicans. Before the board met for the first time on January 1, 1920, it had been the plan of the regular Republicans to nominate for the office of director of the board their new member, Lindsley, who had led the polls.

Even shortly before the meeting began, Hines and Ball had not decided who they would support. As they walked up the courthouse steps at nine o'clock, Hines was stopped by James R. Nugent, the Democratic leader of Essex County and of New Jersey since Woodrow Wilson had left for the White House. Nugent told Hines that the three Democrats would vote for him for director, apparently because of a personal quarrel that had just arisen between Nugent and John Woolston.

Minutes later, by a vote of five to four, Henry C. Hines was elected.

He took advantage of this opportunity to appoint Edwin Ball to every strategic committee of the board. As director, Hines also would be a member of each committee.

In this way the Essex County Republican League secured key positions on the Board of Chosen Freeholders, and Vanderbilt, ten years after his conversation with Elihu Root at President Shanklin's installation, achieved as president of the League entry into the political affairs of Essex County.

III Clean Government, 1920–1938

THE ADVENT OF REFORM

During their first year as freeholders, Edwin Ball and Henry Hines wedged open the problems of the Essex County Board of Chosen Freeholders and began to expose the mismanagement to which the newspapers had often only been able to allude.

Having been named chairman of the building committee by Hines, Edwin Ball, with years of experience in the construction business, was well qualified to examine the status of the county building projects. The construction work on the Overbrook Hospital sewage disposal facilities was the first problem which caught his attention and led to the first of many investigations he and Hines would undertake, investigations that were followed daily by the press and public.

A contract had been let to Mahlon Averill on July 2, 1919, to construct new filter beds at the sewage plant at Overbrook. His bid for the job had been $89,956.50, but on December 1, 1919, less than six months later, he had submitted a request for an additional appropriation of $80,000 to complete the work. Ball's first official act as chairman was to present a resolution on January 22, 1920, to suspend the work at Overbrook pending further investigation. The resolution passed and Ball, Hines, and Frederick Lindsley, the three freeholders who had not been members of the board at the time the contract was awarded, were appointed by the board as a committee to examine the entire project. Vanderbilt was named by the committee as special investigation counsel.

On the morning when the committee and their counsel went to the site of the construction and found several feet of water in the filter beds as a result of a heavy rain three days before, their suspicion that the work was not proceeding properly was confirmed. "If a filter bed will not drain off pure water," they reported, "how can it possibly be expected to drain off the effluent from a sewage disposal plant?"[1] Concrete used in the construction work crumbled in their fingers when they tested its strength. For this work, improperly done and not even half complete, Essex County, with the approval of county engineer Frederick A. Reimer, had paid Averill $90,000.

The committee at once recommended legal action against Averill and the dismissal of the county engineer. In a report that Vanderbilt prepared and presented to the board on April 30, 1920, it was shown that the contract had been improperly drawn, that work had not proceeded according to the proposed plans and specifications, and that the contractor had been highly overpaid for the work he had completed. As a result of these charges, Reimer was removed from office by the board and a successful suit was brought against Averill to recover $90,000.

The exposure of this all too familiar type of attitude among county contractors and county officials and the speedy investigation and prosecution that followed cast the Essex County Republican League into a favorable position for its next campaign, a position further strengthened by the uncovering of two other scandals that same year.

On June 10, 1920, the Board of Chosen Freeholders, with Hines and Ball dissenting, voted to appropriate over $1 million to pave various county roads. The crux of the resolution was that two patented paving formulas would be used to pave the roads, formulas that, oddly enough, had been granted patents even though they consisted merely of mixtures of asphalt and various sized stones. As bidding was restricted to the few local contractors who held the patents, thereby limiting competition and serving only the interests of a paving company, Hines and Ball considered the use of patented paving an unwarranted waste of public funds and stated that they did not think "the County should tie [itself] down to patent pavements for the benefit of road contractors who have no work at present."[2] Although their dissent could not override the approval of the rest of the board, the two freeholders were able to interest the Newark Chamber of Commerce in the situation, and Vanderbilt was again retained as a special counsel.

Investigating the paving contract, he discovered a deal whereby the Democratic assembly delegation had agreed to pass an increase

in the salaries of the freeholders in return for which the regular
Republican freeholders had agreed to allow the Democratic freeholders to name the specific paving formula to be used and thus the
contractor who would richly benefit from the county work. To stop
the paving, Vanderbilt made an application to Chief Justice William
S. Gummere for a writ of certiorari to review the action of the board
in letting the contract. Finding that, by the County Government Act
of 1917, the board could not enter into any contract for county work
whose cost would be financed by a bond issue without first adopting
a resolution to authorize the issue of bonds, Vanderbilt was able to
show the board had illegally assigned the road contract. On October
30, 1920, the chief justice granted the writ and stopped all work on
the roads.

Vanderbilt then took the case to court—first to the state supreme
court and, losing there, then to the court of errors and appeals, which
upheld his contentions. The court declared the paving contract
invalid because sufficient funds had not been appropriated before it
had been let, because agreements with municipalities for sharing the
cost of the work had not been made until after the contract had been
signed, and because the contract provided for paving some roads
which were not even under county jurisdiction.

The roads were later improved with nonpatented pavement, saving the county $330,000. Meanwhile, William H. Parry, a candidate
of the Essex Republican League elected to the state senate in 1920,
was successful in having an act passed which ended the use of such
paving formulas throughout New Jersey.

The third example of unwarranted extravagance became the focus
of the second campaign of the Essex Republican League. On October 16, 1919, the board had awarded the Nugent Construction Company a contract for the construction of new buildings and additions to
the Overbrook Hospital for the Insane. No estimate of the cost of the
construction work was required—a direct violation of law, but a
commonly accepted practice in the county at that time. In the summer of 1920 it became apparent that a cottage for the farmer at
Overbrook which had been included in a blanket contract covering
many improvements had cost the county $45,000. With no specifica-
tions from the board, the Nugent Construction Company had built
the farmer's "cottage" with the following features: ten rooms, an oak-
paneled library, cathedral glass windows, and French doors.

And who is the fairy godmother that built the mansion for the gardener at the
hospital for the insane? [the newspapers asked]. If you must know it is the

Essex County Board of Chosen Freeholders. It is they who waved the wand. It spends $16,000,000 a year of the taxpayers' money. It spends much of it in the way it spent $40,000[3] for a farmer's cottage at Overbrook. It spends it by flagrant violation of the letter and the spirit of competitive bidding. It spends it by exceeding its appropriations, which is contrary to law. It spends it without method, without limit, in any way it pleases.[4]

In the first year that Hines and Ball served on the Board of Chosen Freeholders, similar practices were uncovered and corrected. The resulting improvement in the character of county government was attributed to the two Republican League freeholders.

The approval of the citizens of Essex was noted by the regular Republican organization, which attempted to defeat the League candidates in the September 28, 1920, primary by entering a dummy independent Republican ticket designed to split the independent commuter vote and thereby elect the regular ticket. In addition, there was a "Harding and Harmony" ticket backed by former county chairman Woolston, another group of three, and several independent candidates.

For the Essex Republican League, Edwin Ball induced his friend Billy Mungle, former assemblyman and for fifty years proprietor of an eighth-ward Newark grocery store, to run. He and Henry Hines persuaded Philip Lindeman, a Newark merchant who had never been in politics but who was a leader of Jewish welfare activities, to run on the ticket with Mungle. Zenas G. Crane, a farmer who had had a successful career as mayor of West Caldwell, was run as a representative of West Essex.

Not able and not inclined to establish a traditional political precinct machine, the League depended on the same tactics as in its first campaign, relying on the newspapers to take reform positions and support its candidates. The *Newark Evening News* expressed its willingness to back the League again if its candidates would declare that if elected they would support the policies of Henry Hines and Edwin Ball. "I well remember Mr. Lewis G. Garrison, their political reporter, himself typing such a paper in my office one evening and the three candidates [Mungle, Lindeman, and Crane] gladly signing it,"[5] Vanderbilt recalled. Before the election, however, another major state newspaper, the *Newark Sunday Call*, went on record in favor of the "Harding and Harmony" ticket, thereby dampening the primary prospects of the League, for it now seemed certain that the important Essex commuter vote would be fragmented among the various tickets.

The next day Vanderbilt walked across the street to the office of Wallace Scudder, the publisher of the *Newark Evening News* and a close friend of editor William Thorne of the *Newark Sunday Call.*

[Scudder] had been very kind in the first campaign and I told him just what the situation was. I told him that we had three men who would back up Hines and Ball, but the *Sunday Call* had got itself and us out on a limb.

He said, "What do you want me to do about it?"

I said, "It is rumored that you have some stock in the *Sunday Call.*" Never a word out of him. "It is said Mr. Thorne is one of your very best friends."

He said, "That's true."

I said, "What I want you to do is to get him to change his mind, because two and three makes five, and five is a majority of nine, but two and three kept in separate compartments means chaos."

He said, "I will talk to Mr. Thorne, if you will agree that if he and I decide that his ticket is better than yours, you will not run your ticket."

I must admit that I stared at him. I stared at him for a long time and he looked me keenly in the eye with those light blue eyes of his, and finally I said, "Mr. Scudder, I have a great deal of confidence in you. I'll agree to your terms."

In three days he sent for me and he said, "I have had a talk with Mr. Thorne. I have had two talks with him. There will be nothing [favoring the Harding and Harmony slate] in the *Sunday Call* this week."[6]

Shortly before the primary, the *Sunday Call* swung its support to the League, stating that the three League candidates were the only independent candidates who had a chance to defeat the regular Republican organization. "The independent voters," wrote Thorne in an editorial, "outnumber the supporters of the machine, but they are not so far ahead of them numerically as to be able to scatter their votes and win. They must unite substantially upon three of the nominees and cast their ballots for them or probably lose the battle."[7]

"This is the way Clean Government started," Vanderbilt remarked later, "with these small sums contributed by many citizens, very good candidates, the help of an enlightened press, and a great deal of nerve."[8]

In the primary of September 28, 1920, the three League candidates—Mungle, Lindeman, and Crane—were elected, and in the November election they were swept into office on the crest of the Harding landslide. This was the first election in which women voted, and their vote was strongly pro-League. The total vote cast for the regular Republicans was 41,668 in 1919 and 43,545 in 1920. Whereas the total for the three League candidates in 1919 had been 41,701, in 1920, with woman suffrage, it was 89,056.

The five League freeholders now filled a majority of seats on the nine-member board. The League also succeeded in electing its candidate for state senator, William H. Parry, and eight members to the general assembly. Of this group, George S. Hobart was elected speaker. With optimism now more justified, the *Newark Evening News* heralded these victories and the hope for the future in an editorial of November 3, 1920:

New Day Dawns upon County Government

The election of the Republican candidates for Board of Chosen Freeholders means the redemption of Essex County's Government to the service of its citizens. Messrs. Lindeman, Mungle, and Crane will go into the Board of Freeholders next January as part of the regime that will be obligated by the most solemn pledges that public men can make to the public to cast out the last scraps of a discredited system which too long has held the County administration in a throttling grip. While it has produced wasteful extravagance in the employment of public monies and blighting scandals in the conduct of public business, now for the first time in years the people may look forward to an era of real reform and of genuine business policies in all the County's affairs; such is the pledge and such the bond.[9]

COUNTY COUNSEL

Because of a harmony movement inaugurated between the regular Republicans and the League Republicans before the primary of 1921, the usual primary fight was avoided, resulting in a compromise freeholder ticket composed of one League candidate, one regular candidate, and one candidate acceptable to both factions. After a successful election in November, the nine members of the Board of Chosen Freeholders met on December 15, 1921, for a three-hour conference to select a county counsel. Vanderbilt was appointed by the board to fill the office, according to some because of his general standing at the bar, because of the special study he had made of municipal law as a member of the faculty of New York University, and because of his familiarity with county affairs growing out of his work as special counsel for the investigating committees of Hines and Ball and the Newark Chamber of Commerce. Others viewed his selection as the board's distribution of still another political plum. Reported the *Newark Evening News:* "Repayment of political debts and the acknowledgment of future activities of Mr. Vanderbilt are said to have figured in the decision of the majority of the Board to give him the job."[10]

As both president of the Essex County Republican League, which had now promoted the election of seven of the nine county freeholders, and, by appointment of these freeholders, county counsel, the highest-paid county officer, Vanderbilt had an influence in county affairs ever subject to criticism. He took care to separate his two roles. When questioned in 1927 by Freeholder Elizabeth A. Harris, his most implacable foe on the board, "whether or not, directly or indirectly, he expected to have any part in the selection of county officers in the future,"[11] he responded that, though he had endeavored in his work as county counsel to avoid all political matters of the board—never attending any freeholders' conference without the express request of the director or one or more of the members of the board, maintaining an impartial and professional attitude toward the board at all times, never in any campaign asking any county official for help or support, and refraining from holding any political conference in his county office—he still asserted his right to participate in the Republican League activities. "As County Counsel it is my desire, as well as my duty, to serve the Board and its members in every legal matter consistent with my oath of office and my duty to the Courts. But politically and as a citizen, I am and always hope to be, 'the captain of my soul.'"[12]

That such a distinction could be maintained was more convincing in action than in words. Upon assuming his responsibilities as county counsel, Vanderbilt abolished the offices of assistant county counsel and assistant county attorney, largely because he felt they "would be sure to get in the way,"[13] but the taxpayers welcomed the reorganization of the county legal department and the substantial reduction in its yearly budget. During his first year in office, he inherited thirty suits against municipalities that had declined to make good on cost-sharing agreements on county or municipal roads. Before the advent of the reforms of the Republican League, it had not been considered "good taste" for the county to sue a municipality represented on the Board of Freeholders. After Vanderbilt had successfully terminated all of these suits, the commissioner of internal revenue, perhaps inspired by politics, denied Vanderbilt an exemption for his county counsel salary on the ground that the office was a sinecure. "I had to go to Washington and tell two conferees how hard I had worked. When they demanded to see the evidence, I stepped out into the hall and then came back with four husky porters carrying eight large suitcases full of the records of the various cases I had tried for the County. The conferees threw up their hands and laughed. My squad of porters and I made our way to the station in triumph. Once more justice had prevailed."[14]

He continued to handle the legal affairs of Essex County at a salary of $12,000 a year, a moderate remuneration in comparison with the costs of the legal departments of other major counties in New Jersey and New York.[15] He was reappointed county counsel by the board every third year for twenty-six years, whereas the average term of his five predecessors had been two years. Twenty-six years later when neighboring Hudson County employed eighteen attorneys in its legal department, Vanderbilt was still the single counsel of Essex, receiving the same salary as in 1922.

Nevertheless, his dual position as a politician and an appointed county official led to an ambiguity in his role in county affairs. In a county government like that of Essex, with no single executive head, the legal advisor could wield great influence: the laws and statutes affecting the county could only be extracted by a lawyer, and no important action could be taken without his advice. Although he never attempted to dictate the decisions of the board, Vanderbilt would readily agree that his advice was influential in the decision-making process of the freeholders. Whether this was so by the authority of his reason or by reason of his authority was often, at least in the political columns, an open question.

CONSOLATION PRIZES

On May 31, 1922, William N. Runyon, the candidate the Essex Republican League had supported for governor in 1919, again made formal announcement of his candidacy for the Republican nomination for governor and stated that Arthur T. Vanderbilt of Newark would be his campaign manager. Runyon, at the age of forty-one, had served as a member of the city council of Plainfield, city judge, a member of the New Jersey assembly, Republican leader of the assembly, state senator, president of the senate, and acting governor when Governor Walter E. Edge became a United States senator in 1918.

Runyon's gubernatorial platform included the advocacy of the direct primary, the improved regulation of public utilities to reduce gas and electric rates and trolley fares, equal educational opportunities for children, increased workingmen's compensation, the limiting of night work for women, the expansion of a state highway system, clean waterways, and, in general, stringent economy in the administration of public affairs. But the Democrats forced the spotlight of the campaign on one issue: the Republican position of the "preservation of the Constitution and respect for the law"[16]—the strict enforcement of prohibition under the terms of the two-year-old Eighteenth Amendment, an amendment New Jersey had reluctantly ratified only after every other state except Rhode Island and Connecticut had done so.

Runyon easily won the Republican nomination in September of 1922, but the larger phase of the campaign, the battle for the Senate seat between incumbent Republican Senator Joseph S. Frelinghuysen and Democratic Governor Edward I. Edwards, put a drag on the entire Republican ticket for it was widely rumored that Frelinghuysen was "personally wet and politically dry."[17] The Democrats emphasized the inequalities, disrespect for the law, corruption, and crime that prohibition bred; they called for the "sale and manufacture of light wines and beer under Federal supervision and regulation,"[18] and, if this could not be accomplished under the present laws, for the repeal of the Eighteenth Amendment.

Using the same pledges that had carried him into the governor's office in 1919—"to fight by every lawful means the enforcement of prohibition in New Jersey" and to make New Jersey "as wet as the Atlantic Ocean,"[19] pledges which had led to an abortive Edwards-for-President movement in 1920—Edwards captured the senate seat in November of 1922 by 90,000 votes, pulling his running mate George S. Silzer, a circuit judge from New Brunswick who was equally opposed to the Anti-Saloon League, the Volstead Act, and the Eighteenth Amendment, into the New Jersey governorship in by 45,894 votes.

Several days after the election, Senator Frelinghuysen, realizing that he had been a cause of the Republican defeat, telephoned Runyon's campaign manager. "I can't change the verdict of the polls," the senator said to Vanderbilt, "but I do have some influence with the Harding administration in Washington. Do you think Runyon would like to be named Federal judge for New Jersey?"[20]

Vanderbilt was sure Runyon would accept, and within a month after his defeat he had been appointed. Realizing that his campaign manager had little to show for the busiest year of his life during which he had all but given up the practice of law, Runyon was pleased to recommend Vanderbilt as an able lawyer to Lindley M. Garrison, a vice-chancellor of the New Jersey Court of Chancery, who was searching for a lawyer to be named co-receiver of the giant Virginia-Carolina Chemical Company. Therefore, in February of 1923, three months after the election, thirty-four-year-old Vanderbilt received a call from Garrison offering him the position. He accepted.

With operations extending throughout the southern and midwestern states and with business activities in Mexico and Germany, the Virginia-Carolina Chemical Company had been caught after World War I with large inventories bought at war-inflated prices and with commitments to make more purchases at the same prices. Company sales of $138 million in 1920 had dropped to $87 million in 1921 because of a farm depression and rising competition in its major product lines of fertilizers, chemicals, and cottonseed oil. With continuing declines in sales and a $15 million loss in 1921, and with creditors demanding payments that were impossible to meet, the company agreed in 1923 to allow its president and Vanderbilt to direct and reorganize the company to avoid complete liquidation. The receivers used preferred capital stock to satisfy bondholders and creditors, and raised cash to ease additional obligations by selling subsidiaries and a German potash field and by halting phosphate rock mining in South Carolina and Florida, thus eliminating less profitable operations. Two years later, in 1925, the reorganization was complete, a $19 million fund of working capital had been set aside, and the company was returned to the control of its officers.

In 1925 headlines of New Jersey newspapers reported that Vanderbilt had been paid $100,000 for administering the business of the Southern Cotton Oil Company, a subsidiary of the Virginia-Carolina Chemical Company, and the following year that he had received $75,000 more for terminating the receivership of the parent company. These were among the highest fees ever paid for such work, and an editorial in the *Newark Evening News* condemned them, stating that they jeopardized public confidence in the handling of large receiverships. In a letter to the *News,* Vanderbilt ended the criticism by describing the recovery of the company under the receivership:

To allay such fears on your part, I desire to set the true facts before you. The receivers took over on March 1, 1923, an industrial company with plants located in practically all the Southern States from Virginia to Florida and westward to Louisiana and Ohio. Its financial condition had become very seriously involved, the company having lost over $28,000,000 in the 4 years from 1921 to 1924. In 1920 its common stock sold as high as 80, and in 1924 as low as 1.

During the receivership from 1924 to 1926 the company made a net profit of well over $6,000,000 in contrast with the deficit of the preceding 4 years.[21]

The Virginia-Carolina Chemical Company receivership, which had been the largest industrial receivership in the United States, marked the traditional turning point of a legal career. Vanderbilt was now recognized as one of the leading lawyers in the state. "Up to that time I had been a rising young lawyer, but from that time on I was something else; I was a so-and-so who was trying to steal the business of the older firms. I had broken in on the monopoly."[22]

A DAY IN THE LIFE

A routine day in Vanderbilt's life began before sunrise when he heard one of his children already awake. Together they went downstairs to find their collie and wandered with him through the surrounding woods. On his return to the house, Vanderbilt shaved while eating a sliced apple brought to him by the cook. By 6:45 A.M. he had picked up his secretary at her home and by seven o'clock they were at the office in Newark. Upon reaching the office, his secretary would occasionally discover that he was wearing a mismatched suit or that his tie did not go with his suit. He would then call Floss and ask her to send their caretaker with the proper coat, trousers, or tie.

Free from interruptions for several hours, he spent the early morning dictating correspondence or preparing for a day in court. Politicians learned that, if it was necessary to consult with him, this was the only time of the day they could be sure of reaching his office without being stopped by a telephone operator or squadron of secretaries. The inconvenience of traveling into the city before breakfast ensured that any visitor at that hour had a mission of importance.

As his associates and clerks began to arrive, he planned with them the work of the day and discussed the cases which they were handling. He then set off for court, which consumed the bulk of his day three or four times a week. When he had to go to court in Trenton or Philadelphia or make a trip to Washington, D.C., he took his secretary along on the train and dictated to her, leaving her at the station, where she took the next train back to Newark to type her shorthand notes.

Lunch was often a political or business meeting. If he was in his office, he ordered from the Down Town Club milk with bread in it which he consumed while dictating or talking on the phone or conferring with an associate.

Following an afternoon in court, he returned to his office to meet with clients, to review briefs and trial preparations, and to answer the telephone calls that had piled up during the day. To give his law practice priority over politics, he refused to take political calls until after four o'clock and would ask the receptionist to tell any politician that "Mr. Vanderbilt is out." Despite such efforts, the reception room usually held several political visitors anxious to see him; more than once Vanderbilt was known to leave his office by his second "escape door" if he did not want to meet them and had an engagement out of the office.

He never liked to stay in the office in the evening and so on busy days returned home for dinner with his secretary, afterward retiring to his large second-floor study, where he would dictate until 9:30 or 10:00 P.M., at which time his caretaker drove the secretary home. Two evenings each week he taught at New York University; other evenings were devoted to preparation for trial or to political work; and periodically, either in the evening or on the weekend, he met at his home with all his associates to review the state of pending cases.

With his continuing professional success and with the birth of five children—Jean, Betty, and Lois, and twin sons Bill and Bob—in their first six years of marriage, Arthur and Floss sold their house in East Orange in 1925 and moved to an eighteen-room English Tudor home on two acres of rolling tree-shaded grounds in Short Hills, a residential community of Essex County. Arthur's idea of relaxation was working at home in his study while wearing his black Wesleyan varsity sweater (won for his work as manager of the football team) and sipping a glass of buttermilk or a mixture of Root Beer and cream. Their home was filled with books. Books lined the front hall, the living room, and his study; there were bookcases in the solarium and in all the bedrooms; more books flowed over into the storage rooms on the third floor, into the recreation room, and to the second floor of the garage. These were not only law books and books about the law but history books, biographies, great novels and poetry, essays, art books, and books on political science and philosophy. If he had a hobby, it was surely collecting and reading books, an activity which he felt was especially important for lawyers who were likely to see the pathological side of life and therefore needed literature to restore their balance and to give them perspective.

Once on the Hudson and Manhattan tube train to New York

University, Vanderbilt and his law clerk were discussing the passengers sitting across from them who, from time to time, let their gaze rest on them. "Some people," he said, "are irritated or become nervous when gazed upon. I always maintain a bland expression or 'poker face' which is inscrutable."[23] When such conscious effort was combined with his enigmatic physical features, his personality seemed a mixture of contradictions.

The only characteristic all who knew him agreed upon was his inexhaustible energy and amazing ability to work. His sense of administration and organization, of how to squeeze the value out of every minute of the day, was as legendary as was his ability to appear relaxed in the face of a pressing mass of obligations. A close colleague from one of the busiest periods of Vanderbilt's life observed: "I have never met a man who knew better the value of time and how to control it, or who seemed less rushed than he."[24] There was every indication that the main motivation behind his drive was his complete enjoyment of what he was doing. Despite his unusual diet and meager amount of sleep, he never missed a day of work in twenty-five years because of ill health. It seemed as if he was one of "fortune's favored children." "For them," wrote Winston Churchill, "the working hours are never long enough. Every day is a holiday and ordinary holidays, when they come, are begrudged as an enforced interruption in an absorbing vocation."[25]

Beyond this trait, there was no agreement about the nature of his personality. He was usually even tempered and rarely displayed any great range of emotions. Returning from court, he might call one of his associates into his office and with boyish glee recount how he had won a case or something humorous he had said during the trial. When he was upset, he swore, a habit which he attributed less to his year of work after high school in the engineering department of a railroad than "to his experiences in law offices": " . . . lawyers are much more imaginative in the use of language, I have observed, than even the best of engineers."[26] And on occasions when he was very angry, he threw a pencil or book across his room, much to the fright of any secretary who happened to be with him.

He was a demanding taskmaster. "You expect the impossible and you always get it,"[27] members of his office would often tell him, to which he would respond that he never asked anyone to work harder than he worked himself. Many people who were associated with him discovered that the extent of their abilities and endurance was far beyond what they had imagined, and they were fiercely loyal to him. He had a special skill in infecting others with his enthusiasm and in getting them to work with something approaching his own dedication.

There were those who found his methods ruthless, his style autocratic and uncompromising. It was no secret that he could be caustic and stubborn when he thought people were not performing well. Those who had known him more intimately saw him as a modest, humble man who had a smile or joke for the shoeshine man, the newspaper boy, and everyone he knew on the street as he walked from the station to his office. With his friends he displayed a persistent wry sense of humor. He once told a clerk that it was impolite and not socially acceptable to laugh, that a chuckle was sufficient,[28] but there were times he had to excuse himself from the table or leave the room because he was laughing so hard that it seemed to his companions that "A.T. would split a gut."[29]

Floss, whose affection for Arthur approached adoration, accepted her husband's eccentric work habits with good grace. When he was working at home, she considered it her duty to make certain that nothing disturbed him and that he and his secretary were well supplied with hot coffee cake or candies. During the day, she built her own world around her own interests, which included a variety of community, church, and hospital services and working in her gardens, which were featured in home and garden magazines and which attracted many visitors each spring and summer.

Always ready to drop her own plans, Floss frequently accompanied her husband on his many out-of-state trips. On one occasion he called her at noon with the message that he had to be in Chicago the following morning. He asked her to pack his bag and drive his ancient Packard to Penn Station, where he would meet her with the tickets to make the four o'clock train. On the Newark Turnpike, the car broke down. Abandoning it, she took the suitcase and started running down the side of the highway until she was able to flag a passing truck which got her to the station with several minutes to spare.

In addition to shielding her husband from interruptions, Floss equally saw it as her duty to insist that he take time away from his work. She found that the best way to accomplish this feat was to make plans herself and then to inform him what they were going to do. Saturday afternoon or evening was often spent in New York City at the theater. Twice each month a dancing instructor from the Arthur Murray Studios came to give lessons to the Vanderbilts and some of their friends in their large recreation room. Other nights were reserved for an evening of dinner and dancing, and still others for long drives over the back roads of the surrounding countryside toward Basking Ridge and Bernardsville.

When she perceived that her husband had been working too hard for too long, Floss would schedule a trip far from New Jersey—to their summer home in Maine, to Canada, to Florida, to the Caribbean, or to Europe.

Later in their lives, when both sons and one daughter had become lawyers and two daughters had married lawyers and family reunions were beginning to sound like bar association meetings, Floss quietly insisted that no cases be discussed at the dinner table and that nothing about the law be mentioned in the presence of nonlawyer visitors. In such ways she provided a valuable and necessary balance to her husband's driving life-style.

Vanderbilt had a continuing interest in the smallest details of the activities and experiences of his five children and a continuing desire to offer them advice, though always hesitantly and carefully expressed. A remark like "I hope you won't get me wrong for mentioning one or two things" or "I know you will forgive me if I mention just two little things" would introduce his ideas and suggestions:

> I *would* wear a freshman hat (a) because it costs nothing to conform in *non*-essentials; (b) because other freshmen may think you "big-headed" otherwise, and (c) most important, it makes it easier for you to get to know other freshmen—that's the real reason for them, anyway. When you know all the freshmen and they know you, you can forget it.[30]

Or

> Don't forget to send me copies of your themes. I would suggest that for writing themes you should make a little wider margin on the left, say an inch and one-eighth rather than an inch (it is remarkable what a change in the appearance of a page just a difference of an eighth of an inch there will make), and on the right I suggest setting your carriage to give you a margin of three-quarters of an inch. I should also allow a fair margin at the top and bottom. Not only do these things make for a great improvement in appearance, but they also enable you to spread your work over more pages and the prof gets the notion that he is getting more for his money than he really is.[31]

Or to one of his daughters, agreeing to take her to a hockey game in Boston, a lesson in human nature:

> . . . your saying you want to go to Boston to see the hockey game and also because you think you should know something of Boston reminds me of one of the maxims of our old Dean [Frank W.] Nicholson [of Wesleyan] to the

effect that whenever a man gave him two reasons for wanting to do anything there was a presumption that both of them were open to question. Always pick one strong reason and stick to it. You will find it carries much more weight.[32]

Such advice continued well after all his children had left home and had families of their own. After noting in a joint letter to "My dear Children" that he had achieved only a "low record of 20% success as a propagandist" in convincing them not to smoke, he stated that he had a new crusade "which because it involves no personal change of habits I hope for greater success. I refer to the necessity of safety tubes and tires on your automobiles. Mother and I just do not like to think of you taking the risk of blowouts with ordinary tires. Inasmuch as this is a joint crusade, I hope for much greater success than in my first venture!"[33]

His children were inclined to treat his advice lightly and to poke gentle fun at their father's foibles, which included a real apprehension about an appointment with the dentist or doctor, and a fear of "wild animals," notably a squirrel which he once found sitting on his file cabinets in a third floor storage room, an encounter which sent him racing down the stairs calling to Floss that an enormous rat was loose in the house.

Concerned that his work kept him away from his children too often when they were growing up, he repeatedly made it known to them that he was always available whenever they wanted: "The welfare and happiness of all of you is constantly in my thoughts and I should be quite miserable if I believed that any of you could not talk to me on every possible subject."[34]

A SILK STRIKE AND CIVIL LIBERTIES

Vanderbilt's growing reputation as a lawyer drew many outstanding young law school graduates to his office to work with him as associates, among them Frederick W. Hall and Nathan L. Jacobs, who would be justices on the New Jersey Supreme Court; John A. Ackerman, Samuel Alcorn, Jr., Lawrence A. Carton, Jr., Edward Gaulkin and G. Dixon Speakman, who would serve on the New Jersey Superior Court; James Hunter III, who would be appointed a federal judge; Willard G. Woelper, later the first administrative director of the New Jersey court system; and such prominent members of the New Jersey bar as Marshall Crowley, David Stoffer, and

H. Edward Toner. Together these lawyers formed an effective team. Each was assigned cases in the area in which he was thought to be best qualified—in the field of fire insurance, in estate work, in title work, in the preparation of cases for trial, in research, or in appellate work—receiving the help of the others through a constant exchange of ideas.

With the support of this platoon of "bright young men,"[35] Vanderbilt became an active trial and appellate lawyer, winning all twenty-one cases he argued in the court of errors and appeals between 1928 and 1932, and arguing more cases in the New Jersey state and federal courts than any other counsellor, appearing also before the United States Supreme Court and the Canadian courts. "It has been my privilege as a judge in my circuit to have had many of the great lawyers of my day appear before the court of which I am a member," wrote John J. Parker, chief judge of the Fourth Circuit Court of Appeals, "among others Charles E. Hughes, John W. Davis, George Wharton Pepper, Newton D. Baker and William D. Mitchell. Vanderbilt showed, when he appeared before us, that he was the peer of any of these."[36]

Through the financial success of the law office with insurance, banking, and corporate work—over one half of which was being referred to him by other lawyers—Vanderbilt was able to handle without fee a number of cases that stirred his interest. The first and one of the most famous was a civil liberties case that became a landmark on free speech and unlawful assembly.

On August 1, 1924, six thousand workers of the Paterson, New Jersey, independent local trade union, the Associated Silk Workers, walked out on strike. Although the strike continued peacefully for several weeks, on September 26 the strikers were notified by Paterson chief of police John M. Tracey that no more daily meetings could be held in their headquarters Turn Hall, his alleged reason being his objection to statements a strike speaker had made criticizing local judges and police officers for their activities in restricting picketing. To help reopen their hall, the silk workers contacted the American Civil Liberties Union, which arranged a test meeting. When an A.C.L.U. attorney was unable to procure an injunction from the local vice-chancellor to restrain the police from interfering with the meeting, and when the chief of police and his men surrounded the hall on the evening of the meeting, Roger N. Baldwin, a director of the American Civil Liberties Union, conferred with the strike leaders and decided to hold a protest meeting at the City Hall Plaza, where no issue of obstructing traffic or assembling without a permit could be raised. Feeling certain that the police would arrest the speakers at the meeting, Baldwin hoped to force the issue into the New Jersey courts.

Led by two young women bearing an American flag, between five and six hundred strikers marched to the plaza in front of the Paterson City Hall on the night of October 6, 1924, drawing over a thousand onlookers. The chairman of the strikers, John C. Butterworth, mounted the steps to read the Bill of Rights guaranteeing the freedoms of speech and assembly, but he had said only the words "fellow workers" before a police officer asked if he had a permit to hold a public meeting at that time and place. When he held up the Bill of Rights saying, "This is my permit," about forty policemen burst into the crowd swinging their night sticks, wresting the flag from the two young women who had led the procession, dispersing the onlookers, and arresting the flagbearers, Butterworth, and eight other speakers who had been on the steps of the city hall. The charges against them were disorderly conduct, blocking traffic, resisting an officer, and holding a meeting without a permit. "In all our experience with police brutality in free speech fights, I have never seen so flagrant an exhibition of unprovoked and unnecessary police lawlessness," Baldwin remarked later.[37]

Baldwin voluntarily went to the police headquarters the next morning to assume responsibility for organizing the meeting. Recorded by a *Newark Evening News* reporter who accompanied him, the dialogue that ensued between Baldwin and chief of police Tracey revealed the attitude that lay behind arbitrary police control of strike activities in Paterson—the same attitude that had marked industrial conflicts there in 1913 and 1919 when strikers were also sentenced to jail for exercising their civil rights.

TRACEY: Is your name Baldwin?
BALDWIN: It is.
TRACEY: Boy, you are in wrong!
BALDWIN: Chief, I am not in near so wrong as your men are with me for that disgraceful spectacle last night.
TRACEY: Well, I'm not going to let any communist talk the way that fellow Wicks[38] was talking. We can't have that kind of thing in this town.
BALDWIN: What did he say, Chief?
TRACEY: Why, he was abusing President Coolidge.
BALDWIN: Why, John W. Davis is doing that. Abusing the President isn't a crime. This is the open season for abusing the President.
TRACEY: Well, it's got nothing to do with the strike, and I am not going to allow anyone to talk like that at strike meetings.

BALDWIN: Chief, you talk as if you were the censor of who could talk in this town; what they can say and where they can say it.

TRACEY: Well, I am.

BALDWIN: Say, Chief, you talk as if you were the law.

TRACEY: I am the law.

BALDWIN: I thought there were some courts left over here in Jersey.

TRACEY: Say, you fellows went around yesterday trying to find a chancellor to give you an injunction to open that hall last night, didn't you? Well, you didn't get one. Looks as if I was the law, don't it?

BALDWIN: Well, we'll find out before we get through whether you or the courts control this town. We'll take you to the Supreme Court of the state if we have to.

TRACEY: Oh, you fellows would go anywhere if there was money in it. I know the kind of game you fellows are up to. I wouldn't be surprised if the silk manufacturers in New York are paying you fellows to come over here to stir up trouble to run the Paterson mills out of business.

BALDWIN: That's nonsense, Chief, and you know it. We've been in this business seven years, and we go anywhere there's a free speech issue. We're always after police chiefs who take the attitude you do. Why, we'll defend anybody. We don't care who they are. We have defended the rights of the Ku Klux Klan to hold meetings on private property, and we're as much against the Klan as anyone.

TRACEY: My God, I thought so! But you fellows ain't sincere anyhow.

BALDWIN: Sincere? There's nothing in this for us except trouble.

TRACEY: Well, I'm going to prove whether you are sincere or not. The next time you come over here, I'm going to take you out in front of City Hall and make you kiss the Constitution and the flag!

BALDWIN: You couldn't make me kiss my mother, if I didn't want to. I wouldn't do anything for a police officer just because he told me to.[39]

A month later, in November of 1924, the defendants were tried in the Paterson Court of Special Sessions. The indictment charged that they

together with divers over evil disposed persons to the number of five hundred . . . unlawfully, routously, riotously and tumultously did assemble and gather together then and there with force of arms . . . unlawfully, routously, riotously and tumultously did make a great noise and disturbance . . . and then and there unlawfully, routously, riotously and tumultously make and utter great and loud noises and threatenings [with the purpose and intent] to beat and assault and frighten and intimidate certain and quiet and orderly persons then and there gathered and standing . . . to disturb the public peace and to commit assault and battery upon the police officers, patrolmen and officers of the police department of the said City of Paterson, and to break, injure, damage and destroy and wreck the city hall. . . . [40]

Under a New Jersey statute of 1796 concerning unlawful assembly, a statute that had never previously been enforced but which could always be used, as it had been by Tracy to curtail any meeting which local officials disapproved, Judge Joseph A. Delaney found the defendants guilty as charged. Baldwin was sentenced to six months in the county jail; seven silk strikers indicted with him were fined fifty dollars each. "Teach the out-of-state agitator that Paterson has no need for his bellowing protests and that he is unwelcome here," wrote the *Paterson Evening News* congratulating Judge Delaney on his verdict[41] as the Ku Klux Klan of Passaic County issued a resolution calling for the mayor of Paterson to deport the strikers from the city.[42]

The conviction in the lower court was immediately appealed by the American Civil Liberties Union to the state supreme court. Samuel Untermyer, the famous sixty-nine-year-old partner of the New York City firm of Guggenheimer, Untermyer and Marshall, who for over forty years had been involved in headline cases, volunteered his services upon reading of the conviction. In a decision handed down by that court in 1927, it was held that the strikers had committed the common law offense of unlawful assembly. "The situation created by the defendants presents an analogy to a fire with obvious danger of a conflagration if not checked, and this tendency the principal defendants well knew."[43] The verdict of Judge Delaney was affirmed.

This conviction was appealed in 1928 to the highest court in New Jersey, the court of errors and appeals; and the United Front Committee of the strikers and the A.C.L.U. accepted Vanderbilt's request to make the appeal. Associated with him in the preparation of the brief were former Judge Harry V. Osborn and Dean Frank H. Sommer of New York University.

It was said that Untermyer had lost the first appeal largely through his truculency in court and that Chief Justice Gummere had voted to affirm the decision of the lower court as much because of the behavior of Untermyer as for reasons of principle. (Indeed, the eminent New York attorney had been sentenced to jail for contempt of court, but the order was later rescinded.)

Vanderbilt was as caustic with the court of errors and appeals as Untermyer had been with the supreme court, addressing them in his school-master style and suggesting repeatedly to the sixteen judges on the bench that if they paid more attention to his argument and stayed alert, they would better gather the tenor of it. This time they listened.

In stating the facts of the case, Vanderbilt told how Baldwin's procession had been led by "two beautiful girls carrying American flags." Justice Samuel Kalisch, who was both an admirer of beauty and a stickler for legal precision, looked up to see if he could trap the lawyer.

"Mr. Vanderbilt, I have read the record, and I see no evidence to support your statement that these girls were beautiful."

"Surely your honor will take judicial notice of the fact that any girl carrying the American flag is *ipso facto* beautiful," Vanderbilt answered with an air of studied innocence.

"Quite so, quite so," murmured the justice.[44]

Vanderbilt showed that the facts of the case did not establish that the assembly was unlawful; that the meeting was not illegal for want of a police or other permit, for none was required; that the fact that the police prohibited the advertised meeting in Turn Hall did not alter the lawful character of that proposed meeting or the legality of the subsequent attempt to meet in the square for there was nothing in the constitution or statutes of New Jersey vesting the chief of police with the power to suspend public assemblies at will or to pronounce a meeting illegal; that the meeting did not lay out a program in defiance of the constitutional authorities; and that therefore the conviction should be reversed.[45]

The tribunal unanimously sustained Vanderbilt's position in an opinion handed down on May 14, 1928, holding that, by the New Jersey Constitution, the strikers had a right to freely and peacefully assemble to consult for the common good, to make known their opinions to their representatives, and to petition for a redress of grievances, rights guaranteed through the centuries by the British Magna Charta and the Petition of Right, and the American Bill of Rights. In order to constitute the common law offense of unlawful assembly, it had to appear that there was an intent of the strikers to commit acts which would produce danger to the tranquility of the neighborhood and have a natural tendency to impress rational, firm, and courageous persons with well-grounded fear of a serious breach of the public peace. Wrote Justice Kalisch for the court:

It is rather startling to the most lively imagination that if this meeting was of such a turbulent and disorderly character as described in the indictment, unsupported as it is, however, by the proof, that out of forty policemen only two of them, and they without stating any facts reasonably supporting any ground for fear or alarm which would be entertained by a person of a firm and courageous mind, were seized with fear of a threatened outbreak and breach of the public peace. . . .

From the record before us we find nothing in the statement of the facts contained therein to have warranted the finding by the trial Judge that the accused were guilty of the offense of unlawful assembly.

Judgement is reversed.[46]

The jubilant American Civil Liberties Union, satisfied that "one such victory a year is enough to justify its existence and handsomely justify it,"[47] greeted the decision as "the only liberal state Supreme Court decision in a civil liberties case in recent years," a sentiment repeated in many editorials in papers across the nation which welcomed this "great victory for freedom of speech" and the "end to this disgraceful interference with the rights of the people of this state."[48]

In the early part of the century, although the concepts of freedom of speech and assembly had been treasured as cornerstones of American democracy, in actual practice they were freedoms that could be violated with surprisingly little protest. This paradox had been especially prevalent in West Virginia, Pennsylvania, and New Jersey, where employers supported by local officials and courts were accustomed to repress their workers' free expression of grievances and plans for organization. Thus *State v. Butterworth* was one of the first of a series of cases that helped close the chasm between the theory and reality of fundamental constitutional liberties.

BIG BUSINESS

Professional and financial success provided other opportunities. Recognized as one of the foremost authorities on insurance law and caught up in the golden aura of the end of the decade of the twenties when prosperity still seemed natural and growth inevitable, Vanderbilt in 1928 founded the Public Fire Insurance Company of Newark with a group of prominent insurance experts. The formation of this company was one of the most publicized events in the insurance business that year for it seemed from the start destined to success.

James T. Dargan, Jr., a member of a leading firm of New York adjustors, Windle, Burlingome and Dargan, was named president of the new company; forty-year-old Vanderbilt became chairman of the board. Together they assembled a board of directors composed of the president of the Baird Rubber and Trading Company, the vice-president of the Farmer's Loan and Trust Company, the vice-president of the Central Union Trust Company, the vice-president and general counsel of the Prudential Insurance Company, the vice-president of the Interstate Trust Company, the president of the Savings Investment and Trust Company, and the president of the Virginia-Carolina Chemical Company.

Dargan and Vanderbilt then set about raising funds to start the company, Dargan mining the riches of New York City and Vanderbilt going to his friends among the financiers, public men, businessmen, and lawyers of New Jersey. "To understand the situation," Vanderbilt explained in an interview with the *Eastern Underwriter,* "one must know something about the tremendous wealth with which Northern New Jersey is endowed: the marvelous financial resources of our section of the state; the number of unusually intelligent and powerful men who are at the helm of our finances, business and industry; of the existing courage necessary to embark upon new enterprises; and above all of the wonderful prestige of insurance itself in our community where are located some of the largest and most successful of the insurance companies. The feeling of confidence in insurance in New Jersey is extraordinary. How could it be otherwise when the insurance record there has been so brilliant?"[49]

The ease with which the two men reached, not only their goal of $5,000,000, but an oversubscription of 65 percent with no expenditures for promotional expenses, astounded financial circles. It was reported that, in raising the money, Vanderbilt's talk was of this order: "We are getting up a fire insurance company and expect to have a board of directors of these men. Are you willing to travel along with us and with them? Here is the list of directors who will probably be on the board."[50] One look at the list generally did the trick. A capital outlay of $1,000,000, a surplus of $4,000,000, and a $200,000 equipment fund were quickly established.

Never before had an insurance company been organized on such a solid basis. The remarkable financing of the company and the reputations of the officers and directors constituted sufficient reasons in those days for a scramble for the closely held stock, which climbed in the first several days of trading from $25 to $38 a share.

On May 7, 1928, the Public Fire Insurance Company began operations with headquarters in Newark and New York. In six months it had been admitted to thirty-six states, a rapid expansion made possible by its large cash reserves. By the end of the summer the assets of the company had grown by $2 million. By December, it employed 600 agents. By August 31, 1929, it had assets of $8,702,490 and 1,152 agents who had written nearly $7 million worth of policies. Dargan and Vanderbilt had raised $3 million more to found the Public

Indemnity Company so that their two companies could write practically all forms of insurance.

During the next months as the stock market teetered and began to crash, the two companies continued to prosper, but not for long. Within five years the abundance of metropolitan insurance companies competing for a rapidly dwindling volume of business coupled with the rising number of claims sparked by the continuing Depression forced the Public Fire Insurance Company and the Public Indemnity Company out of business.

Vanderbilt's feelings about the brief life of his two companies— whether he had planned to devote all his time to them or whether they were to remain one of several interests, whether he had hoped to accumulate considerable wealth, how he must have felt in having rapidly risen to financial prominence in the same city where he had grown up in a family of limited means, and how he reacted to this first major defeat in his life—are difficult to gauge for later he rarely mentioned his short career in big business or the losses he had suffered. The experience dealt him a severe financial blow in the early days of the Depression because of the amount of his own savings he poured into the formation of the company, into the purchase of its stock during the initial days of the crash to show his confidence in its stability, and later into helping settle the obligations of the companies. To avoid personal bankruptcy, he was forced in 1933 to borrow from the National State Bank of Newark $600,000 which he was to repay over a ten-year period.

It can well be assumed that the financial straits in which he found himself during the Depression years considerably altered any political ambitions he might previously have been nurturing. In late August of 1929, at the pinnacle of his business fortunes, when his activities and travels were being recorded daily by the public press, he was asked to run for the United States Senate.

I can imagine that I would fit quite well in the rogues' gallery, publicly known as the United States Senate, and I rather fancy that I could have a good time along with the other boys messing things up for the country in general. There are, however, several insuperable difficulties which I may briefly enumerate: —

1. A wife who, I think, would much prefer Short Hills to Washington.

2. Five children who have to go to school in a civilized community.

3. Some political associates in the state who need my constant watching and guidance.

4. Some large notes in various local banks which also require considerable watching and cultivation by way of periodical interest payments not to mention an occasional reduction.

I might add others, but I think the final one is controlling and completely disposes of the matter. I realize, of course, that some of the boys from time to time have taken advantage of bits of information which they have acquired at the front to clear off various notes and mortgages, but I understand that this went out of fashion with the retirement of Mr. [Albert B.] Fall. . . . So, to use the language of our distinguished Ex-President, I must say that "I do not choose to run" in 1930; at least I may say that I do not choose in 1929 to run in 1930.

His negative response, however, seemed to become less definite as he continued:

If it should happen that the aforesaid notes and mortgages are properly marked "paid in full" and "cancelled of record" and I should unexpectedly find myself in a position to retire from the active practice of law, I can think of no more interesting way to spend one's days than to follow the course outlined by you. I am therefore asking you to take this merely as a qualifying refusal of the nomination, applying only to the current year and subject to revival, on my part at least, at such time as circumstances of the patient's case make it seem desirable for him to seek new forms of excitement.[51]

Despite the continued financial success of his law practice, which enabled him to pay off the $600,000 loan in several years, and despite his growing political power in New Jersey, he thereafter humorously brushed aside all proposals to run for governor or senator. The collapse of his business ventures—which eliminated his chance of quickly fulfilling his high school prophecy (. . . senator . . . May-be!) and also Floss's prophecy ("Miss Althen has lately had her fortune told. Her fates decree she shall marry a millionaire. . . ."[52])— would be the first of several twists of fate which kept him from high national office. It was also, however, an event which would focus Vanderbilt's energy and talents increasingly into the law. And the experience of managing a large business concern, of developing and applying methods of organization and control to a far-flung enterprise, would later provide the theoretical framework for the revolution he sparked in applying principles of business administration to the administration of justice in the nation's courts.

THE BOSSES

The shadow of defeat began to slip into his life from another quarter during the early 1930's, perhaps in part because his active law practice, coupled with his effort to build the insurance companies, had drawn much of his attention away from county politics. Throughout the decade of the twenties the Essex County Republican League, still without possession of the county committee machinery and without ever receiving the assistance of the Republican organization of the city of Newark, had continued to elect many of its assembly and senate delegations and to control the Board of Chosen Freeholders. With the collateral patronage accruing to the League from its legislative and county successes and with ready allies in the neighboring counties of Burlington, Passaic, Bergen, Middlesex, Mercer, and Union, the insurgent movement had become a force to be reckoned with in New Jersey politics. It was therefore surprising that in 1931, for the first time in twelve years, the candidates for county freeholder chosen by Vanderbilt and backed by the League lost the primary election to the regular Republican organization. The reason was Jesse R. Salmon.

Sporting $500 panama hats, stocky, cigar-smoking, sixty-eight-year-old Jesse Salmon, who had been elected county chairman of the regular Republican organization of Essex in 1921, looked the part of a city boss and reveled in his reputation as one. Only once had Salmon and Vanderbilt met in the interest of party harmony—in 1921 to produce the compromise freeholder ticket between the two Republican groups. Each following year was marked by open combat between the two strong-willed Republican leaders, making the history of Essex politics from 1922 to 1935 the history of a running battle between Salmon and Vanderbilt.

It was commonly suspected that Salmon was involved in bootlegging operations, that he received a cut on every truckload of whiskey that was transported through Essex County, and that he was helping to support his Republican organization through his illegal profits. In the fall of 1923, the Anti-Saloon League filed a petition for an investigation of the source of the regular Republican organization's campaign funds, and the Essex Republican League at the same time asked Salmon to tell publicly the story of his primary campaign financial transactions. As was his habit when his affairs were under investigation, Salmon disappeared. A month later the newspapers chronicled the rescue of several men from a burning cruiser off the coast of Florida; one of the men on the rescue list: Jesse R. Salmon.[53]

The Republican League regularly continued to challenge the county chairman to reveal the source of his large campaign funds, challenges to which he never responded beyond dismissing them as "the quintessence of political asininity."[54] During the next primary

campaign, in September of 1924, Vanderbilt attacked Salmon and his
"mysterious money" in a humorous speech that the *Newark Evening
News* reprinted and that the Essex commuters talked about for days:

> Early in July a group of estimable men decided to take a cruise in the good
> ship "Mysterious Money," Captain Jesse R. Salmon commanding. They
> thought they were out for a jolly trip, sailing somewhere between [United
> States] Secretary of State Hughes' 12-mile limit and Senator [Walter] Edge's
> 3-mile limit, but at all times close enough to shore to be able to take to the
> long boat in event of storm.
>
> In August storm warnings were sent out, but our jolly adventurers failed to
> heed them. They were busily engaged in constructing an immortal docu-
> ment, which they called a platform, that would be comparable in their
> rollicking minds with the Mayflower Compact. The only difference of course
> is that the Mayflower Compact is immortal because it says something;
> whereas the storm-tossed platform is memorable only because, when read
> and reread, it says absolutely nothing.
>
> Then on Wednesday evening of this week the searchlight of public
> opinion was turned on the good ship "Mysterious Money" by the Essex
> County Republican League. The captain and his crew, who are his candi-
> dates on the Essex County Republican organization ticket, were clearly
> exposed to the public view. On Thursday, a leading newspaper of the
> County repudiated not only the candidates on Captain Salmon's organization
> ticket, but also condemned the leadership of the captain, as well as ridicul-
> ing their immortal platform of 1924 for taking absolutely no stand on any of
> the issues of the campaign.
>
> What does this carefree crew of candidates do? Some would ask the
> captain to jump overboard. Some, more panic stricken than the others, would
> throw him overboard. They interviewed the captain. He refuses to walk the
> plank. They consider heaving him overboard. They debate all night. They
> decide he is too big for them to throw overboard. What shall they do? With
> one chorus the jolly fellows cry, "Let's leave the ship. Let's take to the long
> boat." So, strapping the captain to the mast as he sleeps, they fill the long
> boat with provisions ready to take to the open sea.[55]

Despite these charges and the fact that they caused Salmon to
disappear more than ever from the public eye, the Essex County
Republican League failed for several years to substantiate its suspi-
cions.

Throughout the decade of the twenties, Salmon had little voice in
county Republican matters and lean patronage pickings because of
the strength of the League. Nevertheless, regardless of the rumors
and allegations about his personal-profit leadership of the party, he
continued to draw the support of many respectable Republican

businessmen and citizens of Essex who had always backed the regular Republican organization and continued as county chairman. Eventually, his day came. In 1931, a great number of county employees who resented their first salary cuts made necessary by the continuing Depression shifted their support from the League Republicans to the Salmon organization, which seemed to have more money to dispense than ever. This shift helped carry the Salmon slate to victory in the primaries, but to little avail for in the November elections three Democratic freeholder candidates were elected for the first time since 1918.

In 1932, although Vanderbilt staged a strong campaign for the League candidates, they were badly defeated by the Salmon ticket in the primaries, as was the League's attempt in November to capture a majority of the county committee seats to displace Salmon from the chairmanship.

When in 1933 Vanderbilt entered no ticket, it seemed to many that he and the League had finally lost the firm grip they had held on the county government. Even his position as county counsel seemed precarious when a Salmon effort to defeat his reappointment in 1932 almost succeeded. Vanderbilt later wrote: "I for one, was so discouraged by the seeming apathy of the public as to whether they had decent government or not, so worn down by the continual misrepresentation of my motives for simply doing my plain duty as a public officeholder, so depressed by the chronic cynicism of the press as to every effort to improve political conditions, that I was almost convinced that it would be folly to attempt another fight against entrenched political corruption in our party."[56]

Ironically, it was Jesse Salmon who played the lead role in sponsoring Vanderbilt's rally. At a Republican political dinner attended by many of the most prominent citizens of the county at the Essex Club in Newark on December 28, 1933, Salmon boasted in an informal after-dinner talk that "he had not waited for opportunity to knock at his door but that he had kicked the ——— door down himself and had crashed through to make seven hundred thousand dollars with the bootleggers."[57] Many of the guests were astonished to hear Salmon himself admit what had before been only the subject of gossip and speculation, and immediately pledged their support to the Essex Republican League.

With a group of followers that included new additions like William H. Seely, a former editor of the *Newark Evening News*, president of the Newark Board of Education and an influential businessman in the city, Everett Colby, a founder of the New Idea movement, and the Reverend Lester H. Clee, the dynamic pastor of the large Second Presbyterian Church of Newark, Vanderbilt in 1934 reorganized his independent Republican group, changed its name from the Essex County Republican League to the simple title "Clean Government" to underscore the continuity of the two organizations—which Salmon ridiculed as the "Sanitary Squad"[58]—and prepared a platform and slate to defeat the Salmon organization.

Sommer's New Idea movement had failed to take root years earlier because its leaders, in their idealism, had neglected the practical side of politics. If the Essex League was to continue as an effective movement, as Clean Government, Vanderbilt reasoned, it had to be the only Republican organization in the county. A good cause and good candidates were not enough; the only way in which organized political control could be continually combatted by independent forces was through carefully planned effort, matching the party machine with a militant organization, close contact with the editors of the daily papers, and an old-fashioned door-to-door registration campaign.

The new strategy paid off. At the primary on May 17, 1934, the Clean Government candidates for the freeholder and assembly seats won to a man. "The smashing victory of the Clean Government slate demonstrates that the Republicans of Essex County went to the polls with a grim determination to end machine domination," reported the *News*. "They had ample reason for their course and they did a fine job."[59] And the next day the weekly magazine *The Oranges* praised Vanderbilt's work:

The margin by which his ticket swept to victory is so commanding as to leave no doubt in the minds of anyone who is responsible for it. The movement was Vanderbilt from beginning to end. It was he who picked the ticket, encouraged those selected to run, took the brunt of the campaign and deserves the reward of victory. After facing three disastrous defeats in succession, any man without supreme confidence in himself would have given up leadership of the opposition to others. The persistence and the skill he has shown cannot be overestimated. If I do not mistake, New Jersey has at last got what she has needed for years: a Republican boss who has intelligence enough to know that a political party cannot steal its way to victory, and honor enough at least to give the public a chance in its eternal fight with political cut-throats.[60]

As the 1934 general election approached, Salmon pledged his support to the Democratic slate to cut into the Republican vote, proclaiming that if he got nothing else in the campaign, he was going to get Vanderbilt. On a Tuesday morning, within an hour of each other, two prominent Newark attorneys with regular Republican affiliation came to warn Vanderbilt of Salmon's intentions. "Both said they had not slept and they looked it. They told me that the order of the High Command was 'Smear Vanderbilt,' that there was no hope for the organization ticket unless Vanderbilt was destroyed once and for all."[61]

Every night for two weeks a speech was made by a Salmon Republican denouncing Vanderbilt as the "lily white statesman," "the political renegade," and "the million dollar prize receiver," and accusing Vanderbilt of a "lust for power," of a desire to be county chairman, of innumerable conflicts of interest between his positions of county counsel and Republican politician, of filing briefs for private clients and then, as county counsel, sitting down to advise the Essex County Board of Taxation how to decide the cases, of improperly assuming the administration of lunacy estates as county counsel, sometimes turning the handling of them over to his brother, Leslie Vanderbilt, of having the bonds in these lunacy cases written by his Public Indemnity Company, and of soliciting $1 million worth of county policies for his Public Fire Insurance Company. "Let Mr. Vanderbilt tell the citizens of Essex County how he, the Moses of the so-called Clean Government group, secured $925,089 worth of insurance on public buildings for the company which he sponsored. . . . Does Vanderbilt stand for clean government or does Vanderbilt stand for government that pays Vanderbilt well in many and devious ways?"[62]

Vanderbilt publicly set forth the facts surrounding each accusation and stated that if the county freeholders found anything illegal or unethical in his conduct, he would "forthwith resign as County Counsel. . . ."[63] Each charge was later proved false, but the fight continued viciously to election day. Wrote Vanderbilt late in October: "I have never been so busy in my life—in court every day and politics after court and evenings, not to mention law school. The campaign will be over three weeks from tomorrow. . . . I think we are going to win because the public is a little fed up on bosses hereabouts and is ready for any kind of change. As usual, I have been taking my poundings in the press, but ultimately I hope to even things up a bit."[64] In the November election he did; the complete Clean Government slate won handily, delivering the first fatal blow to Salmon's Republican organization.

The next year the Clean Government group launched another

campaign against Salmon to wring from him the chairmanship of the Republican county committee and the remnants of his county influence. To carry weight in state politics, it was necessary to show that the group could run the party organization in Essex, for measures sponsored by Clean Government in the legislature were often stymied when other counties would recognize only the official county Republican organization. Clean Government therefore nominated candidates, not only to the county, assembly, and senate seats, but also to a majority of the seats of the county committee, a committee of 1,152 consisting of two delegates from each of the 576 election districts. When the entire slate won the 1935 primary nomination, Jesse Salmon announced his retirement as county chairman. A Vanderbilt candidate, Stanley S. Nauright, was elected to replace him.

From then on, Clean Government, never for many years in danger of defeat at the polls, assumed an increasingly active role in state affairs, and Vanderbilt, as its leader, became a figure of increasing political importance. Always something of a rarity in the practical world of New Jersey politics, Vanderbilt played a role in the political operations of the Hall of Records in Newark and of the State House at Trenton that was the subject of continued debate during the twenty-eight years of his leadership. Not dependent on politics for his living, he spent at most several hours a day on political matters even at the height of the campaigns. He rarely attended political dinners and meetings, even less frequently made public speeches, and had little time to spend in social contacts.

Beyond being a delegate to the 1936, 1940, and 1944 Republican National Conventions, Vanderbilt never ran for public office because, as he joked, he did not have "the back slapping qualities required for election to popular office,"[65] and with his distinguished name he could never have convinced the voters that he was "just a poor boy off the farm."[66] In a more serious vein, when asked in 1933 to run for governor, he had stated that he "would be utterly unwilling to sacrifice my present political independence for any elective post for I know full well that most of the real things in our political life are not accomplished by the men holding official positions but by those who have groped and struggled mentally with the problems that always confront one in politics and which constitute a large part of its joy and fascination."[67]

The words with which he later described his responsibilities as the leader of the Clean Government party summarized his role as clearly as the pages of speculation of the political columnists: "I ran the Essex Republican Organization, with plenty of advice, but with the ultimate decisions my own."[68]

His primary concern in managing Republican affairs was in finding citizens who would run for office under the Clean Government banner. The candidates selected were citizens who he felt could win and maintain the confidence of their constituency, men and women who would work to create an honest, effective government in the public interest, from Mahlon S. Drake, the president of the Irvington National Bank, to Mrs. Edith H. Colby, a leader in the New Jersey women's suffrage movement, to Ralph DeCamp, the proprietor of the DeCamp Bus Lines—all amateurs in the sport of politics but men and women who brought to the game high ideals and enthusiasm, and the intelligence, time, and financial security to hold public office as a duty but not as a business.

It was Vanderbilt's conviction that in those communities where lawyers, doctors, and the leading businessmen were taking their part in local government, there would be a decent, self-respecting government, but in those communities where the natural leaders were too much concerned with their own affairs and too absorbed in their own business, there would be a poor, inefficient government. "It is not so much that the men nominated by the machine are not good men individually," the *Newark Evening News* once noted about Salmon's candidates, "but they represent a system which when the showdown comes, the men's loyalty to the machine comes ahead of loyalty to the taxpayers."[69]

The Clean Government candidates who filled the seats on the Board of Chosen Freeholders and in the legislature were the types of people who on their own volition probably would never have entered politics. Vanderbilt's annual responsibility was to induce them into running for office, a race from which he found most men would shrink despite the fact that they were not called upon to put up campaign contributions and despite the fact that, by running on his ticket, they were almost sure to be elected.

He discovered that a major stumbling block in recruiting candidates was the woman of the household, who dreaded the rough and tumble to which her husband would be exposed. He learned from experience how to overcome this feminine opposition. "When the good lady begins to hesitate, you just ask her, 'Won't you pray over it?' No woman can turn you down on that. Then the next step is to say, 'Why shouldn't we pray right now?' If you can get them to pray right on the spot and make your appeal a very personal one, you will find that there are very few women who have the courage to turn God down."[70]

He found he rarely had to encourage a freeholder or assemblyman to run for reelection. They all wanted to.

Although Vanderbilt received the advice of delegates from the different municipalities, he would make the final decision of who would run on the Clean Government ticket. On the morning of the last day for filing nominating petitions, he would call a breakfast meeting at the Robert Treat Hotel in Newark, a meeting attended by the township chairman of the Republican organization in each of the suburbs and some of the ward chairmen from the sixteen wards of Newark. The candidates would be presented, and the delegates asked for an endorsement of the ticket. While perhaps not democratic, this political device had the advantage of making it almost impossible to file petitions in opposition and so held together the loosely molded organization. The candidates were of such caliber that—from the standpoint of selecting the best men and women for office, rather than the most expedient political choices—it was difficult to criticize their credentials. The endorsement of the ticket was always unanimous.

It was hard to convince many Democrats and some Republicans that these hand-picked Essex politicians were not Vanderbilt puppets responding when the wires were pulled. Two factors made such a political relationship improbable. The first was that, with the range of his legal and professional responsibilities, Vanderbilt did not have the time to oversee the affairs of a county of 900,000. "I have always wanted primarily to be a good lawyer and one cannot be a good lawyer and still have the time to be a political boss, minding everybody else's business for him."[71] The second factor was that the candidates selected were the type of people who were jealous of their political independence, who would not act on any basis but their own reasoning. While it was inevitable that the freeholders and assemblymen selected shared Vanderbilt's basic political philosophy as espoused by the Clean Government movement and thus were often united on fundamental issues, the degree of dissension among the Clean Government officeholders indicated that they were not blind loyalists.

The voters learned that they could rely on the campaign promises of the League and Clean Government candidates and depend on their devotion to the county once in office, for the years beginning with the election of Henry Hines and Edwin Ball to the board were marked by a constant vigilance of county business affairs. Contractors were held strictly to their bids despite claims that they had made mistakes in their estimates or neglected by oversight to include certain costs. If a contractor failed to meet his promise, all future bids from him were rejected. Agreements were reached with municipalities in Essex for cost-sharing programs. A legal assistant was added to the prosecutor's office to collect the fines and forfeitures which had previously been disregarded. Appointive positions were consolidated; sinecures, such as the position of county veterinarian and county supervisor of roads, were abolished. The expense accounts of the members of the board were cut to a realistic minimum, putting an end to trips all over the United States at county expense.

During the 1920's as the waste and extravagance that had plagued the county were being reduced, the resources of Essex were reallocated and channeled by the board into constructive directions to improve the standard of living of the county. Among other services, the county government was able to finance a program of welfare relief to help cover the cost of hospitalization of indigents, to provide old age assistance, and to aid dependent and handicapped children; to finance the construction of three large vocational schools, a modern highway system to accommodate the onslaught of automobile traffic, and a Hall of Records to consolidate the county offices; and to finance the rebuilding or renovation of every county institution, including the hospital for contagious disease, the tuberculosis sanitarium, the county penitentiary, and the hospital for the insane.

During the years of the Essex Republican League and Clean Government, the financial conservatism of the Board of Chosen Freeholders allowed an expansion of services and an improvement of roads, parks, and institutions but at a cost well within the ability of the people to pay. This was in contrast to the many counties that went deeply into debt during the days of easy government spending in the twenties and then found themselves bordering on disaster during the Depression years.

The first ten years during which the League controlled the board, from 1921 to 1931, were years of growth in Essex County as the population swelled from 652,089 to 833,513. While the population was increasing, the tax rate decreased from $6.22 per thousand in 1920 to $4.71 per thousand in 1935. Yearly the county debt declined from a high of $47,085,000 in 1931. The elected officials of Clean Government, individuals whose diverse ideas and temperaments often led to the same kind of bitter disagreements that could arise on any board, were at least united in their attempt to realize a sound financial administration of the county government by adhering to the simple formula of weighing every proposed expenditure against its effect on the tax rate. Through cautious business sense, the board was able to provide superior county services for a large metropolitan population at less cost than similar counties in New Jersey or New

York, a fact which the appreciative taxpayer did not fail to recognize on election days during the difficult years of economic turmoil.

Even as the population of Essex shifted throughout this era from a solid Republican county to a narrowly held Republican county and despite the great Roosevelt avalanche in 1936, when he carried the county by 33,000 votes, the voters of Essex never failed to return their Republican freeholders to office. Democratic Governor Charles Edison in 1945 appraised Vanderbilt's role in Essex politics: "We should distinguish between bosses who are in it for personal power and profit and political leaders. Leadership is necessary in political parties. Arthur Vanderbilt is sometimes called a boss, but his leadership has produced the best government in any county in the state."[72]

With the rise of Clean Government and an assembly delegation of twelve from Essex—the largest delegation of any New Jersey county—Clean Government assemblymen, never defeated in any election after 1936, held a veto power over all New Jersey legislation and fought for the same goals of governmental economy in the state that had been achieved in the county. From 1935 to 1942, only one state bond issue was able to pass the legislature, a $21 million issue for unemployment relief in 1939 that the Essex delegation pared down from a proposed $100 million. In the same period, the bonded debt of New Jersey fell from $109,765,000 to $58,888,000. The Essex delegation opposed unnecessary borrowing for state purposes, supported legislation regulating municipal government borrowing which helped reduce local government debt from $1,080,000,000 in 1935 to $856,000,000 in 1941, and opposed any new forms of taxation. It was at the forefront of the battle for honest elections in New Jersey—securing the establishment of an office of superintendent of elections and commissioner of elections, and campaigning incessantly for the introduction of voting machines in every county—and advocated a thorough revision of New Jersey's antiquated constitution.

The Clean Government representatives were never popular in state politics because of their drive for government economy and because of their willingness to cross party lines to advance their goals. It was, however, the opposition they met that led to the continued vitality of the Essex group movement, just as the laxity of the Republican Old Guard from 1917 to 1919 had made possible the emergence of the insurgent League and just as Salmon had been the ogre that the League and Clean Government could annually parade before the voters.

Much of the opposition to the statewide measures Clean Government sponsored arose from the machine of the powerful boss of Hudson County, Mayor Frank Hague of Jersey City. "Politics," Mayor Hague had said in an interview with *Collier's* in 1938, "is a business. That's what the reformers don't get. They think it's a sort of revival meeting, with nothing to do but nominate some bird who's never seen a polling place, make a lot of speeches about clean government, and then sit back and wait for voters to hit the sawdust trail. It's a laugh. You got to have organization, and not just for a few weeks before election, but all the year round. Understand?"[73]

Politics had always been a business for Hague. Raised in the Horseshoe of Jersey City—a poor Irish immigrant neighborhood that had been gerrymandered by a Republican legislature to isolate all the Democratic voters in one assembly district—Hague had grown up in an environment where ward politics was the only ladder out of the slums and where taking care of one's friends was considered a basic function of government. Dropping out of school after the sixth grade with an ambition to be a policeman, he became a Jersey City constable at the age of twenty-one, in 1897. Forthright and efficient in his work, he later became deputy sheriff, sergeant-at-arms, city hall custodian, street and water commissioner, director of public safety, and, in 1917, with some intricate political maneuvering,[74] mayor of Jersey City.

Bordering Essex County on the Passaic River, across the Hudson River from downtown New York, Hudson County was a major eastern railroad center with nine trunk lines terminating in the county and with almost one-third of Jersey City composed of railroad terminals, warehouses, and freight yards. To meet the growing payroll of his political organization, Hague hoped to increase the assessments on the railroads by $93 million above the $67 million they were already being taxed. The State Board of Taxes and Assessments denied his request and allowed an increase of only $185,870. Hague concluded that the only way for him to survive as a politician was to gain control of the State Board by helping elect a governor who would repay the political debt by appointing a compatible Board. Therefore, in 1919 almost immediately after his appeal for higher assessments was refused, Hague announced that Edward I. Edwards, a fifty-five-year-old self-made man who was president of the First National Bank of Jersey City, would seek the Democratic nomination for governor. When Edwards defeated James R. Nugent in the September primaries and won the governorship in the general election, Hague succeeded Nugent as the Democratic leader of New Jersey. Every commissioner on the State Board of Taxes was replaced, and the new board immediately approved Hague's railroad property assessment.

Simultaneously, politics more than ever seemed to become a business for Hague, and a profitable business. Although his annual salary as mayor never exceeded $8,000 and although except for his public office as mayor he had no other gainful occupation, in 1919 Hague acquired property in Jersey City for $12,000. In 1921 for $63,000 he bought more land on which the Duncan Hall Apartments were built; the same year he bought property for a summer home in Deal, New Jersey, for $18,000 and 150 shares of stock in the First National Bank of Jersey City for $37,500. In 1922 he acquired 100 shares of stock in the Trust Company of New Jersey for $34,500. In 1926 he purchased property on Gifford Avenue in Jersey City at a cost of $27,500, also buying 34 more shares of the Trust Company of New Jersey for $8,469 and an ornate Spanish castle at Deal for $65,000. In 1927 he improved his home and property at Deal for $59,520 and bought 68 more shares of the Trust Company of New Jersey for $23,826. He bought 134 more shares the following year for $13,500.

Mayor Hague, his wife, and their son Frank, Jr., were living like millionaires. They had a cook, two maids, and a handyman to care for their fourteen-room apartment in Jersey City, a chauffeur to drive their armored Cadillac and a retinue of bodyguards to travel with them, several servants and two gardeners at their palatial estate on the Jersey shore. They took yearly voyages to Europe, winter vacations at their oceanside home on Florida's Biscayne Bay, and had annual leases on suites at the Waldorf-Astoria in New York City.

Hague's sudden conspicuous affluence and the fact that all his financial transactions were in cash was enough to cause the legislature of 1928 to appoint a joint committee to probe the affairs of Jersey City and Hudson County.

The [Clarence] Case Committee was able to determine that political revenue was being raised in Jersey City by several unusual means: through condemnation proceedings in which Hague, through a front, would buy property which Jersey City would soon condemn and buy from him at several times the price he had paid; through proprietors of movie theaters in Hoboken and Jersey City who paid large sums of money to induce municipal agents of those cities to refrain from enforcing the Sunday closing laws; through bus franchise fees which were illegally manipulated; through a "three per cent club" which Hague initiated, a system by which 3 percent of the annual salary of each Jersey City employee was taken out of his paycheck by taking 3 percent of the city treasury funds and budget appropriations held for salaries and using these resources for political purposes; and through "Rice Pudding Day," the annual day for contributions to the Democratic machine which were a condition to obtain or retain public employment.

Calling 335 witnesses whose testimony filled 8,200 pages, the Case Committee seemed ready to initiate legal action against Hague that would end his political career and put him in jail. The Committee subpoenaed Mayor Hague in September of 1929 and, after a preliminary examination, asked him ten questions concerning his bank accounts and his methods of financing his real estate and stock purchases. Upon Hague's refusal to answer each of the questions, the New Jersey legislature ordered him arrested for contempt. Hague submitted himself for arrest to vice-chancellor John J. Fallon, who before being elevated to the New Jersey bench had been the county counsel of Hudson County and an important member of Hague's political organization. The vice-chancellor concluded that Hague's arrest was without legal justification and ordered him immediately released from custody.

Fallon's action was promptly challenged by the senate and general assembly, which charged that the vice-chancellor was biased and prejudiced in favor of Hague; but the chancellor decided in the case of *In re Hague,* 103 N.J. Eq. 505 (1928), that prejudice growing out of business, political, or social relations was not sufficient to disqualify a judge. The real ground was cut from under the Case Committee when the court of errors and appeals held in a six-to-six decision in *In re Hague,* 123 N.J. Eq. 475 (1930), that investigations of alleged violations of the criminal law by public officials were strictly judicial in nature, and that under the New Jersey Constitution the legislature had no power to conduct such an investigation. Hague therefore could not be held for contumacy as a witness for, according to the ruling, which ran counter to federal court decisions, he had no obligation to testify before the legislature.

The Case Committee was therefore unable to prove conclusively the existence of a conspiracy of Jersey City Democratic politicians which was wasting the public money under cover of legal forms and through the extortion of the 3 percent tax, or that financial gains were accruing to Mayor Hague and other politicians involved in his Democratic machine at the expense of the public treasury.

That there was a well-oiled political machine in Hudson County controlled by Mayor Hague, that the price of doing business with the city government came to include, as a matter of routine, kickbacks to the leadership, was never a secret. As public needs were neglected and private fortunes amassed, many of the scars of this type of political system began to mark the city. When Hague had come to power in 1917, Hudson County and neighboring Essex County were similar in population, in assessed valuation, in their total tax levy and levy per capita. During the same years that the Board of Chosen Freeholders was managing the finances of Essex County, Hague was pursuing a different economic route in Jersey City and Hudson County. Figures taken from the reports of the New Jersey State Tax Department show that in the first twenty years of his leadership, the tax rate in Jersey City tripled, assessments doubled, the city budget went up 450 percent, the city debt increased 500 percent, and the debt charges soared 725 percent. Taxpayers in Jersey City paid at least four times as much for their local government as the taxpayers in any city of comparable size in the United States, and Jersey City owed more money than any municipality with anywhere near its population.[75]

What the highest-taxed city in the United States received in return was an invincible political machine. The city and county were organized for political purposes into a clear chain of command, from precinct workers to precinct captains to ward lieutenants to ward bosses to Mayor Hague. Food, clothing, and coal were distributed to the poor, and an endless array of city payroll jobs were created to reward the politically faithful, including such improbable full-time occupations as picking up boxes that fell off trucks on a one-block stretch of roadway, keeping ballot boxes in repair, "foreman of vacuum cleaners," "cuspidor cleaners," and "supervisor of sinks."

As supporters of the Hague machine found themselves favored by the munificence of the city, so the disloyal were taught a lesson. Mail could be withheld or opened before delivery. Telephones could be tapped. Business licenses could be suspended. Theaters and apartment houses could be condemned as fire or health hazards. Tax assessments could be raised. Citizens could be jailed or deported from the city.

Hague's retaliation against the city's major daily newspaper, the *Jersey Journal*, which had repeatedly criticized his regime and exposed his financial deals, provided an example of his strong-arm methods. Any city or county employee caught reading that paper was summarily fired. The *Journal's* property was reassessed and a heavy tax increase imposed. Malicious public charges were made against the owners of the paper. Firemen and policemen distributed door-to-door leaflets denouncing the paper. *Journal* delivery boys were arrested for violating child labor laws. Businesses found it prudent to discontinue their advertising in the *Journal*. Then the police and firemen returned on their door-to-door sweep through the city soliciting subscriptions for the *Journal's* rival. Finally, the *Jersey Journal* realized that it had not been fair to the mayor. Favorable articles about Hague and his administration regularly began to fill the pages. Stores resumed their advertising. Charges were dropped against the owners of the paper. And city employees were once more allowed to read the *Journal*.

But even the assured votes of all his supporters were not enough for statewide political purposes. Hague's ability to conjure up great majorities in the gubernatorial elections with his "one day Democrats" was as notorious as his practice of losing the poll books by fire after elections to destroy evidence of ballot fraud. In Jersey City, more people were registered as voters than there were adults eligible to vote. "Apparently," stated an exposé of Hague's regime in the *New York Evening Post*, "in Jersey City babies crawl from their cribs to register, the insane escape from asylums, the sick leave their beds, the dead rise from their graves and thousands of persons materialize out of nowhere."[76] When such weapons were launched against the state Republican party, which often found itself wracked by factionalism, Hague was easily able to elect most of New Jersey's governors from 1920 until 1940—Democrats Edward I. Edwards in 1920, George S. Silzer in 1923,[77] A. Harry Moore in 1926, 1932, and 1938, and Charles Edison in 1941. Even the two Republican exceptions, Governors Morgan F. Larson in 1928 and Harold G. Hoffman in 1935, soon found themselves seeing eye to eye with Mayor Hague. For example, Hoffman's campaign pledge of "No Additional Taxes" was broken the day after his term began when he sent a lawyer to Albany to get sample forms for a sales tax, an income tax, and a corporate franchise tax which he and Hague in alliance attempted to impose on New Jersey.[78]

Since the governors appointed the members of the state administrative agencies, boards, and commissions, the county prosecutors, the attorney general, and all county and state judges, it proved difficult to bring charges against Hague in court, as the Case Committee had discovered. Some state judges, a remarkable number of whom were from Hudson County and had been loyal supporters of the mayor before their elevation to the bench, aided the Hague machine by ruling in favor of Hague and his followers in the litigation in which he was involved. The most publicized example of his circle of patronage occurred on February 20, 1939, when Governor

A. Harry Moore announced that he had appointed Mayor Hague's son, thirty-four-year-old Frank Hague, Jr., who had failed to graduate from either of the two law schools he had entered, to a judgeship on the highest tribunal in the state, the court of errors and appeals, because, Moore stated, he knew the appointment would "make his dad happy."[79] As a letter to the *New York Times* put it, "When Big Hague says, 'I am the law,' Little Hague can answer from the bench, 'You tell 'em Pop.' "[80]

Although both houses of the legislature were Republican throughout Hague's career, except in 1932, and might have formed an effective balance to his power, he seemed to be able to exert a subtle influence on the state legislators. There existed in the senate and general assembly what the editorial writers called "Hague Republicans"—Republican legislators who in their public statements vigorously decried the graft and corruption in Hudson County but who never used their power to check Hague's control over New Jersey. By the late 1920's, Hague's power was seen as "infiltrating through insidious means into every corner of the state."[81]

Clean Government first clashed with the Hague machine in the gubernatorial election of 1937. Elected to the general assembly in 1934 as a Clean Government candidate, Reverend Lester Clee had become its speaker in 1935 and a state senator in 1936. Running for governor in 1937, the popular Clee rolled up a vote of 281,000 in the Republican primaries to beat incumbent Governor Harold G. Hoffman. The unprecedented majority of 45,000 that Essex gave to Clee was in part the result of the evenings that Vanderbilt had spent at the telephone for several months personally obtaining the pledges of 1,000 committeemen and committeewomen to get out the vote as they never had before.

When the extent of Clee's support in the primaries became evident, Hague persuaded A. Harry Moore to resign from the United States Senate and return to New Jersey to run for a third term as governor, for it seemed that no other Democrat could beat the Republican candidate. Although in the general election on November 3, 1937, Dr. Clee won every county of the state except one by a total margin of 84,000 votes, he was defeated by A. Harry Moore through the vote that Hague piled up in Hudson County, a vote that turned out to be only 1,000 less than the 130,000 vote majority Hague had promised to give Moore before the election.

Clee claimed he was robbed of the governorship by the fraudulent vote of Jersey City and set about to prove it. The total vote in Jersey City was 145,000. Giving the city every benefit of the doubt, Clee's counsellors calculated that, if as many as 90 percent of all eligible voters had registered and 90 percent of the registered voters had voted, Jersey City could have produced at most a vote of 119,336. Added weight was given to the charge of ballot fraud by superintendent of elections John Ferguson, whose job it was to insure that honest elections were held throughout the state. Ferguson testified that in the Moore-Clee gubernatorial election in Jersey City "[I]ntimidation was the order of the day. In front of one polling place I counted two police captains in uniform, a captain in plain clothes, two detectives in plain clothes, one Jersey City Commissioner and ten uniformed policemen. Of what earthly value were my two election deputies there? The police officers laughed at them, the police officers swore at them and told them that if they opened their mouths they would wake up in the hospital."[82] Many of Ferguson's election deputies signed affidavits that they had been bribed, intimidated, arrested, and even beaten and confined to jail on election day by Hague's police. Further, from a brief inspection that investigators had been able to make of two Jersey City poll books, it was found, for example, that in the first district of the first ward, there was a vote of 433 for A. Harry Moore and 1 for Lester H. Clee, a result which seemed unusual because in the primary elections 103 Republican votes had been cast. David H. Wiener, one of the counsel for the investigating committee, remarked, "I want to point out to the Committee ballot number 434, apparently the only Republican vote counted. . . . It appears to have been counted only because it was marked with a red pencil and could not have been erased without doing definite damage to the ballot. . . ."[83]

Clee and his counsellors challenged the Hudson vote several days after the election, and Mayor Hague in turn challenged Clee to proceed with an investigation:

Ever since I have been in politics, which is many years, all I have heard from Republican leaders is fraud and corruption in Hudson County. . . . I say to Senator Clee and his cohorts: Now is the time for your recount. I dare you to come into Jersey City or any other city in this county and proceed with your recount. Let me make a special request, that you come into Jersey City and open every box in order that you and your followers will be silenced forever. . . . I cannot too strongly say to Senator Clee and the Republican Party: I dare you to come into Jersey City. . . .[84]

Hague was confident that Clee could not raise the money necessary for the recount, but when the $9,795 was produced, Hague thereafter charged that the proposed recount was a "sinister" attempt to force the use of voting machines in Hudson County. Clee's attorneys petitioned Chief Justice Thomas J. Brogan—previously one of Mayor Hague's personal legal assistants, his counsel when he appeared before the Case Committee, the selection of Governor A. Harry Moore as associate justice of the New Jersey Supreme Court in 1932 and as chief justice in 1933—for permission to review the poll books to examine and compare the signatures contained in the poll books with the signatures of the alleged registered voters contained in the signature copy register. Clee's attorneys showed Chief Justice Brogan the results of the partial recount of just two poll books: men in the insane asylum had voted; a rabbi who had not lived in Jersey City for three years had voted; votes had been cast in the name of citizens who had moved out of the district; these citizens who had moved signed affidavits that they had not voted in Hudson County in the election; people who were known on election day to have been on their deathbeds had voted; ballots had been torn, had tobacco juice on them, showed unmistakable signs of erasure, and others showed that where voters had failed to vote for the proper candidate, their errors had been corrected, not always with the same kind of pencil or pen. Chief Justice Brogan declared in *Lester H. Clee v. A. Harry Moore*, 119 N.J.L. 215 (1937), that the supreme court lacked power to permit the requested full examination in advance of the trial between Clee and Moore contesting Moore's victory.

On January 17, 1938, a month after this decision was handed down, the New Jersey Assembly authorized an investigating committee to get the poll books from Jersey City, but commissioner of registration Charles F. Stoebling, the Hudson County political leader who kept the books, suddenly fell ill, his physicians refused to let the committee question him, and Jersey City police put his apartment and office under twenty-four-hour guard. The committee sought the aid of the state police, but the attorney general of New Jersey, David T. Wilentz, an appointee of Governor Moore, would not let the police enter Jersey City except on the request of the mayor of the city or the governor of the state, requests that were not forthcoming from Hague or Moore.

With Clee's second petition to challenge the Moore victory in court, Chief Justice Brogan held in *In re Clee*, 119 N.J.L. 310 (1938), that the statement in the petition that illegal votes were cast for the successful candidate—a statement based upon comparisons of the signatures in the poll books with the register of voters in a single district—was insufficient, too vague and uncertain to warrant a consideration of the charge. In addition, the chief justice refused to order a grand jury investigation, a refusal based on the argument that it was the duty of the courts to uphold an election unless it clearly appeared that it was illegal, and on the argument that fraud was a conclusion of law and therefore could not be charged in general terms, that it was necessary to state specific facts from which fraud could be legitimately concluded.

Shortly after Chief Justice Brogan's opinion was delivered, it was announced by Jersey City officials that the poll books from the Moore-Clee election had been lost in a fire.

IV Jersey Justice, 1930–1939

JUSTICE DENIED

In New Jersey in the early decades of the twentieth century, the effects of rapid industrialization, urbanization, and population growth were overburdening the state's colonial judicial system. The result was a labyrinth of confusion and delay in the courts that came to be known as "Jersey justice." Lawyers and litigants alike told of their experiences with the New Jersey courts, epitomized in the story of one attorney who argued a case before a vice-chancellor of the court of chancery who consistently delivered his opinions years after trial. After several years, the vice-chancellor sent his clerk to the attorney to inform him that his decision in this case would be handed down on the following Monday. When the clerk returned and reported that the attorney had not seemed interested and that he had said the vice-chancellor could "go to hell," the outraged judge called to demand an explanation.

"No, sir, I didn't say that," the lawyer explained. "I said that my client is dead, and so far as I know everyone else who was interested in the case is dead, and I suspect they have gone to hell for what they said about you."[1]

It was the collision of one of the most rapidly developing states with the nation's most archaic state judicial system that made problems which would soon plague many courts first obvious and critical in New Jersey.

The conglomerate organization of the judicial establishment which in part accounted for the backward state of the courts was the result of the historical origins of New Jersey's judicial system. By an order of 1702 from Queen Anne to Edward, Lord Cornbury, the royal governor of the province of New Jersey, the Supreme Court of New Jersey was patterned after the courts of the Queen's Bench, Common Pleas, and Exchequer. The six other courts of colonial New Jersey— the justice's court, the county courts of sessions and common pleas, the vice-admiralty court, the prerogative court, the chancery court, and the highest court, even above the supreme court, the court of appeals, consisting of the governor and the legislative council—were also structured to resemble their English counterparts.

On May 15, 1776, the Continental Congress of the American colonies recommended that each of the thirteen colonies promulgate a constitution to provide a basis for the conduct of its affairs after the removal of its royal governor and for the duration of the Revolution. With reports that General William Howe was landing at Sandy Hook and with British invasion imminent, the New Jersey constitution was drawn with understandable haste. On June 24 a special committee was instructed by the Provincial Congress to draft the document, two days later it was complete, and on July 2, two days before the Declaration of Independence was signed, it was adopted.

The constitution made as few changes in the form of government that had existed in the colony as were consistent with the contingencies of the Revolution. So uncertain was the future as these men drafted the document and prepared to flee from their homes that they had secured the incorporation of a final conciliatory declaration: "Provided always, and it is the true intent and meaning of this Congress; That if a reconciliation between Great Britain and the colonies should take place, and the latter be taken under the protection and government of the Crown of Great Britain, this charter shall be null and void. . . ."[2]

The colonial courts as they existed in New Jersey at the beginning of the American Revolution were thus incorporated into the New Jersey Constitution of 1776, although there was little direct reference to the court system in that six-page document. As Article XXII indicated, in no substantial way was New Jersey's legal system altered from what it had been for three-quarters of a century: "The common law of England, as well as so much of the statute law, as have been heretofore practiced in this colony, shall still remain in force, until they shall be altered by a future law of the legislature. . . ."[3]

Continuing to function with a judicial organization which it attempted to mold to meet the requirements of a territory whose needs were quite different from those of the mother country, New

Jersey was one of the few colonies that did not rewrite its provisional revolutionary constitution soon after reaching statehood.

Limitations of the judicial article of the constitution began to appear almost at once. With the upper house of the legislature as the court of last resort, there was no check that the legislature would not pass an unconstitutional law. As it was structured, the New Jersey court system could fall under political manipulation; if a judge handed down an unpopular opinion, it was possible that he would be denied reappointment by the legislature.[4] Of the court of appeals, Chief Justice Joseph C. Hornblower declared in 1844: "In more than half of the cases which have been decided in that court for forty years past I say with boldness and confidently that *causes* have not been tried, but *the parties* or *the tribunal* from which the appeal has come."[5] With the tenure of the judges left to the pleasure of the legislature and with the chancellor of the court of chancery (the governor) subject to annual change, the court system could be neither independent nor stable. In 1840 Governor William Pennington recommended that the state constitution be revised to separate the office of governor and chancellor: "The increase of business in the court of chancery has been so great that it now requires the whole attention of the chancellor and the nature of his duties call for permanency in office."[6] Pennington added about the judicial system in general that the practices of some of the courts "are so little familiar to our bar, and our statute laws are often so vague and uncertain, that the whole subject presents a wilderness of perplexity to the practitioner."[7]

Movements for constitutional revision arose in 1790, 1797, 1819, 1827, and 1840, but each was unsuccessful. Finally, in 1844, sixty delegates were elected to meet in convention to frame a new constitution for New Jersey. The convention continued from May 14 until June 29, and the constitution was ratified by the people of the state on August 13, 1844. Even with the changes wrought by this convention, much of the 1776 constitution was preserved. The only important changes affecting the judiciary were the creation of a court of errors and appeals without executive or legislative members, and the transfer of the power to appoint judges from the general assembly to the governor. The colonial court system still remained.

This judicial system clashed with the realities of a modern state in the first decades of the twentieth century. The 1844 court system under which Vanderbilt was practicing had been prescribed at a time when New Jersey was primarily an agricultural community, when the population of the state was 373,306 and the population of the largest city was 17,298. By 1930 the population of New Jersey was 4,041,389, and Newark alone had 442,337 inhabitants. As an aggregation of separate agricultural communities had become a complicated industrial state, the annual cost of running the state government had risen from $100,000 to $100,000,000. Between 1900 and 1930 the population of the state increased 168 percent, the tax ratables 593 percent, the number of actions begun in the state supreme court 935 percent. It was a wonder that the judicial machinery had not yet suffered a complete collapse, that it was able to function at all.

By 1930 the New Jersey court system had become a hydraheaded monster of confusion for litigants and a legal maze for lawyers. As the amount of litigation passing through the courts increased explosively, more courts were established by the legislature. To the court of errors and appeals, the supreme court, the court of chancery, the prerogative court, the court of common pleas, the circuit court, the orphan's court, the surrogate's court, the court of oyer and terminer, the court of quarter sessions, and the court of special session were added other county courts by legislative enactment: the juvenile and domestic relations court, the civil district court, the criminal judicial district court, the small cause court, the county traffic court. To these were added more municipal courts: the police courts, the magistrate courts, the mayor's court, the justice of the peace courts, and the family courts. It was said that "one must know a great deal of legal history before he can learn even the meaning of the names of some of the courts of New Jersey, and a law student must have read his Blackstone intelligently, and have asked many questions . . . before he can begin to understand the functions of the various courts and their relation to one another."[8]

The distinctions between the courts were ambiguous, their jurisdictions overlapping. Litigants often discovered that they had to resort to several courts before their case could be settled. Of the total number of opinions filed in the chancery courts and law courts each year, as many as a third were being decided on jurisdictional questions. For example, in *Metropolitan Life Insurance Company v. Urback* (127 N.J. Eq. 253 [E. & A. 1940]; 127 N.J.L. 585 [E. & A. 1942]; 130 N.J.L. 210 [E. & A. 1943]; 138 N.J. Eq. 108 [E. & A. 1946]), a Mrs. Urback, the beneficiary of a $2,500 insurance policy on the life of her husband, started a suit at law on the policy shortly after her husband's death in 1938. After nineteen months of litigation in the law courts and chancery court and the court of errors and appeals, the judges could not make up their minds whether the case belonged in the law courts or the equity courts. In the eight years after the litigation was begun, the case passed through the courts of law four times, the chancery court twice, and the court of errors and appeals four times before Mrs. Urback was awarded in 1946 the $2,500 specified in the insurance policy.

In another instance, litigants were compelled to go through five hearings in various courts only to find themselves back in the court where they had started (*New York Sash etc. Inc. v. National House etc. Inc.*, 131 N.J.L. 466 [E. & A. 1944]; 135 N.J. Eq. 150 [E. & A. 1944]).

Each court was independent. Each judge was king, holding court at his pleasure. Each was self sufficient, unwilling to brook control or supervision, for the time-honored doctrine that a judge must be independent in his judicial determinations had led to the assumption that a judge must be independent in matters of administration as well.

The two separate systems of courts inherited from England, law and equity (which England had merged in 1873 by creating a single High Court of Judicature), which by 1930 remained in only two states, New Jersey and Delaware, had different formalized rules of pleading. Practice and procedure in each court was determined by a diversity of statutes relating to the specific court, by rules adopted by each court and, to a degree, by the rules adopted by the different divisions of the courts sitting in the twenty-one counties. The inherent weakness of a primarily legislative system of judicial procedure was that it was susceptible to multitudinous amendments, many of which were passed to correct the supposed defects of procedure involved in individual cases. As a result, generations of amending legislative tinkers had produced a body of rules of pleading, practice, and evidence in which certainty of detail was developed to such an extent with exceptions and provisos that all simplicity was lost.

The court of errors and appeals was composed of sixteen members: the chancellor, the chief justice, the eight associate justices of the supreme court, and six lay judges whose purpose it was to bring a commonsensical, nonlegal approach to the judicial process. It was odd that this court of last resort in New Jersey—described as being "a little bigger than a jury and a little smaller than a mob"[9]—was so large when the New York Court of Appeals consisted of seven members and the United States Supreme Court consisted of only nine justices; odd until one realized that all of the judges of the court of errors and appeals had other duties to perform. The chancellor not only sat on the high court but also directed the vast administrative machinery of the court of chancery, acted as the surrogate general in the prerogative court, and sat as a member of the court of pardons. The supreme court justices also sat for the three terms of the supreme court and supervised the administration of the court of common pleas, the orphan's court, the court of oyer and terminer, and the court of quarter sessions. The six lay judges divided their time between their work on the court of errors and appeals and their work on the court of pardons in addition to engaging in private business.[10]

While this scattering of authority might have suited the needs of the small farming communities of the nineteenth century, in a bustling twentieth-century manufacturing and commercial state it resulted in a diminution of judicial efficiency, in chaos and delay in the disposition of the business of the courts. More judges were added to the growing judicial system to meet the backlogging litigation. By 1930 the court of chancery, the province of the governor-chancellor before 1844 and of one chancellor after 1844, consisted of ten vice-chancellors, twelve standing advisory masters, and several hundred special masters. Yet the court was unable to handle the growing volume of litigation.

To the great majority of citizens, a conception of the judicial process reflected, not the actions of the appellate court of last resort, but rather the impressions they received in the courts of first instance where they were most likely to appear. What they experienced in the justice of the peace courts, the police courts, and the traffic courts they quite naturally tended to project to all the courts; and what the people saw and heard in these courts created a dubious impression of justice. In 1786, after ten years in office, Governor William Livingston's major complaint about New Jersey's government had concerned these courts of first instance: "I have seen justices of the peace who were a burlesque upon a magistracy, justices illiterate, justices partial, justices groggy, justices courting popularity to be chosen assemblymen, and justices encouraging litigiousness."[11] In the century and decades that had followed, the situation had not improved.

Under the influence of the popular revolt of the second quarter of the nineteenth century, the Jacksonian Revolution, the New Jersey Constitution of 1844 had provided for the popular election of justices of the peace with no thought of imposing any standards of qualification on the office. The compensation of these judges depended on the number of their convictions, a situation that darkened the reputations of their office. The advent of the automobile in the twentieth century further increased the opportunities for plunder when the fixing of tickets became an accepted practice.

In some counties, these lower courts were as integral a part of the political system as of the judicial system. Police judges were often so closely associated with political organizations that if, for instance, a lawyer was a Hague man, he was quite likely to get a favorable decision from a Hague judge regardless of the merits of the case. Police judges sometimes did not even preside over their courts in person, but appointed their clerks, without any authority in law, as "acting judges." The judges of these courts rarely wore robes, and many held court in the back rooms of stores or in private homes. Under these conditions, the self-respect of the judges and the respect of the litigants, witnesses, and spectators for the law, was minimal.

In these ways the judicial machinery in New Jersey was breaking down, giving rise to the epithet "Jersey justice." Between 1900 and 1930, the amount of litigation started each year in many of the courts had leaped by almost 1,000 percent. In 1930 in the county courts, 17,200 cases remained untried, whereas in 1920 the number of untried cases had been 3,600 and in 1910 it had been 1,600. Equally severe conditions existed in each of the other courts. Judges in every court were obliged to undertake a volume of work they knew was impossible to handle, a volume of work they knew could never be brought to date as they saw, week after week, more cases being added to their lists than they would be able to try. The early deaths of some of the judges were attributed in part to these strains and frustrations they experienced weekly. More clearly attributable to the congested calendars was the careless attitude assumed by many judges in the face of their insurmountable work. Judicial delay had become a comfortable way of life for judges and lawyers and a fact of life for litigants who languished in jail, untried month after month, or who waited, often under adverse circumstances, for the financial restitution that a trial could bring.

Calendars were clogged. Litigants faced interminable delays to get into court. After cases were tried it was not uncommon to wait two to four years for a decision, with some trials and opinions drawn out over the course of a decade or more. New Jersey lawyers suggested to their clerks that they read Dickens' account in *Bleak House* of the nineteenth-century English Court of Chancery and of the never-ending case of *Jarndyce v. Jarndyce* to help them adjust to the tempo of the New Jersey Chancery; and after making their way through the twisted course of a trial, many citizens could feel along with the litigants Dickens described that it was better to "suffer any wrong that can be done you rather than come here." D. W. Brogan commented in *The English People* in 1943: "The most indisputably English export to the United States (apart from the basic language) was the common law, but if you want to see the old common law in all its picturesque formality, with its fictions and fads, its delays and uncertainties, the place to look for them is not London, ... but in New Jersey. Dickens, or any other law reformer of a century ago, would feel more at home in Trenton than in London. ..." The New Jersey judicial system came to be known as "the most antiquated and intricate that exists in any considerable community of English speaking people."[12]

In 1930 the English Court of Criminal Appeals was disposing of its cases in a matter of days; in the court of last resort in Connecticut, opinions were handed down within two months after argument; in the New York Court of Appeals, in two to six weeks after argument; in the Supreme Court of Ohio, in three to four weeks after argument; in the court of last resort in Pennsylvania, within four weeks after argument; in the Supreme Court of the United States, in two months. In New Jersey, the amount of time it took to dispose of each case could run into years.

Such problems as the amalgam of courts; the division of the judicial system into distinct courts of law and equity; the minutiae of practice and pleading based on an agglomeration of precedent, rules of court, fictions, and statutes; the deciding of cases upon mere points of practice and procedure; the lavish granting of new trials; the scattering of the duties of judges among various courts; the absence of any power to assign judges to those courts where they were most needed; and the complete lack of an administrative system to control the operation of the courts—all meshed to delay trials and decisions, to cause many decisions to be rendered on jurisdictional issues rather than on the merits of the cases, and to encourage trials to become battles between opposing counsel based on technicalities, delay, and surprise.[13] Counsellors were advising their clients, no matter how strong their cases, that it would be simpler and less expensive for them to avoid going to court than to fight their way through the complexities of a New Jersey trial. And lawyers with corporate connections knew that businesses were being kept out of New Jersey by lack of confidence in the state courts.

These conditions bred a fear, a distrust, of the judicial process. Popular dissatisfaction with the law centered, not on the substantive principles of the law and not on judicial opinions, but rather on the mechanisms of applying the law, problems in the administration of justice which were delaying and denying justice to citizens of the state, but problems which, theoretically, were the easiest of remedy.

THE NEW JERSEY JUDICIAL COUNCIL

Concerned that the unjustifiable delays of the law, the intricacies of outmoded procedure, and the inefficient utilization of cumbersome judicial machinery were making the enforcement of the law increasingly inadequate and were threatening to make legal rights inoperative, several members of the New Jersey Bar Association took action to establish a judicial council for New Jersey that would conduct a continuous study of the state judicial system and devise ways and means to improve its operation. Founded in 1930, the New Jersey Judicial Council was modeled after the councils of twenty other states which had been organized throughout the 1920's in response to Chief Justice William Howard Taft's warnings about the growing backlog in the courts. It consisted of judges from the various New Jersey courts, the majority leader of the senate and assembly, the attorney general, the president of the state bar association, and five counsellors at law selected by the president of the state bar. One of the appointed counsellors was Arthur T. Vanderbilt, who had been instrumental in the formation of the council and who was elected chairman at its organizational meeting.

The first report of the council, submitted to the governor on December 15, 1931, outlined the problems of the New Jersey courts and collected and evaluated all available data that illustrated the present state of litigation in the courts as well as the growth of the volume of litigation since 1900. With these facts and figures, the council made known to the bench and bar, the legislature, and the citizens of New Jersey the deplorable condition of the courts from the standpoint of congested calendars. The gravity of the situation it discovered led the council to a consideration of the fundamental rights of the litigant which it formulated as follows:

1. A prompt and efficient trial of his case;
2. At reasonable cost;
3. Represented by competent attorneys;
4. Before impartial and experienced judges and competent juries;
5. With the privilege of a review of the trial court's determination by an appellate tribunal composed of similar judges who will

render a final decision within three or four months after the
appeal is initiated.[14]

The council then made recommendations for the realization of these
rights. Lacking any legislative authority to implement its recommendations, it depended on the willingness of the governor and legislature to adopt the measures it proposed. This first report included
eleven recommendations to expedite appeals. Each was introduced
as a bill in the legislature and, of these, five became law. All five
remained within the framework of the existing court structure.

Each succeeding year as the statistics flowed in from the courts, it
was evident that more judicial work was accumulating. Moreover,
these statistics indicated that there was a reduction in the volume of
business the courts were conducting while the cost of running the
judicial system was increasing. Although the judicial council in its
first year of operation had decided that it would not attempt to
propose any constitutional amendments to revise the state judicial
system, it soon became clear that the crazy quilt of New Jersey courts
was not improved by slight annual patchwork alterations. Council
recommendations and legislative acts could alleviate some of the
problems of the courts and stave off a total breakdown, but no lasting
solution could be effected without the passage of amendments to the
judicial article of the New Jersey Constitution to overhaul, modernize, and streamline the entire judicial system. Confidence was shown
in the work of the council, which was being recognized as one of the
most active in the nation, when the legislature in a joint resolution of
April 27, 1931, directed the council to "make a complete study of the
status of the judicial system of the State and report and submit to the
next Legislature its findings and recommendations as to amendments to the Judicial Article of the State Constitution."

Accordingly, the council developed a plan for fundamental court
reform. In 1932 in its third annual report there appeared a model
judicial article for the New Jersey Constitution designed to speed up
the trial of cases and to provide for the prompt disposition of appeals
through the organization of a modern court system and the specialization of the duties of each judge. None of the principles the council
incorporated in the article were startling innovations. All were matters of common sense and sound business practice. Many had
already proved successful in other state court systems: the division of
labor of the courts and judges; the assignment of a single function to
each judge; the preclusion of judges from the practice of law and
from politics; the right of every litigant to one trial and then to one

appeal; the organization of the courts into a more coherent system through consolidation of courts like the court of common pleas, orphan's court, court of oyer and terminer, court of quarter sessions, and court of special sessions into a single county court in each county; the designation of an administrative head for each court to oversee the work of that court, and the designation of the chief justice as the administrative head of the state court system with power to transfer judges and to regulate practice and procedure in the courts.

The council invited committees from the New Jersey Press Association, from the State Chamber of Commerce, from the State Federation of Labor, from the State League of Municipalities, from the State Federation of Women's Clubs, and from various other organizations, including the colleges and universities of the state, to study the constitutional amendments it had prepared and to make suggestions and revisions. When the legislature studied the amendments, they would therefore represent, not the work solely of lawyers and judges for the benefit of lawyers and judges, but rather the work of lawyers, judges, and laymen designed for the benefit of litigants.

The amendments received support from these organizations and the approval of the state bar association, the conference of county bar associations, and every county bar association in the state. There was no opposition voiced by any member of the bench or bar during the period of a year and a half when they were before the legislature. But although the amendments passed the senate without any opposition, they failed to pass in the assembly by a narrow margin.

The amending clause in the 1844 constitution required that constitutional amendments be passed by two successive sessions of both houses of the legislature and only then submitted to the vote of the people at a special election. Other obstacles arose when the possibility of passage of the judicial council's amendments became too likely. One year a respected member of the bar assisted the council in drafting the amendments, only to fight against their adoption when the amendments came up for vote in the legislature. On another occasion the judicial council assented to a change in the composition of the supreme court in a proposed amendment on promise of forthcoming support, only to discover that the support never materialized. These were not isolated occurrences. Vanderbilt remarked after years of fruitless effort:

We prepared draft after draft of a revision of the Judiciary Article of our Constitution in an effort to placate various interests and at the same time bring about a measurable improvement. We learned to our sorrow that some of the interests who pretended to be satisfied with our successive drafts once they had got what they asked for, did not hesitate to oppose our entire effort when the draft reached the floor of the Legislature. Then strange things ensued: one year our amendments did pass in the House only to be defeated in the Senate; the next year they did pass in the Senate only to be defeated in the House. You will recognize, of course, the old legislative run-around.[15]

It would later become clear that behind much of this runaround was the opposition of Mayor Hague of Jersey City to any type of judicial reorganization that might threaten his power over the New Jersey judiciary, and also, perhaps equally, the opposition of lawyers and judges to any alteration of the system under which they worked, the same type of opposition Frank Sommer had encountered with the promulgation of the Practice Act of 1912. Whether motivated by mere inertia or apathy, by fear that changes in procedure would jeopardize their learning in the field or lessen the advantage older lawyers had over younger members of the bar, by antipathy to learning new rules of practice and procedure, by an unwillingness to alter a system under which they were comfortable and prospering, by fear on the part of weak judges that proposals for judicial reform included their own elimination from the court system, by the desire of strong judges to maintain the edge they held in experience or ability, or by the aversion of lawyers to support positions they believed their judges disfavored—professional inability to see the need for any kind of change in the law made judges and lawyers formidable opponents to the proposals of the judicial council. Laymen, unsure in the specialized world of law, were either indifferent to the problems of the courts or certain that they could offer no assistance.

Each year for ten years Vanderbilt was reelected chairman of the council. Yearly his advocacy of a modern court system became more insistent as calendar congestion worsened while judges and lawyers, professionally responsible for its cure, and governors and legislators, a majority of whom were lawyers, sat idly by as if the disease were incurable or as if they were not responsible for it.

Lawyers wondered how, as an active counsellor, Vanderbilt dared to be such a vocal advocate of court reorganization. Daily he had to appear before judges who knew he was recommending such controversial measures as a bill providing that, if a judge did not decide a case within two months after it had been submitted to him, he could not draw his pay until he did decide; or a bill that, when decisions were dependent upon the actions of several judges and the judges were unable to decide a case within two months after the appeal had been argued, the presiding judge had to certify that fact to the governor, who could, if he thought the public good required it, appoint special judges to help the courts catch up in their work. Although Vanderbilt never feared that his proposals would threaten his efficacy as a counsellor before the New Jersey bench, he did admit to a friend in 1947 that his fight for judicial reform "has literally cost me hundreds of thousands of dollars in fees which did not come my way because it was known I was working for a new court system—you know how those things go. . . ."[16]

Forty-two years old and still youthful-looking when he was first appointed to the newly formed judicial council in 1930, Vanderbilt would not reach his goal of a streamlined, businesslike court system for his state until he was almost sixty, when he said, "[M]ost of my gray hairs were not acquired in the trial courts or in the appellate tribunals, but rather by seventeen years of vexatious activity in an effort to secure a sound system of judicial administration in New Jersey."[17] In comparison with what lay ahead, his work on the judicial council was merely the opening skirmish of the seventeen-year siege.

THE AMERICAN BAR ASSOCIATION

In its attempts to find solutions to the problems of Jersey justice by studying the judicial systems of other states, the New Jersey Judicial Council began to discover the growing deficiencies in the adminis-tration of justice throughout much of the United States, a trend which was confirmed when Vanderbilt was named chairman of the National Conference of Judicial Councils in 1933. This organization was faced with the same limitations as the state councils; its proceedings, its votes, its resolutions carried no legislative authority. But during his four-year term, the National Conference was active in encouraging the formation of judicial councils in other states and in securing grants from the Carnegie Corporation which made possible a num-ber of comprehensive studies of problems in judicial administra-tion.[18]

It was through the American Bar Association that Vanderbilt first gained access to a forum to bring the problems of the American courts to nationwide attention. Since 1920 he had been active in the

New Jersey Bar Association, serving on its board of trustees, and as its third, second, and first vice-president. He led the movement to coordinate the activities of the local bar associations into the general council of the state association to meet more effectively the problems of legal and judicial reform, and had sponsored the organization of a junior bar conference for New Jersey. In 1937 he declined the nomination to the presidency of the state bar association because of his prospective duties in the American Bar Association.

The New Jersey member of the House of Delegates of the A.B.A., the founder and first chairman of the section of insurance (which became the largest single section of the Association), a member of the Board of Governors, and chairman of the budget committee, Vanderbilt, on January 5, 1937, was nominated to be president of the American Bar Association. "While he is known in Essex County chiefly for his political activities and leadership of the Clean Government," the newspapers reported, "Arthur T. Vanderbilt has been regarded by the legal fraternity as an outstanding figure for judicial reform in New Jersey."[19] Forty-eight years old when nominated president and forty-nine when elected at the meeting in Kansas City on September 22, 1937, Vanderbilt was one of the youngest presidents in the sixty-year history of the Association.

At a meeting of the Board of Governors shortly after Vanderbilt had been nominated, elder statesman Newton D. Baker, the president of the American Judicature Society, asked what he wanted to accomplish during his term. Vanderbilt said that he hoped to convince the profession that archaic court systems and procedures, unbusinesslike delays of the law, and problems of judicial administration, rather than defects in substantive law, were undermining the public's respect for the law, and that immediate remedial action by members of the legal profession was essential to stem popular criticism of lawyers and courts. Mr. Baker replied, "Vanderbilt, if you will stick to that and nothing else, you have a real opportunity to make a genuine contribution to the profession and to the public."[20]

In his opening address before the American Bar Association in Kansas City on October 1, 1937, he sounded the cause that would carry him across the country as he challenged the profession to face the issue of improving the administration of justice in the courts and the administrative tribunals:

... Will the Bar tackle this herculean task? It will, if it can be induced to turn away from the swarm of petty problems we are attempting to meet, and to look at black shadows resting over many countries in four other continents,—

countries in which law has been replaced by despotism, where liberty, without which the spirit of man cannot survive, has perforce been banished, where courts, so-called, are in bondage, where law is one man's or one clique's whim, and where the Bar is debased or exiled.

The shadow can never grow here. The spirit that answered the tyranny of colonial governors, that wrote the Declaration of Independence, that cautiously framed the Articles of Confederation, that in due time forged the structure of the Constitution, and that, as our frontier moved West, decade after decade, carried with it the doctrine of liberty under law, can and will in these times when we no longer have a frontier, solve these paramount problems of judicial and administrative justice in a commercial and industrial era. We will solve them, because our duty to our profession and public opinion alike demands that we start to solve them and to solve them now.[21]

During his year as president, Vanderbilt traveled 72,000 miles visiting thirty-nine states, England, and Canada, discovering the extent of the common problems in the administration of justice, and spreading and selling the idea of judicial reform. At bar association meetings, law schools, conferences with leaders of the profession and government, receptions, luncheons, dinner meetings, judicial conferences, commencements, inaugurations, and hearings, he stressed the need for judicial reorganization and advocated the benefits of the unification of court systems, the modernization of court administration, and the simplification of court rules.

He assailed the "quaint professional notion" that courts existed primarily for the benefit of the judges and lawyers and only incidentally for the benefit of litigants. He supported the need for improving the caliber of judges, jurors, and lawyers. He warned of the dangers of granting subordinate judicial powers to independent administrative agencies which, as he said, made the rules of the game, played the game as one of the teams, acted as umpire, and then wrote up the newspaper reports. He warned of the commissioners of these tribunals who, without the qualifications of judges, often handled issues of more far-reaching importance than those that appeared in the traditional courts, and of the political atmosphere in which these commissioners were obliged to work. He condemned the lack of administration in judicial tribunals, the lack of judicial safeguards in administrative agencies, the election of judges, oversized appellate courts, limited judicial tenure, involved trial proceedings, delayed decisions, and clogged dockets. Time and again he explained how an efficient administration of justice would preserve and strengthen the taproot of freedom in a democratic society, the right to a fair trial, which was, in the last analysis, the most fundamental of all rights for, without it, all other rights were empty and meaningless. Of what real value was a suit for a breach of contract or a libel action for injury to one's reputation if the judge on the bench or the jury in the box or one's attorney at the counsel table was either incompetent or corrupt, or if the system of procedure under which they attempted to work was dilatory, cumbersome, exceedingly expensive, or unduly restricted the search for truth? The delay, expense, and protraction and duplication of causes could result in as effective a denial of substantive rights as if these rights had never existed.

In February of 1938, he sailed for England to study the English judicial system, which was widely recognized as a model system of administering justice. Many of the changes he was recommending had been implemented in England the previous century as a result of popular pressure and had proved successful in modernizing the courts. Visiting the Court of Privy Council at Downing Street, Vanderbilt asked one of the barristers how soon the court would decide the case that was then being argued. The Englishman looked very surprised.

"Why, at the end of the argument. They will have a short consultation about it, and one of them will be assigned to write the opinion. He will bring it back next Monday, and it will be printed in the newspapers next Tuesday or next Wednesday at the latest."[22]

"Of course, they do have their delays over there," Vanderbilt reported when he returned.

The businessmen are up in arms and are filing petitions in Parliament because they have gotten so far behind that trials are not heard sometimes for three or four months after issue joins, and businessmen think that it is perfectly terrible and outrageous, and they say if something is not done about the courts, there is going to be a rebellion. When I explain to them that the gentlemen who practice law in Boston think it is wonderful that their cases are reached for trial within three years, they are again sure that America is a barbarous land.[23]

It was, however, another experience in England that most convinced Vanderbilt of the necessity of a sound judicial system, of the importance of improving the administration of justice in the state and federal courts. On February 20, 1938, the day that Anthony Eden resigned as Secretary of Foreign Affairs in protest to Neville Chamberlain's efforts at appeasement with Hitler and Mussolini, a bleak Sunday shortly before Vanderbilt was to leave England, he was the guest of Lord Chancellor Maugham. The Lord Chancellor had no

sooner returned home from one cabinet meeting than he was summoned to another. Two cabinet meetings on a Sunday made it a day
without precedent in English history. The sense of impending danger was insistent. The Scandinavian countries, the Low Countries,
and France were all that lay between England and the states in
which law had been replaced by despotism.

That afternoon while Vanderbilt waited for his host to return, as
the possibility of a second world war was becoming a stark reality, as
he searched for causes of how Nazism, fascism, and communism had
arisen, he felt certain that nothing would do so much to preserve a
democratic form of government as a judicial system that held the
confidence of the people. It was the law alone—and its effective
administration—that was the guarantee of freedom.

. . . I venture as my deepest conviction in the field of public life that, if our
American form of government should fail, it will be because we have
neglected our responsibilities for perfecting the processes of justice in our
traditional courts, in our newer administrative tribunals, and in our legislatures which were the source of the administrative tribunals.[24]

If people had confidence in the courts, their respect for the law
would survive the shortcomings of every other branch of government. "But if they lose their respect for the work of the courts," he
wrote later, "their respect for law and order will vanish with it to the
great detriment of society, for it surely does not have to be argued
that respect for law is all important for the survival of popular
government."[25]

It was with a renewed commitment to the necessity of judicial
reform, spurred by the problems he was observing in the nation's
courts and by the impending world war, that he drove harder to
spread his warning that immediate steps had to be taken to avert a
breakdown in the American system of justice.

The pace was frenetic, but he never displayed traces of the pressure under which he lived or the real apprehension he felt each time
he stood up to make an address. The *Seattle Daily Times* reported on
April 28, 1938:

Hotel rooms in which Arthur T. Vanderbilt, president of the American Bar
Association, plans to stop should be wired for sound several days in advance.

Mr. Vanderbilt himself should be equipped with mechanical stage effects
capable of emitting faint clouds of smoke and steam at proper intervals. It
would make Mr. Vanderbilt a much more logical figure at first sight, and
enable those who visit him to see him as they have imagined him.

Anyone who has studied his itinerary since he was elected to the presidency of the American Bar Association last autumn must visualize him as a sort of human pinwheel, fizzing around the continent with fluttering coveys of mail winging desperately in his wake. He has traveled 45,000 miles in a little more than four months, has appeared at countless meetings and dinners, and has answered between one and two hundred letters a day.

It is a little unbelievable to walk into his hotel room and find a calm, self-possessed man with an easy wit, moving and talking slowly as though he had nothing more strenuous before him than a stroll in the park. All he had to do was answer his mail, visit attorneys, keep a luncheon engagement and address an evening banquet at the Washington Athletic Club. . . .

It is only when the conversation turns to the legal reforms for which the American Bar Association has fought for three decades that he gets up out of his chair and talks on his feet moving slowly with the court-room prowl of a trial lawyer.[26]

While Vanderbilt's primary aim of the year was to alert the profession to the seriousness of the growing crisis in the courts, he also took action to lay the foundation for the massive task of modernization that lay ahead.

During his presidency, the Section of Judicial Administration of the American Bar Association was established. With the help of its chairman, Senior Judge John J. Parker of the United States Court of Appeals for the Fourth Circuit, Vanderbilt persuaded the American Bar Association to adopt a major program of reform. Judge Parker organized seven committees to formulate and recommend minimum standards of judicial administration—realistic and practical standards to insure that the administration of justice in the states could meet the changing conditions of the contemporary age. Parker designated as the heads of these committees lawyers, law professors, and judges who were the recognized experts in particular fields: Circuit Judge Joseph A. Moynihan of Detroit, improving pretrial procedure; Judge John P. Dempsey of Cleveland, methods of selection of juries; Federal Judge W. Calvin Chesnut of Baltimore, improving trial practice; Dean John H. Wigmore of Chicago, improving the law of evidence; Professor Edson R. Sunderland of Ann Arbor, simplification of appellate procedure; Ralph M. Hoyt of Milwaukee, control of state administrative agencies; and Judge Edward R. Finch of New York, improving judicial organization and administration.

The completed committee reports, approved by the Section of Judicial Administration, were distributed to every member of the American Bar Association in advance of the annual meeting at Cleveland in July of 1938. "Note well the words 'minimum' and 'practical,' " Vanderbilt wrote in the foreword:

The reports of these seven committees make no attempt to scale the heights of perfection or to reach out for the idealistic. They are entirely utilitarian in their objective. They were prepared with a realistic consciousness of the very genuine difficulties involved in inducing our judges and our lawyers to change any of their working habits in the field of judicial procedure. Hence the recommendations of the seven committees are limited in number to those matters which are absolutely essential if the administration of justice in America is to be responsive to the needs of our times. . . . Some day—and, I hope, in the not too distant future—a more enlightened generation will look back on these reports and wonder that it should have been necessary to write them, necessary to agitate for the recommendations set forth in them, and necessary, perhaps, in some states to invoke the aid of enlightened and farseeing laymen to bring about their adoption.[27]

At the close of Vanderbilt's term in 1938, the sixty recommendations contained in the seven reports received, with one minor exception, the unanimous approval of the House of Delegates. The Association approved a resolution directing the state committees of the A.B.A. to press for the adoption of these recommendations. Judge Parker was named chairman of a special A.B.A. committee on Improving the Administration of Justice which was created to help bring the recommendations to the attention of the bench and bar of the forty-eight states. During the next several years, Parker named seven advisory committees from every state to gauge how their states measured up to each of the minimum standards, and took it upon himself on behalf of the special committee to travel to many states to arouse the profession, press, and public to the importance of implementing the minimum standards.

Vanderbilt's campaign to focus attention on the limitations of the administration of justice in the courts and Judge Parker's work to draft and advocate the Minimum Standards of Judicial Administration were among the first steps taken on a nationwide basis to sweep away public criticism of the bar and to attempt to bring about a carefully conceived and coordinated program to modernize the American judiciary. As clearly as "The Causes of Popular Dissatisfaction with the Administration of Justice," Roscoe Pound's address before the annual meeting of the American Bar Association in 1906, was "the spark that kindled the white flame of progress" in the field of judicial administration, so was the work of the American Bar Association in 1938 the bellows that blazed that flame into a practical program of reform. Within the next ten years, the Administrative Office of the United States Courts, the Administrative Procedure Act, the Federal Rules of Criminal Procedure, the amendments to the

Articles of War which laid the groundwork for the Uniform Code of
Military Justice, the procedural reforms in a number of states based
on the Federal Rules of Civil and Criminal Procedure, the piecemeal
acceptance of the Minimum Standards of Judicial Administration by
the several states, and the complete reorganization and modernization of the New Jersey judicial system would mark initial results of
the gradual awakening of the profession to the needs of adapting the
law, the courts, and the administration of justice to the realities of a
changing, modern society.

"I AM THE LAW"

Three months before Vanderbilt's term as president of the American Bar Association ended, an incident occurred in Jersey City that
crystallized many of the issues he had been espousing that year.
Norman Thomas, a Presbyterian minister and socialist leader who as
a member of the American Socialist Party had been a candidate for
governor of New York in 1924, for mayor of New York City in 1925
and 1929, and for president of the United States in 1928, 1932, and
1936, was barred from speaking in Journal Square and deported from
Jersey City by Mayor Frank Hague on the night of April 30, 1938.
This denial of free speech and assembly in New Jersey seemed to
Vanderbilt an ominous reflection of the politics of the fascist regimes
in Europe: "It seems there is little use of fighting for democracy if we
are to tolerate our tiny Hitlers and mouselike Mussolini's at home."[28]
Of what real worth were the fundamental rights guaranteed in the
federal and state constitutions, he had argued all year, if they could
not be enforced in a fair trial? He volunteered his legal services to
Thomas, and at the sixty-first annual convention of the American Bar
Association on July 25, 1938, presented once more, with a new
immediacy, the ideas he had worked to spread:

Man does not live by law alone. Law is only tolerable because it makes
individual liberty possible. Without law, liberty would be non-existent
except for a favored one or a favored few. Liberty, then, is the chief concern
of the bar as it should be of democratic government. . . .

We must recognize the fact that all of the unreasoning destructive forces
that wrought such havoc to the courts and to the profession a century ago are
again at large, some of them in aggravated form. If democracy is to survive
and with it law and liberty, it will be because our people have faith in the
integrity of our courts, from the highest to the lowest. The people must have

such confidence in the efficiency, the integrity and the wisdom of all of our courts as a matter of everyday experience that in times of stress they will instinctively feel safe in resorting thereto for the vindication of their rights. . . .

Some leaders in public life seem to be unable to distinguish between freedom of speech, freedom of the press and the right of lawful assembly on the one side and treason to government on the other. We have reached the point where suggestions for concentrating one's opponents in Alaska are seriously advocated in open court by men claiming to carry the banner of democracy. Such declarations sound strangely alien in the America of George Washington, John Adams, Benjamin Franklin, Alexander Hamilton and Thomas Jefferson. Yet, there are many people to whom this philosophy of intolerance for views they dislike has a strong appeal. They fail to realize that it necessarily precludes intellectual freedom, religious freedom, and political freedom. They fail to comprehend that under this philosophy of intolerance America never could have become free. To the credit of the Bar let it be said that it has never failed to realize the essential relation between law and liberty, between the independence of the courts and the maintenance of our constitutional guarantees of individual freedom—the age-long struggle for popular government. The challenge of intolerance the organized Bar will meet by uniting to perfect the process of judicial administration, in both our traditional courts and in the newer administrative tribunals and by insisting on the maintenance of their independence and integrity.[29]

The deportation of Norman Thomas had been a climax of Mayor Hague's fight for "Americanism" in Jersey City. Hero, demagogue, rascal, and benefactor to the people of Jersey City, Hague was a magnetic figure who both molded and reflected the moods of his constituency. Sixty-two in 1938, tall, erect, with a vigorous step and a quick Irish temper, Hague portrayed his regime as a crusade to win the continual struggle he saw between nationalism and communism, between Catholicism and atheism. The slogan of his Jersey City administration was "No vice, no crime, no racketeering." At his frequent Americanization Day parades with their rallies, flags, and speeches, he never failed to recount—along with the stories of his rise from the Horseshoe slums, of his distribution of jobs and Thanksgiving and Christmas baskets to the needy, and of his work to construct the Jersey City Medical Center, where Jersey City patients were admitted and treated at little or no cost—his victory in keeping the taxi dance halls, cabarets, red light districts, night clubs, speakeasies, and burlesque shows out of his city. "Jersey City," he was fond of saying, "is the most moralest city in America."

This view was not shared, however, by J. Edgar Hoover of the

Federal Bureau of Investigation, who since 1935 had refused to accept for publication the crime statistics forwarded to him from Jersey City because of his belief that the city administration was distorting the statistics to make them conform to its slogan.

To maintain the moral fiber of the city had, in Hague's view, necessitated both the largest police force of any American city of equivalent size and the innovation of a number of curious measures: the passage of an anti-leaflet ordinance to control the distribution of printed matter; the removal by the police from every newsstand of magazines and newspapers with articles condemning Hague's administration, such as the February 7, 1938, edition of *Life* with its article on Jersey City sweatshops, and the periodic editions of the *New York Post* in 1938 that contained an exposé of the Hague regime; the frequent use of the New Jersey Disorderly Persons Act of 1936, which permitted the arrest of any person "on foot or in any automobile, vehicle or public conveyance who cannot give a good account of himself."[30]

These and similar methods were used by Mayor Hague to silence critics, to eliminate strikes—a move he felt necessary if he was to draw new business to his highly taxed city—and to rout the frequent invasions of the "long-haired reds" from other states, the "undesirables," the "subversives," the "radicals," the "agitators," the "labor organizations," the "communists," and even the people who came to Jersey City who looked like "Jews from New York."[31] "This is one of the real American cities of the nation," Hague proclaimed at one rally. "'America first' is the byword of Jersey City. This is America; the communists must be smashed."[32]

When the Congress of Industrial Organizations had attempted to establish itself in Jersey City in November of 1937, Mayor Hague, believing it a communist organization, had prohibited it from meeting. "As long as I am Mayor of this City," he had told the local chamber of commerce, "the great industries of the city are secure. We hear about constitutional rights, free speech and the free press. Every time I hear these words, I say to myself, 'that man is a Red, that man is a Communist.' You never hear a real American talk in that manner."[33]

By distributing leaflets explaining the law, the C.I.O. attempted to inform Jersey City wage earners of their rights under the National Labor Relations Act of 1937, an act designed to encourage collective bargaining for the betterment of terms and conditions of employment. The C.I.O. was notified by the city in November of 1937 that its distribution of literature violated the anti-leaflet ordinance. When the organization made known its intentions to continue to distribute the leaflets, police officers stationed at the Hudson Tubes stopped all persons coming into Jersey City who were identified as C.I.O. workers, seized and searched them without warrants, confiscated all C.I.O. literature, arrested some of the workers, and forcibly placed others on ferries headed back to New York.

When the workers returned to Jersey City that same day with more circulars, the police transported the workers outside of the limits of Jersey City. Subsequently, the C.I.O. tried to hire halls in Jersey City to explain the National Labor Relations Act and to discuss unionization, but private halls were denied them as was a permit for an open-air meeting.

On December 17, 1937, the American Civil Liberties Union, interested in the trouble, applied for a permit for an open-air meeting in Jersey City at any place in the city on any one of a number of days to discuss civil rights under the Constitution. When protests against holding this meeting were made to Mayor Hague by the Jersey City Chamber of Commerce, the Association of the Sons of Poland, the Jersey City Lion's Club, the Jersey City Real Estate Board, the Ladies of the Grand Army of the Republic, and the Italian War Veterans, and when the Catholic War Veterans of Jersey City announced that if the "Reds" continued their attempt to "invade Jersey City," their organization would be forced to "take the law in [their] own hands" and drive them out, urging each veteran to come to any future meeting of the C.I.O. armed with "two feet of rubber hose,"[34] the director of public safety of Jersey City, Daniel Casey, denied the permit. His denial was based on a Jersey City ordinance that gave the director of public safety the authority to prohibit public meetings to "prevent riots, disturbances, or disorderly assemblages."[35] Later Mayor Hague went on radio to praise the veteran groups for their Americanism in the defense of the Jersey City against the current red menace.

On June 14, 1938, in the New Jersey District Court hearing to restrain the mayor from denying the C.I.O. demonstrators permission to assemble in Jersey City, Hague amply demonstrated his feelings about the organization, and, without hesitation, revealed the intolerant and repressive spirit of his administration. Mayor Hague was asked by Dean Spaulding Frazer, attorney for the C.I.O.:

Q. Do you believe that persons who believe in the doctrines of Stalin, Hitler and Mussolini should go back to those countries?
A. Do I believe what?

Q. That persons who believe in the doctrines of Stalin, Mussolini and Hitler, should go back to Russia, Italy and Germany?

A. I believe that anyone who comes here and is displeased with the methods of our country and government, and feel that it is necessary for them to set themselves up as objectors to the form of government that we enjoy here and find that this country is apparently not pleasing to them, they should be driven back, not go back, driven back.

Q. Driven back?

A. Yes, sir.

Q. Suppose they were born in this country, should they be driven back then?

A. Well, I think we ought to establish a camp in Alaska there and house them there and keep them away from the American people, and if they don't believe in our form of government, and are opposed to our methods and our form of government, I think there should be a remedy for this.[36]

Later in the trial when Hague was asked, "But you don't believe much in these civil rights, do you?" he again repeated his firm conviction: "Whenever I hear a discussion of civil rights and the rights of free speech and the rights of the Constitution, always remember you will find him with a Russian flag under his coat; you never miss."[37]

Shortly after the C.I.O. and the A.C.L.U. had been denied permission to assemble by the Hague government, the American Socialist Party applied for a permit to hold a meeting in Jersey City to test Hague's power. Norman Thomas would be the speaker. Hague's director of public safety again refused to grant a permit on the grounds that Thomas's request was an attempt "instituted by the C.I.O. and the alleged red, Communistic groups to invade Jersey City, tear apart its industries and businesses, destroy lives and interfere with the peace and happiness of the people of Jersey City, and, that therefore in [the opinion of the director of public safety] the granting of such a permit would lead to serious disturbances and disorderly assemblage, inevitably resulting in riot."[38]

Thomas nevertheless decided to speak. He believed the denial of the permit to speak in Jersey City was discriminating, un-American, and unconstitutional and meant to test it in the only practical way: by going to Jersey City, making a speech without a permit, and carrying the ensuing case to the courts—if necessary, to the United States Supreme Court.

A crowd of two thousand cheered when Thomas arrived in Journal Square in Jersey City on the night of April 30, 1938, but, within minutes after leaving the automobile that had brought him, he was forced into a waiting car by Hague's police and driven along back roads to the Jersey Central Ferry landing. "Do you consider it an arrest when a police officer puts [someone] in a car and takes [him] somewhere not the police station?" Hague was asked in the C.I.O. trial. "No," he answered, "I think he is doing them a favor."[39]

Later in the resulting litigation concerning these events in the New Jersey Supreme Court, Thomas testified to the events of that night:

Two officers got out of the car . . . and talked to the officer on the landing. I asked about that time for the names of the officers or their shield numbers. They all refused and the only uniformed officer covered his shield. I could not see it. I then said, "Since I am not under arrest, I am leaving this car." Whereupon, the two officers in the car in front said, "No you don't," and the uniformed officer who was driving, hastily jumped out and shoved shut the door, which I had partially opened. He stood by the door, holding me in the car [until another officer returned and said] "Come along." I said I was not going voluntarily. One officer took me by one arm and another by another, and led me onto the ferry boat, and one officer stayed on the ferry boat until just at the point of its departure, when he got off. By this time, as I have already said, there were several officers, and they lined up along the brink, as if fearing I might climb over the iron gate after the boat was pulling out, to see what would happen, as if I was going to jump. They lined up with their arms outstretched and their hands that way [indicating] to repel me. I did not jump. I did not particularly care for swimming around there, and enough force had been used to make it perfectly plain that I, an American citizen, was being deported from an American city, without being arrested and without my will.[40]

In a radio address several days after his deportation, Thomas asked President Roosevelt to censure Hague's actions: "You are hero and leader to millions of Americans. You have repudiated for yourself, your party and your country, the degradation of lands where men are slaves of dictators. . . . Is it only foreign dictators whom we are to fear and fight?"[41]

Hague, however, had been vice-chairman of the Democratic National Committee since 1924. As floor manager of the Alfred E. Smith forces in 1932, he had toured the Middle Atlantic states to line up anti-Roosevelt delegates, issuing an early statement before the Democratic National Convention at Chicago on June 24, 1932, that Governor Roosevelt could not carry a single state east of the Mississippi River, and if nominated, had "no chance of winning in the November election."[42] When Roosevelt won the party nomination, Hague swiftly switched sides and promised that if Roosevelt would come to New Jersey to open his presidential campaign, Hague would "provide the largest political rally ever held in the United States."[43]

Roosevelt went to Sea Girt, New Jersey, on August 27 to address the mammoth outdoor rally Hague had organized, estimated to have been attended by 100,000 to 115,000 people. "If it wasn't the biggest rally in history up to that time, it must have been very close to it,"[44] wrote James A. Farley, Roosevelt's campaign manager. Roosevelt said, "There is no general who could have assembled such a host but my old friend, the mayor of Jersey City."[45]

From the time of Roosevelt's inauguration, every New Jersey federal patronage matter, including appointments of district attorneys, of officers to state agencies, and of judges to the federal courts, passed through Mayor Hague's office. In 1936 when Roosevelt returned to Jersey City to lay the cornerstone of a new hospital in the Hague Medical Center, it was reported that a quarter of a million cheering onlookers lined the streets to greet him.[46] With Hague therefore a tolerated—though perhaps not a respected—figure within the Roosevelt administration, it was not surprising that the President took no action in response to Thomas's radio challenge in 1938.[47]

The Socialist Party of Newark decided to hold a public meeting at which Norman Thomas would explain what had happened in Jersey City on April 30 and also deliver the speech he had been prevented from giving in Journal Square—an attack on Mayor Hague's violation of the constitutional rights of the C.I.O. in depriving members of the freedom of speech, the freedom of the press, and the freedom of assembly in their attempts to organize Jersey City workers. As Thomas rose to speak before the Newark meeting in Military Park on the evening of June 4, 1938, there appeared a twenty-five-piece brass band hired by Hague blaring "Hinkey-Dinky Parlez-vous," "Over There," and "Tiger Rag" to drown out Thomas's voice.

The band was followed by Hague's veterans, Legionnaires, Central Labor Union men, and Legion wives and children who waved small American flags with one hand, chanted "We want Americanism—Not Reds," and with the other hand threw rotten vegetables, eggs, and light bulbs at Thomas. Others carried placards similar to those that had been displayed in Jersey City: "Norman Thomas, Roger Baldwin and Stalin—One For All And All For One, KEEP OUT!" and "The Working People Of Our City Are Content—REDS KEEP OUT!" Thomas refused to be intimidated, insisted on continuing his speech, and called on the Newark police for protection, but the police felt they were unable to control the crowd and stopped the meeting.

In the C.I.O. litigation, Hague proudly testified about his militant veterans, most of whom were public employees or relatives of public employees, and how they would move at his command as they had in these recent events:

A. Now, as far as the veterans is concerned they move very rapidly; they are minute men. So don't be surprised if you find them in action two days after the receipt, or the publication, of any communication because they can muster three or four thousand veterans in twenty-four hours.

Q. Unquestionably.

A. They work fast over there [in Jersey City].

Q. You have no difficulty in marshalling veterans when you want them for your parades, do you?

A. No, I don't.

Q. Do you think you could have prevailed upon the veterans to have been a little less aggressive if you had asked them to?

A. Well, I wasn't desirous of asking them that.[48]

To demonstrate support of Hague's actions against the C.I.O. and Norman Thomas, an Americanization Day Parade was held in Jersey City on the night of June 6, 1938, announced by posters put up throughout the city featuring Hague's picture and the words, "Stand Shoulder to Shoulder with Mayor Hague and Keep the Communists Out." The *New York Times* reported that that night "a parade of National Guard troops, representatives of the A.F. of L., union, civic, fraternal and veteran groups flowed through Journal Square while the Mayor smiled approvingly from a reviewing stand. . . . At least half of the persons who lined the mile-long parade route and filled the square waved American flags, while overhead aerial bombs exploded and fireworks lighted the sky. . . ."[49]

The people cheered lustfully when Hague declared: "This is the voice of the American people speaking; this is the American way of doing it. Nobody should ever hesitate to take their cause to the people. The people of Jersey City are sustaining their mayor in opposing any invasion by those Reds."[50]

It was reported in the press that Hague had been strongly advised by his legal counsel not to become enmeshed in pressing the free speech and assembly issue with the C.I.O. and Thomas, advice he probably disregarded because of his inability to understand the implications of his actions or the way they were being viewed by much of the nation. At any rate, he was soon over his head in litigation.

While Hague appealed in the United States Circuit Court the district court decision which held that the Jersey City permit power had been used as an instrument of arbitrary suppression of the free expression of views, Vanderbilt brought three court actions on behalf of Norman Thomas. Two of the actions were against the Jersey City police—a charge of kidnapping under the Lindbergh Law and a civil suit for assault against Thomas. The third action was for a writ of mandamus from the state courts ordering Hague to permit Thomas to speak in Jersey City.

The Supreme Court of New Jersey rejected each of these actions in October of 1938 when it stated that Thomas "has no more right to speak in public places in that city, such as highways and parks, without a permit than he has to invade a citizen's home without invitation. The Director of Public Safety knows the temper of the people he serves. . . . The public is entitled to their tranquility, and the discretion to issue the permit in question is vested with the chosen representative of the city."[51]

To many, however, the findings of the extended trial in the state supreme court had shown a deliberate policy of the Jersey City officials to discriminate against the C.I.O., the A.C.L.U., and Norman Thomas in any possible way to prevent the public expression of their ideas in Jersey City. This suppression was defended under the plea of the maintenance of public order. Some considered this excuse specious in both the C.I.O. case and the Thomas case and believed that, if allowed, it would place the rights of free speech and assembly at the mercy of any political faction, would mean that such rights could be sacrificed to intimidation. The denial of the rights of speech and assembly was essentially a manifestation of intolerance, that the views of the C.I.O. and the American Civil Liberties Union and Thomas—critics and detractors of Hague's administration—were unacceptable to the authorities of Jersey City. The law alone could not instill that degree of tolerance upon which democratic political, religious, and educational institutions rested, but the courts could, in concrete cases, aid in preserving free institutions by forbidding definite acts that suppressed lawful free expression.

The C.I.O., now fighting Hague in the Third Circuit, along with Thomas and Vanderbilt, who had appealed the New Jersey Supreme Court holding in the New Jersey Court of Errors and Appeals, attempted to corner Hague in the state and federal courts by testing the legality of the Jersey City permit ordinance he had applied on the two occasions to deny the rights of free assembly and speech.

To the court of errors and appeals, Vanderbilt submitted a brief for the reversal of the supreme court decision on the grounds that the right of free speech and peaceable assembly, under the United States Constitution and the New Jersey Constitution, extended to public places and could not be subject to previous restraints; that the Jersey City ordinance permitted the denial of a permit to Thomas upon the basis of anticipation of riot, disturbances, and disorderly assemblage and was therefore unconstitutional and void; that a permit to speak in a public place could not be constitutionally denied in order to maintain the public tranquility; that, assuming the ordinance was constitutional, the issuance of a permit thereunder was not discretionary, and Director of Public Safety Casey's refusal to issue a permit to Thomas was arbitrary; and that, assuming the issuance of a permit under the ordinance was discretionary, Casey's refusal to issue a permit constituted a clear abuse of discretion.

After Vanderbilt had submitted his brief but before oral argument, the Circuit Court of Appeals handed down its opinion in *Committee for Industrial Organization v. Hague* (101 F. 2d 774 [1938]), holding the ordinance under which Hague had acted in the C.I.O. case, and hence the Thomas case, unconstitutional. This decision was appealed by Hague, but was upheld by the Supreme Court of the United States in a landmark opinion delivered on June 5, 1939, agreeing that the rights of freedom of speech and of peaceable assembly were protected against infringement by state action by the due process clause of the Fourteenth Amendment, and that a municipal ordinance requiring the obtaining of a permit for a public assembly in or upon the public streets, highways, parks, or buildings of the city was not a valid exercise of the police power. Such a permit system based on the decision of the director of public safety as to whether a meeting would lead to "riots, disturbances, or disorderly assemblage . . . can thus, as the record discloses, be made the instrument of arbitrary suppression of free expression of views on national affairs, for the prohibition of all speaking will undoubtedly 'prevent' such eventualities." (*Hague v. C.I.O.*, 307 U.S. 496, 511 [1939])

"We owe you far more than we can ever pay for the service you have given to Civil Liberty," Thomas wrote to Vanderbilt, "and it is somewhat ironic to see it suggested that you are doing it for big fees. Would you like me to give evidence to the contrary? Or would you rather that I should keep still?"[52]

Vanderbilt replied, "I don't think there is anything to be gained by carrying on newspaper controversy with the Mayor who has nothing to lose and considerable to gain by continuing the barrage."[53]

The first major battle had been won against the mayor who had declared on more than one occasion, "I am the law," the mayor whom Vanderbilt had more than once called the "two-bit Hitler on the Hudson."

CHAIRMAN OF THE BOARD

As a trial and appellate lawyer, Vanderbilt had represented the political right and left, the corporation and its employees, the county and its citizens. From his defense of Norman Thomas, which had branded him a "communist," at least in the eyes of Jersey City authorities, he turned to the management of a major business concern in the largest corporate case of his practice.

One day in October, 1938, shortly after Vanderbilt's term as president of the American Bar Association was over, Chancellor Josiah O. Wolcott of Delaware had called him long distance.

"Mr. Vanderbilt," he said, "I am looking for a lawyer with two qualifications: he must be a diplomatic administrator, number one, and number two, at the same time, extremely courageous if the occasion demands it."

"Your honor," Vanderbilt responded, "I doubt if such a man exists. Diplomacy and courage can't be part of the same individual. But I will try to think of some names to fit your bill as closely as possible. Could I call you back in an hour?"

"Damn it, Vanderbilt, I didn't call to get a lecture in psychology or a list of lawyers. I called to offer you a job."[54]

The Loft candy and beverage concern had won a $48 million suit against Charles G. Guth, the president of the Pepsi-Cola Company, who was unable either to raise this sum in cash or to secure the necessary $96 million bond issue. As a result, Chancellor Wolcott had taken over the two Delaware concerns and had contacted Vanderbilt to help resolve the dilemma.

Guth, a former president of Loft who had been dissatisfied with Loft's business arrangement with the Coca-Cola Company, had bought the Pepsi-Cola Company in 1931 with Loft capital and had plowed more Loft money into the failing soft drink company, turning Pepsi-Cola into a highly profitable corporation with the novel introduction of a twelve-ounce bottle of the soft drink for a nickel. When Guth was driven from Loft in 1935 because of his one-man manage-

ment of the concern and by the failing finances of the company
caused by his mismanagement of its resources, he took with him 91
percent of the Pepsi-Cola stock. The other 9 percent was held by his
friends and family. A suit was brought against Guth by Loft to gain
control of this stock since all the risk of failure in the purchase of the
Pepsi-Cola Company had been Loft's, not Guth's; and as Loft
resources, not Guth's, had been poured into the company, Loft
believed it deserved the rewards of the now profitable company.

A massive proxy fight followed. As the battle proceeded to court,
Loft was staving off bankruptcy. It was losing so much money each
year that its only hope for recovery was the suit against Guth, which,
if successful, would bring it 91 percent of the Pepsi-Cola stock.
Chancellor Wolcott, in his opinion of September 17, 1938, had held
that, in building the Pepsi-Cola Company, Guth had "used Loft
executives, Loft personnel, Loft equipment, Loft facilities, Loft mer-
chants, Loft money, Loft credits,"[55] and so the results did indeed
belong to the candy concern. All of Guth's stock, the money he had
received as loans and dividends, and the profits earned were to be
turned over to Loft.

Guth believed that, as Pepsi-Cola had been developed partly by
his own efforts, he was entitled to the stock and Loft was entitled
only to an equitable adjustment based on its contribution to the
success of the Pepsi-Cola Company. He therefore appealed the
decision to the state supreme court.

Pending the court's decision, the management of the Pepsi-Cola
Company was put under a provisional board of directors. Three
members of the board were to be named by Guth, three by the
president of Loft, and a seventh, the deciding vote in all matters of
controversy—which inevitably would be every matter—was to be
named by Chancellor Wolcott. It was at this point that Wolcott had
called Vanderbilt.

During the next eight months, over the course of thirty meetings,
the business of the board was to keep the company running, and
Vanderbilt's job as chairman was to act as a buffer between the two
factions in order to preserve the stability of the company. That this
was a formidable task was evident in the fact that neither group could
trust any secretary to record accurately the minutes of these meetings, and so a court reporter was retained to transcribe every word
spoken, immediately type the transcripts of the meetings, and present a copy to every member of the board. As chairman of a board of
directors that could never agree on any policy, Vanderbilt, by casting

each deciding vote, ran the company for a year according to his own judgment.

It was soon discovered that, as the interim board carried on its work, Mr. Guth, fearing the appellate court decision, was preparing an escape route by secretly carrying out plans to launch another cola drink company, Noxie-Kola. Moreover, he was planning to take with him many of the executives of Pepsi-Cola and its bottlers, and, using his same raiding tactics, was starting this operation with Pepsi-Cola funds. On March 13, 1939, the interim board of Pepsi-Cola removed him from office as general manager of the company and appointed a committee of one Pepsi-Cola board member, one Loft board member, and Vanderbilt to manage the Pepsi-Cola Company.

A month later, the Supreme Court of Delaware affirmed the decision of the court of chancery, holding that the purchase of Pepsi-Cola was a corporate opportunity available to Guth only because of his association with Loft. Therefore, the stock belonged to Loft. The Loft shareholders were paid with an exchange of Pepsi-Cola stock. Vanderbilt stepped down as chairman and became chief counsel for Pepsi-Cola and a member of its board of directors.

The dispute with Loft was not the only conflict in which Pepsi-Cola was engaged in 1939. For many years Pepsi-Cola had been fighting a vigorous and expensive legal contest with the Coca-Cola Company, which had claimed an exclusive trademark right to the word *cola*. Wishing to terminate the drawn-out legal battle, Vanderbilt directed the litigation in over thirty lawsuits in the United States and several more in foreign countries, winning favorable decisions in the courts of the United States and then in Canada. Coca-Cola appealed the Canadian decision to the British Privy Council, whose decision would be binding throughout the British Empire, but Pepsi-Cola, handling its case through British associates, on March 19, 1942, won final approval for the use of the Pepsi-Cola trademark throughout the world.

A MOMENT IN MAINE

As he woke early and worked seventeen-hour days practicing law, teaching at the law school, leading the Clean Government movement, and promoting judicial reform projects, Vanderbilt knew that Maine was always there. Leaving the Eastern Airlines terminal at La Guardia Airport in New York, he could be in Boston in less than two hours, then, by shifting to Northeast Airlines, arrive in Portland, Maine, in another hour. During the summer months Floss would be waiting for him at the airport to drive him up Route 1 and on to Brunswick thirty-two miles away. Passing Bowdoin College, they followed a country road eight miles through pine woods out Harpswell Neck, driving by only an occasional farmhouse or cottage. Finally they turned at their stone wall and on slowly down the twisting dirt driveway past the fields of blueberries and scrub growth, past the caretaker's cottage, around the granite and shale outcroppings and through the forest of pines, past the barn and apple orchard and then the stand of maples and birch. Three-quarters of a mile from the road, the drive turned to the left, the woods opened up, and there before them was "At Ease," their large white Georgian colonial home with dark green shutters, a row of ancient oaks in front, and a lawn that rolled slowly down toward the bay. The expanse of Casco Bay, the black ledges and silent islands, and the sunsets behind Mount Washington and the Presidential Range a hundred miles in the distance were more beautiful than anything Arthur or Floss had ever seen, and there they went each summer, and occasionally in the spring and fall, to rest.

Each morning as Floss worked in her sunken garden and cutting gardens and as the children were leaving to explore the islands or to sail down toward Mere Point for the races, Vanderbilt called his office to talk to his secretaries and associates in order to oversee his law practice without returning to Newark too often during July and August. The rest of the morning and some of the afternoon was spent on the side porch with his Soundscriber, answering correspondence which would be transcribed daily in Newark by three secretaries. When it seemed to his children at the saltwater pool in a field by the shore that if their father didn't hurry up the afternoon would soon be over, one of them would run up to the house to tell him it was time to go swimming, the one form of exercise he enjoyed. Later in the afternoon he worked on any writing projects with pressing deadlines, read some of the books he had brought with him, or sat with Floss and the children in chairs under the oaks.

Although he began each summer with every intention of accomplishing all the projects he had put off during the busy year, shipping ahead to Maine wooden crates of books and cartons of files, he came to believe that other aspects of his long summer vacation were just as important. Maine, he believed, could preserve his health and make it possible for him to continue to carry an amount of work that otherwise would have become an impossible burden years before. He retreated to Maine in the summer, physically overextended. He came to relax and regain a sense of fulfillment and life.

Sailing in their racing sloop, the *Bunny*, out on the bay in the Chris-Craft cruiser, or walking in the evening with his family through the paths in the woods and down to the shore where the wind waves splashed on the rocks began to put in perspective the problems which could become easily distorted and out of proportion in the din of the city and the rush of a crowded life. And the chug of a lobster boat up the bay in the early morning fog and the quiet breezes moving in the leaves of the oaks in the night seemed to restore his stamina and health. By the end of the summer in Maine, he was again anxious to get back to work.

V The Crowded Years, 1938–1948

THE WHITE FLAME OF PROGRESS

The work of the American Bar Association in 1938 focused attention on the deficiencies in the administration of justice in many state and federal courts and helped pave the way for the subsequent passage of several important Congressional acts which simplified and integrated the federal judicial system.

That the time was ripe for such legislative action was evident in the history of the campaign for the passage of the first of these measures, the Federal Rules of Civil Procedure. Whereas in actions in equity, federal procedure was governed by Supreme Court rules, procedure in actions at law conformed to the procedural rules of the state in which the federal court sat. Because there were wide variations among the states, there could be no set of uniform rules in the federal court system. This situation created great confusion in determining the applicable procedure of a particular federal court from an array of state statutes, rules of court, judicial decisions, and state constitutional provisions.

In 1912 Thomas W. Shelton, appointed chairman of the American Bar Association's Committee on Uniform Judicial Procedure, had begun a twenty-two-year campaign to introduce a bill in Congress that would give the United States Supreme Court the same rule-making power in actions at law that it had long exercised in equity. Despite the support of successive presidents and attorney generals, Shelton's bill was always blocked by the adamant opposition of the chairman of the Senate Judiciary Committee, Senator Thomas A.

Walsh, who did not believe lawyers should be required to be familiar with two different procedural systems in actions at law, one for the state courts and one for the federal courts. After Shelton's death in 1930, the committee was discontinued. But in 1933, after Senator Walsh died, an interest was shown in Shelton's proposal by Attorney General Homer S. Cummings, who directed various studies to be made in the Department of Justice and who in 1934 put the resulting bill through Congress.

The legislation served as an enabling act, delegating to the Supreme Court the authority to draft rules regulating civil procedure in the federal courts. Chief Justice Charles Evans Hughes appointed an advisory committee headed by former Attorney General William D. Mitchell and the dean of the Yale Law School, Charles E. Clark, to prepare rules that would constitute a uniform code of practice and procedure for the federal court system. Soliciting the suggestions of individual judges, lawyers, and law professors throughout the country and the recommendations of committees organized by every state bar association, the advisory committee drafted a set of rules which incorporated the best practices of the states.

The Federal Rules of Civil Procedure became effective on September 16, 1938. In merging law and equity into one procedural system, in standardizing federal procedure, in introducing in the federal courts the most simplified and modern procedural system in the United States, in serving as a model for procedural reform in the states, in utilizing the assistance and experience of the legal profession in the process of drafting, and in opening the way for additional comprehensive acts to improve the administration of justice throughout the federal court system—the Federal Rules of Civil Procedure remain the greatest single landmark in American procedural reform.[1]

Largely because of the success of the Federal Rules of Civil Procedure, the passage of additional reform measures seemed as swift as the battle for simplification of civil procedure had been prolonged.

The second bill, passed in 1939, created the Administrative Office of the United States Courts.

Although the Judiciary Act of 1789 had established the basic framework of the federal court system, thereafter the judiciary had grown as a hybrid with no attempt to mold it into a centralized system. By the twentieth century, any integration or cohesion had all but disappeared.

The administration of this unwieldy string of courts scattered across the nation lay in the hands of the Justice Department in the person of the attorney general, who, as incongruous as it seemed, was also counsel for the chief litigant in the federal courts, the United States. In 1938 in a communication to Congress, Attorney General Cummings emphasized the need for an office of the courts to take over the financial and administrative work of the federal court system, an idea which the Conference of Senior Circuit Judges had been advocating for over a decade:

I am convinced that the function of the judiciary cannot be performed efficiently and expeditiously unless the courts are equipped with proper and adequate administrative machinery which they themselves can control and for which they will be responsible. The independence of the judiciary would seem to require that its administrative work should not be handled by one of the executive departments, or be under the control of the chief litigant in the Federal Courts.[2]

Cummings appointed Vanderbilt chairman of a commission of five lawyers—George Morris, former chairman of the House of Delegates of the A.B.A.; Herschel W. Arant, president of the Association of American Law Schools and dean of the Ohio State University Law School; and Gordon Dean and Alexander Holtzoff of the Department of Justice—to confer with a committee of five senior circuit judges appointed by Chief Justice Hughes—Judges Manton, Parker, Evans, Stone, and Groner—to draft a bill for the establishment of an office to separate the executive and judicial branches of the government in the field of court administration. Their proposed bill received the unanimous approval of the House of Delegates of the A.B.A., and, after hearings before the House of Representatives and Senate, was enacted by Congress on August 7, 1939.

The legislation created an administrative department for the judicial branch of the federal government to supervise the personnel of the courts, to examine the state of the dockets of the various courts, to serve as a clearing house of information as to where judges were needed for temporary service and as to what judges were available for such service, to prepare and publish statistical data for the use of senior circuit judges, to prepare and present the budget of the federal courts to Congress, to disburse the moneys for the operation of the courts, and to make recommendations for improving judicial business practices within the federal circuits.[3] Thus, the Administrative Office attended to the necessary housekeeping functions of the court system while scrutinizing the work of the courts to discover more efficient means of promoting promptness and efficiency in the disposition of litigation.

As the act was the first in the history of the United States to provide a distinct agency for the businesslike administration of the courts, it was, in the words of Judge John Parker, "the most important piece of legislation affecting the judiciary since the Judiciary Act of 1789."[4] The Administrative Office proved so successful in showing that courts could utilize modern methods of business management without jeopardizing the integrity of the judicial process that in 1948 the Section of Judicial Administration of the American Bar Association would take steps to promote the formation of similar offices in the several states. Ten years later, seventeen states, the District of Columbia, and Puerto Rico would have their own administrative offices.[5]

As a result of several years of agitation by the committee on administrative law of the American Bar Association, by the President's Committee on Administrative Management, and by the committee on administrative agencies and tribunals of the Section of Judicial Administration of the A.B.A., Attorney General Frank Murphy in February of 1939 appointed a twelve-man committee headed by Dean Acheson to study the new profusion of federal regulatory agencies and to investigate the need for procedural reform in the field of administrative law.

Thirty-five administrative agencies that exercised executive powers and subordinate legislative or judicial powers to determine, either by rule or decision, private rights and obligations had arisen between 1776 and 1930. With the nationwide depression of the 1930's demanding nationwide remedies, more power was concentrated in the executive branch with the birth of seventeen additional agencies. More than two hundred emergency agencies would mushroom during the years of the Second World War.

As the adjudication of controversies and statements of rights by administrative agencies far exceeded the output of the traditional courts—so that, for instance, one agency alone, the Federal Board of Tax Appeals, decided more cases each year than all the federal courts—the growth of administrative law had created a host of new problems in the administration of justice. Most of the agencies were created without regard to the existence, functions, or jurisdiction of the others, leading to uncertainty and disagreement as to the scope of their powers. Their work was largely adjudicatory in nature, yet they were neither bound by the judicial structure of courts nor bound to observe the fundamental procedural safeguards that were essential to the preservation of private rights. Each had its own peculiar procedure and methods—from an attorney's right to appear in a matter for his client up to the perfection of an appeal—with enough variations between them to be troublesome to the practitioner.

This divergency of procedure, coupled with the failure of some agencies to formalize and publicize their procedures or to make known promptly their regulations and decisions,[6] made it impossible in many instances to determine the existing law of an agency, a situation that discouraged lawyers from appearing before them. Instead, lawyers advised their clients to retain as counsel experts on the particular agency with which they were engaged in litigation.

The most serious fault of the administrative agencies was that each combined legislative and judicial functions. The same agency and sometimes the same men served in the same matter as rulemaker, investigator, prosecutor, and judge. As the 1937 report of the President's Committee on Administrative Management recognized, "Commission decisions affecting private rights and conduct lie under the suspicion of being rationalizations of the preliminary findings which the Commission, in the role of prosecutor, presented to itself."[7] This situation limited the check of judicial review and weakened public confidence in the fairness of the commissions.

With the aid of a squad of young lawyers who had complete access to the federal agencies, the Attorney General's Committee on Administrative Procedure spent two years studying the administrative establishment, investigating and dissecting the procedures of twenty-seven of the more important federal administrative units, discovering the common traits of the administrative process and the defects in that process, and devising proposals to remedy them. In 1941 it submitted to the attorney general a report which analyzed the need for corrective legislation.

A minority report was filed at the same time by three members of the committee—Carl McFarland, the chairman of the American Bar Association's Committee on Administrative Law; E. Blythe Stason, the dean of Michigan Law School; and Vanderbilt—who, while agreeing with the basic principles of the majority report, insisted on strictly applying standards applicable to judicial tribunals to the administrative agencies. The minority believed that a recognition that administrative adjudication was judicial in nature would help lead to the elimination of prejudiced examiners, of *ex parte* hearings, of biased reports based on improper or insufficient evidence or no evidence at all, of the habit of "dipping into the record" as the basis of decision, and of executive or political influence on the administrative mind.

The majority and minority differed on three basic propositions. The first was the necessity for a legislative statement of standards of fair procedure, which was favored by the minority and opposed by the majority. The minority believed that a legislative statement of the fundamentals of fair play would help to eliminate much of the mystery and variability of the administrative process and in this way alleviate the distrust felt by many litigants and lawyers who came in contact with the agencies. The majority believed that such a statement of principles could never encompass the great range of agencies and that it would interfere with the flexibility of the administrative process—one of its most important attributes.

The second split concerned how the legislative, executive, and judicial functions of the agencies could best be separated. The majority advocated an internal separation by isolating those engaged in rule-making or legislative responsibilities from those engaged in judicial tasks. The minority, citing the traditional division between prosecutor and trial court in ordinary criminal litigation and the Bureau of Internal Revenue and the Board of Tax Appeals as examples of a successful division between rulemaker and prosecutor on the one hand and judge on the other, proposed the complete separation of functions, with the division of all agencies into two independent groups of agencies.

The third question on which the members of the committee disagreed concerned the scope of judicial review, an issue that the minority argued was interrelated with the question of the separation of functions. Until complete external separation of functions was provided, the minority believed that judicial review had to be given a wide scope so that abuses of concentrated power from the merging of legislative, investigative, prosecuting, adjudicative, and appellate powers in a single agency could be remedied by the balance of judicial review regarding all aspects of the administrative process. The majority felt that too broad a grant of judicial review could seriously hamper administrative efficiency and the vitality of the agencies as an independent means of determining private rights.

Bills patterned after the recommendations contained in both the majority and minority reports were introduced in Congress in 1941, but the Senate Judiciary Committee, after holding extensive hearings, suspended action in consideration of the emergency of World War II.

With the crop of agencies that sprouted during the war years,

Congress exhibited apprehension at the mounting power of the executive branch and so reopened its hearings on the bills. The final result, the McCarran-Sumners Bill, which came to be known as the Administrative Procedure Act and which incorporated some of the views of both the minority and majority reports, passed the Senate on March 12, 1946, and the House on May 24, 1946, and was signed into law by President Truman on July 11, 1946.

As with all legislation, the Administrative Procedure Act involved compromises. It did set forth the procedural principles by which Congress expected the administrative agencies to operate, conforming to a considerable degree to the suggestions of the minority report. The administrative agencies with combined prosecuting and adjudicatory powers, however, seemed too strong a tradition for Congress to overcome. The complete separation of functions was not instituted, although safeguards to ensure a real internal division were provided for, including measures providing that hearing officers be independent of any officers engaged in investigative or prosecuting functions, and that the appointment and tenure of the hearing officers be under the control of the Civil Service Commission, to free them further from agency influence. Concerning the third disagreement between the majority and minority reports, Congress did not give judicial review as wide a scope as the minority had hoped, but rather provided that persons adversely affected or aggrieved by any agency action should be entitled to judicial review in statutory form, or, in the absence or inadequacy thereof, by any applicable form of legal action. The courts were to defer to administrative findings of fact if there was substantial evidence to support them, reviewing only questions of law.

In incorporating aspects of both of the model bills, the Administrative Procedure Act dispelled much of the fog that had surrounded the work of the administrative agencies, helped to protect the individual litigant from the hazards of uncertain administrative procedure which could result in unfair or arbitrary action, and at the same time preserved the flexibility and resourcefulness of the agencies that made them important additions to the traditional legislative, executive, and judicial units of government.[8]

Immediately after the Federal Rules of Civil Procedure had become effective in 1938, the Section of Criminal Law of the American Bar Association had recommended a bill authorizing the Supreme Court to bring about complete procedural reform in the administration of federal criminal justice, which still was based on the diverse systems of procedure of the various states. President

Roosevelt offered his support: "Much has been accomplished in recent years in the direction of simplification of civil procedure and coordination of the operations of the courts, especially in the Federal field. Much still remains to be attained in the realm of criminal law and penology. I am hopeful that Congress will make provisions for the regulation and simplification of Federal criminal procedure by means of judicial rule-making similar to that made by it several years ago in respect to Federal civil procedure."[9] An enabling act was passed by Congress on June 29, 1940, forming the last link in the chain of statutes needed for complete federal procedural reform through the Supreme Court's rule-making power.

　　In February of 1941, Chief Justice Charles Evans Hughes appointed Vanderbilt chairman of an advisory committee of eighteen members of the legal profession—lawyers, judges, prosecutors, and educators—to draft rules of procedure in criminal issues for the federal district courts. Committees of lawyers in each state were appointed by senior circuit judges and district judges to cooperate with the advisory committee, and similar groups were formed by every state bar association to recommend the best practices of the several states. A research staff was set up to study the recommendations and to prepare an initial draft following as closely as the subject matter permitted the order and form of the Federal Rules of Civil Procedure. Every member of the advisory committee studied the draft individually and then as a group. During the course of four years, there were ten separate drafts, two of which were examined by the cooperating committees, as well as discussed at the judicial conferences of the separate circuits, at bar association meetings throughout the country, and at the annual meeting of the American Bar Association. A final draft was submitted to the justices of the Supreme Court, who studied and revised it and then presented it to Congress. On March 21, 1946, the Federal Rules of Criminal Procedure were promulgated by Congress.

　　Federal criminal procedure had become mired in the same overgrown, technical, expensive, and dilatory system that was straining much of the law. Wrote Attorney General Tom Clark:

At the very inception of criminal cases the ends of justice have all too frequently been defeated by a bewildering array of pleas in bar, pleas in abatement, motions to quash, motions to dismiss and demurrers. No prosecutor desired to face such a barrage of technicality and few defense counsel enjoyed the prospect of preparing a series of tedious motions and pleas. The only benefactor of this confusion was perhaps the wily defendant to whom expense was immaterial, but to whom delay was paramount. Further chaos was encountered in the many procedural steps which until now were regulated by a strange mixture of Federal laws, state laws, common law, and rules and decisions of courts, both state and Federal. These diverse points of view resulted in a legal "wilderness of single instances" utterly devoid of reason and uniformity; procedure varied from court to court so that an attorney from one state often found himself virtually unable to try a case in the Federal court of another state.[10]

The Federal Rules of Criminal Procedure, designed "to provide for the just determination of every criminal proceeding" and to "secure simplicity in procedure, fairness in administration, and the elimination of unjustifiable expense and delay" established a brief, uniform code of procedure to expedite trials from verdict to appeal and to give undue advantage to neither defendant nor state. For example, there were rules that provided: that the old type of indictments couched in several pages of ponderous Elizabethan English be replaced with a simple form requiring no more than five lines; that a defendant could obtain an effective change of venue either within or without the state where the alleged offense was committed if the court felt that local prejudice could prevent a fair and impartial trial; that indigent defendants receive additional protection such as subpoenas at government expense for witnesses located anywhere in the United States; that warrants of arrest be valid throughout the United States instead of only in the issuing district; that defendants no longer be able to obstruct the progress of a prosecution by the filing of pleas in abatement, demurrers, and motions to quash; and that all preliminary objections be included in a single motion.

The advisory committee reduced to sixty rules which took less than three-sixteenths of an inch of shelf space the statutes and decisions governing criminal procedure which had occupied over sixteen feet on the bookshelf. The new rules were recognized as models of simplicity and flexibility and were later adopted in whole or in part by states intent on improving their system of criminal procedure. Moreover, the importance of the rule-making power— that the judiciary be enabled to regulate its own procedure—gained further acceptance with the passage of the Federal Rules of Criminal Procedure and became thereafter a dominant principle of federal and state procedural reforms. No longer would the federal courts have to wait for a procedural problem to become critical before a state legislature would attempt to correct it. With the new rule-making power of the Supreme Court, the task of effecting changes in the federal procedural machinery, when the need arose, was simple.[11]

On March 23, 1946, Vanderbilt was appointed by Secretary of War Robert P. Patterson as chairman of the War Department's advisory committee on military justice. The committee was composed of Walter P. Armstrong, Joseph W. Henderson, and Jacob M. Lashley, former presidents of the American Bar Association, retired Chief Judge Frederick T. Crane of the New York Court of Appeals, United States Circuit Judge Morris A. Soper of Baltimore, former Chief Justice Floyd E. Thompson of the Supreme Court of Illinois, William T. Joyner of the North Carolina bar, and Judge Alexander Holtzoff of the United States District Court of the District of Columbia.

The purpose of the committee was to study the Army courts-martial system, which had fallen under attack and was under investigation by both houses of Congress at the end of World War II, and to recommend methods of reform conforming to the American conception of justice and fair play.

The existing system of military justice, based on the Articles of War which had last been revised after World War I, was defective in its lack of checks and remedies. Too many commanding officers attempted to control or interfere with courts-martial proceedings, to influence the courts they had appointed to force findings of guilt, to override the recommendations of the staff judge advocate, or to pressure the staff judge advocate to change his recommendation. The accused was in a relatively helpless position when confronted with the power of the government, a disparity of strength accentuated when the interest of the government in a case was strong enough to tempt the prosecutor to strain to convict, or when legally unskilled officers conducted the proceedings. There was such variability and severity in the impact of the system on the accused as to bring military courts into disrepute among the large body of drafted men accustomed to the safeguards and protections of the civil court system.

The advisory committee based its findings on the study of hundreds of briefs and memoranda submitted by laymen and lawyers, most of whom had served on courts-martial during the war, on testimony taken at nine months of regional hearings throughout the country at which scores of witnesses appeared, on a two-day hearing in Washington at which high-ranking Army officers and representatives of veteran organizations testified, and on recommendations solicited from the nation's legal profession.

While the committee decided that the Army could not operate successfully under a civil judicial system and that a civilian entering the Army had to surrender as many of the safeguards which protected his civil liberties as was consistent with the operation of the Army, it disagreed with the testimony of many officers who argued that military justice should be left a function of command. It was essential, the committee believed, that enlisted men realize that if charged with an offense, their case would not rest entirely in the hands of their accuser, but that rather with the help of competent counsel, they would have the opportunity to present their evidence to an impartial tribunal with the right to impartial review.

The advisory committee therefore recommended: that any interference or attempt to influence the court or reviewing authority be prohibited and that any actual attempt be punished; that all judicial officers of the courts-martial be members of the Judge Advocate General's Department and appointed by the Department, both to provide for the adequate legal structure of a trial and to place key personnel beyond the influence of the commanding officer; that the final review of all general courts-martial be placed in the Judge Advocate General's Department; and that a board of officers be appointed to consider other changes in the Articles of War and the *Manual of Courts-Martial* concerning areas which interested the committee but about which it did not feel qualified to express opinions.

The recommendations of the advisory committee and of the special review committee which succeeded it became the basis for substantial amendments to the Articles of War passed in 1948, and laid the groundwork for the Uniform Code of Military Justice enacted into law on May 5, 1950.[12]

BACK TO WESLEYAN

As Vanderbilt's work on the committees drafting legislation to improve the federal judicial system took him to Washington each month during these crowded years, so the problems his college fraternity, Delta Kappa Epsilon, had begun to encounter took him monthly to Middletown, Connecticut.

During the Roaring Twenties, the scholastic and moral standards of the Deke house had collapsed. The fraternity had assumed the atmosphere of a country club; the brothers had little interest in Deke or Wesleyan affairs and even less interest in their courses. The grade-point average of the Deke house was the lowest of any of Wesleyan's thirteen fraternities and was well below the college average.

When Vanderbilt was elected alumni president of the fraternity in 1935, this situation was brought to his attention. "Five years ago last Fall," he wrote in 1940, "[a Deke brother] shocked me by telling me that he felt he had made a mistake by letting his son go Deke when he might have gone either Alpha Delta or Psi U. Professor [George] Dutcher confided in me that not only was our scholastic standing very bad—in fact, the worst—but the morale at the House was equally low, not that the boys were bad, or anything like that; they were merely wasting their time, and that, in my humble judgment, is a crime, in college or out. . . . It is our job, I think, to make it clear to them that the greatest happiness is to be found in making the most of themselves."[13]

With the help of several other alumni, Vanderbilt decided to try to restore the chapter. For the rest of his life, he traveled to Wesleyan ten to twenty times each year to talk to the brothers about their studies, encouraging them to call him by his college nickname "Art Van," joining the Dekes in night "bull sessions," listening to their complaints and questions, and advising them as he was able. He tried to instill in them a sense of the importance of their college work and to help them look ahead to plan their careers. He talked with Wesleyan administrators and professors to see how he could assist the members of the chapter. He invited group after group of Deke brothers to have dinner conferences with him in New York and to go to the theater afterward. Finding leadership and responsibility lacking, he initiated a plan whereby seniors were to act individually as advisors to freshmen, following their work, consulting with their professors, checking their records before and after each midsemester examination, and helping them plan their activities, scholastic and extracurricular. Gradually, the chapter's attitude toward scholastic achievement started to change. The grade-point average of the fraternity rose, the Dekes began to win a number of Wesleyan's awards and prizes, and the bonds between the members of the fraternity strengthened.

At the same time, the alumni members of the fraternity began to take great interest in the chapter's scholastic accomplishments and the rising prestige of the house on the Wesleyan campus. Vanderbilt seized this opportunity to eliminate the large mortgage on the fraternity house which had been taken out when the Depression prevented many alumni from fulfilling their pledges toward the construction of the house. In a series of trips, meetings, dinners, and after-dinner talks with the Deke alumni and through a voluminous correspondence, he encouraged all the Deke brothers to develop closer contact with the undergraduates and to help reduce the mortgage which hung heavy over the chapter.

Within several years, DKE had risen in scholastic standing at Wesleyan from thirteenth to second place, a rank it continued to maintain; and on the seventy-fifth anniversary reunion of the fraternity in 1942, the $45,000 mortgage on the Deke house was burned.

Vanderbilt maintained a close relationship with each succeeding fraternity class. His secretaries and associates were amazed at the amount of time he spent on the telephone with officers of the fraternity, reviewing the scholastic standing of each member of the house, suggesting steps that could be taken to help those who were having trouble, and encouraging those who were doing well. It seemed unbelievable to them that a person with so many matters constantly pressing for attention would have the interest to concern himself with the details of the lives of the brothers of his college fraternity. "It is a great thing to come back and be treated as an equal—" he explained, "called by your college nickname—be argued with, not submitted to. Years roll off your shoulders. . . . I used to like to come back to Middletown as an escape, as a sanctuary, if you please. . . . And so, Middletown as an escape seemed almost as essential as home. . . ."[14]

THE MAYOR AT WORK AGAIN

By 1940 the annual proposals of the New Jersey Judicial Council for revising the judicial article of the state constitution had still not passed both the general assembly and the senate in a single year. Undoubtedly, this "legislative run-around" would have continued had it not been for Mayor Frank Hague. Correctly perceiving that the modernization of the state courts would be a breach of the judicial Maginot Line he had constructed around his Hudson County bailiwick, Hague attempted to terminate all work for court reform.

It was only when the incoming president of the New Jersey State Bar Association, Milton M. Unger, announced his intention in 1940 of reappointing Vanderbilt as a member of the judicial council for another five-year term, that his predecessor in office revealed that he had just filled the only two vacancies on the council, a fact of which the state bar had not been informed. The New Jersey Bar Association found this move "peculiar," and the *New Jersey Law Journal* charac-terized it as "a rather extraordinary attempt to quietly dump Vander-bilt."[15] Vanderbilt was just as blunt: " ... Mayor Hague, whom I have never met for I learned early in politics that it was as important not to know certain people as it was to know certain others, decided that I was becoming too expert in the arts of agitation so he had me disassociated from service on the Judicial Council by the very simple expedient of having one of my good friends, who was president of our State Bar Association and who had the power of appointment of the lawyer members of the Judicial Council, simply fail to reappoint me."[16]

Although with this move Hague had hoped to end all the talk of court reorganization and constitutional amendments, his maneuver instead brought to a boil a situation that had simmered for years. At Vanderbilt's prodding, Governor Charles Edison put through the legislature an act to set up a Commission on Revision of the New Jersey Constitution to draft a model constitution for the state. The commission was to consist of seven members: two appointed by the speaker of the house, two appointed by the president of the senate, two appointed by the governor, and one appointed by the members of the Commission.

To block Vanderbilt's being appointed, the speaker of the house and the president of the senate, both Republicans, but both political adversaries of Clean Government, appointed other men, confident that Governor Edison's two appointments would go to Democrats. "My old friends in the Legislature thought they had it so arranged that I would not be a member of the Commission," Vanderbilt wrote in retrospect, "but Governor Edison, then a Democrat, fooled them by appointing me, a Republican, to the Commission, a stratagem for which the Republican majority of the Legislature never really for-gave him."[17]

Charles Edison, the son of inventor Thomas A. Edison, had resigned as secretary of the Navy in 1940 to run for governor of New Jersey. Edison, whose candidacy had been urged on Mayor Hague by President Roosevelt, focused his campaign on the need for court reform and a new constitution for New Jersey and on attacking the Hudson County political machine: "If you elect me, you will have elected a governor who has made no promises to any man. You can be sure that I'll never be a yes-man except to my conscience."[18]

Hague, confident that such declarations were merely campaign rhetoric, was unconcerned. In the November election he delivered to Edison a plurality of 108,000 votes over Republican candidate

Robert Hendrickson, enough to carry Edison to victory by a state-wide margin of 44,000 votes. With such an impressive showing from Hudson County, Hague was certain that he still held considerable sway over the governor's office.

That this was not so was soon made clear. On Edison's first day in office as governor, he was shown a special telephone that Governor A. Harry Moore had installed to connect directly with Mayor Hague's office. Edison ripped it out of the wall.

Within his first week in office, the new governor again was able to demonstrate his political independence by appointing to a vacancy on the supreme court Frederic R. Colie, a Republican lawyer from Newark who had led the state bar association's fight against the elevation of Frank Hague, Jr., to the court of errors and appeals.[19]

Mayor Hague called Edison from Miami.

"Charlie," he cried, "you've turned out to be just the kind of governor I thought you'd be, you ——— Benedict Arnold! Do you know what I'm going to do to you for this? I'm going to break you, Charlie, if it's the last thing I do. And don't get the idea that Mayor Hague is going to fight you out in the open where you can grab off a lot of fancy publicity. I'm going to cut you from underneath in ways you won't discover until too late. I'm going to ruin you, Charlie, because you are a ——— ingrate."

He continued raging. At one point he exclaimed, "I could understand it if a Republican governor did this to me, but a Democrat? Charlie, have you lost your mind?"

Edison replied that he did not think so.

Hague demanded, "Look, here's what I want to know: can you count on this ——— in a pinch?"

"I'll never know that, Mayor," Edison answered, "because I'll never ask him for a favor. I'm appointing a judge, not a stooge."[20]

Edison's Commission on Revision of the New Jersey Constitution to draft a model constitution was one element of his program to break Hague's power in New Jersey. Senator Robert C. Hendrickson as chairman, Judge Walter J. Freund, *Trenton Times* editor James Kerney, Jr., Senator Crawford Jamieson, Professor John F. Sly of Princeton University, Arthur T. Vanderbilt, and Judge Walter D. Van Riper made up the commission.

"When we first convened," Senator Hendrickson recalled, "I had never met seven members with more divergent views on the theory and principles of government, and that applies to all branches of the government, judicial, executive, legislative and administrative."[21] But after five months of deliberation during their meetings at the

University Club in New York City, where they spent each weekend, the committee unanimously agreed on a draft of a constitution that favored court reorganization. Furthermore, unlike the New Jersey Judicial Council, which had attempted for ten years to retain the support of the leaders of the bench and bar and legislature by consenting to a watering down process of its amendments, the new commission, isolated from the whirlwinds of New Jersey politics, decided to forget compromises and simply to draft the best judicial article and state constitution within its power. It would depend on the reasonableness of the draft to win support for its acceptance.

The commission included no Hague representatives, an omission that did not fail to stir the apprehension and ire of the mayor. Several days after the composition of the commission was announced, the *Jersey Journal* had warned that it would be dominated by Hendrickson and Vanderbilt "for the purpose of revising the constitution to suit themselves and the interests they represent: the railroads and other malefactors of great wealth."[22] Edison in the meantime had kept up his attack on Hague, repeatedly appointing anti-Hague men to state positions and making public statements designed to infuriate the mayor. For example, in the spring of 1942, Edison stated that he planned "to separate as many Hague Democrats as possible from the state payroll and to try to keep any new ones from catching on."[23] The thought of Edison's appointing judges to a new set of courts or of reorganizing the executive department—possibilities if a new constitution was approved—was not conducive to lulling Hudson County into passivity, a tactic which might well have speeded the cause of constitutional revision. Instead, such actions antagonized the mayor, who began to prepare his arsenal of political weapons to impede any progress toward constitutional change.

On May 18, 1942, the commission presented to the governor, legislature, and people of New Jersey its draft of a new constitution. Included with it was a proposal for a referendum, to be held at the September primary, authorizing the legislature to revise the model constitution and submit it to the vote of the people in the 1942 general election.

Hague went into action. He lined up all the Democratic legislators against the Hendrickson constitution and won loyal allies among the Republican legislators of rural New Jersey, who had always feared that revision would result in legislative reapportionment and thus weaken their disproportionate power in the state senate, which could be controlled by representatives of 15 percent of the state's population.[24] A joint legislative committee blocked the Hendrickson referendum by revising its timetable, stating that no further action for change of the New Jersey constitution would be taken until after the termination of World War II.

But the next year, under the leadership of Clean Government assemblyman Dominic Cavicchia of Essex County, the new majority leader of the assembly, the assembly on April 2, 1943, unexpectedly passed a bill submitting the constitutional revision referendum at the general election in November, 1943.

With Governor Edison nearing the end of his three-year term, the state Republican party was anxious to find a gubernatorial candidate who would not only carry forward Edison's work for constitutional revision and his fight against Hague, but who would also be able to win against Democrat A. Harry Moore, who Hague had decided would run for a fourth term as governor.

Seventy-three-year-old Walter Edge, a leading New Jersey statesman who had been governor of the state from 1917 to 1919, a United States Senator in the 1920's, and an ambassador to France, was quickly agreed upon as the best candidate after he publicly promised Vanderbilt that he would not cooperate with Hague and that he would assume leadership of the movement for constitutional revision. Very much an astute politician, Edge called a meeting of the Republican senators and stated that, unless the state senate passed the Cavicchia bill calling for a referendum to authorize the 1944 legislature to revise the model constitution, he would refuse to run for office. While Edison had struggled in vain to move the bill through the senate, the legislators were anxious to have the patriarch of the state Republican party run against Moore and so quickly passed the bill.

Several months before the election, A. Harry Moore, much to the displeasure of Mayor Hague, decided he did not want another term as governor and retired from politics.[25] It was a combination of this event, the ability of the various factions of New Jersey Republicans to rally behind Edge, and the introduction of voting machines in New Jersey with the passage of a bill sponsored by Clean Government assemblymen after the Clee defeat in 1937[26]—that let Edge emerge the victor of the 1943 gubernatorial election. At the same time, the constitution referendum was approved by the citizens of New Jersey.

"It [Election Day] was a great day for the Republicans in this state, and particularly in this County," Vanderbilt wrote. For the first time in his political career the gubernatorial election had not fallen under Mayor Hague's magical spell. "We gave Edge in Essex over 45,000 of the state majority of 130,000. With the referendum on Constitution Revision there was a statewide majority of 130,000 to which Essex contributed a majority of 65,000. That is just half the total. All in all, I think we have done quite a job. . . ."[27]

Vanderbilt was designated by Governor Edge in January of 1944 a special assistant attorney general to defeat in the courts an application that had been made through Hague to overturn the referendum of November. The application asserted that the difficult amendment process authorized in the New Jersey Constitution of 1844 was the only available method of constitutional change. "It became my embarrassing duty to tell the court that it was without jurisdiction, the matter being a political issue." Nevertheless, Vanderbilt felt that

. . . the Borg case [*In re Borg*, 131 N.J.L. 104 (1944)] was worth working on, because Judge Porter's decision on Monday denying the application to set aside the vote of the people for a new constitution is the first real success I have had in a fourteen year fight to improve our judicial setup. . . . Mr. Frank Hague, of course, is the real party in interest, and they renewed their application again on Saturday before three Justices. After a lengthy argument, court adjourned and told us to come back after lunch and the three Justices, Parker, Perskie and Heher, decided in our favor.[28]

This decision of the court delivered in January legitimatized the legislature as a constitutional convention. "Now," Vanderbilt realized, "we are faced with the more difficult task of getting the Legislature to prepare a right kind of Constitution. . . . For the next three or four weeks, it will mean night and day work preventing some of the bad boys in the Legislature from sliding into the Constitution little weaseled words that will defeat some of the legitimate objectives we have in mind."[29]

In January and February of 1944, the New Jersey legislature sat as a constitutional convention to prepare a document based on the model constitution drafted by the Commission on Revision of the New Jersey Constitution. In addition to the reorganization of the judiciary, several provisions which the commission had incorporated into the draft which the Republican-dominated legislature was now considering made it certain that any new constitution would be obnoxious to Mayor Hague: a provision that ten years of legal experience be a condition to appointment to the state's higher courts—a qualification which would have made impossible the appointment of Frank Hague, Jr., and have eliminated the lay judges on the court of errors and appeals which Hague customarily packed with Hudson

County reliables; a provision that the legislature have broad constitutional powers to investigate the conduct of state and municipal officials—a provision which would have overturned the decision of *In re Hague* (123 N.J.Eq. 475 [1930]) and made a thorough investigation of the Hague regime by the Republican legislature inevitable; and a provision that would have altered the method of railroad property taxation and greatly decreased the tax revenues for Jersey City which had always been the foundation of Hague's machine. With these provisions and with Governor Edge actively snipping away at his power, Hague viewed the movement for a new constitution as a fight for his political life.

Mayor Hague appeared before the legislature on February 18, 1944, the last day of the public hearings, to express his views, which were then reiterated throughout the day by eleven of the fourteen other speakers, each of whom was a representative of Jersey City veteran organizations.[30] Although the Hudson County speakers developed many specific criticisms of the new constitutions, the thrust of their argument was an emotional plea not to change the Constitution "while the boys are away at war."[31]

At the completion of the hearings, the legislature on March 3, 1944, approved a revised constitution with a vote along strict party lines. The new constitution would be submitted to the vote of the people in November.

Several circumstances made the prospect of public acceptance of the constitution less than favorable. With the news of the invasion of Europe after D-Day and the excitement of a presidential campaign filling the headlines, press coverage of the work of the state legislature was relegated to the inside pages of the newspapers. The proposed constitution was so closely identified with the state Republican party that widespread bipartisan support was not forthcoming. And the smaller rural counties continued to believe that constitutional change was against their best interests.

Hague was in no mood to count on these circumstances to defeat the constitution at the polls. He began his own work to make its rejection certain and overwhelming.

He took out full-page advertisements in the state newspapers and covered highway billboards throughout New Jersey with messages proclaiming that the new constitution would take away the rights of such groups as farmers, veterans, sportsmen, women, and civil service employees. He obtained confidential lists of the names and addresses of all New Jersey men and women in the services and sent them literature attacking the proposed constitution. He sent a personal letter to each Democratic committeeman and -woman in New Jersey, stating that the proposed constitution "will virtually result in the wiping out of the Democratic party in New Jersey," and asking the workers "to do everything possible to defeat this proposed constitution and to hold our Party intact."[32] Hague himself made speeches up and down the state, venturing outside of Hudson County for the first time in over ten years to participate in an election campaign.

His smokescreen of propaganda and false issues proved effective in obscuring what was inherently a complicated subject. "As fast as one direct misrepresentation was answered," Governor Edge complained, "two more leaped up in its place."[33] Reported the *New York Times:*

> Appealing to special interests whenever a seed of skepticism could be planted, the Mayor's forces succeeded ... in creating enough confusion to split the ranks of war veterans, police and firemen, civil service employees, [and] farmers. ... To his critics, the Hague tactic was simple yet vexingly difficult to combat. Its design, they charged, was to frighten one group and then another with sensational falsehoods—falsehoods that Hitler and Goebbels would admire because they were so difficult to nail down.[34]

Shortly before the election, as a finishing touch, Hague spread rumors that the broad investigative power that would be given to the legislature would be used to violate the seal of the confessional, and that the new constitution would place the tax-exempt status of church property in jeopardy.[35] Shortly, the Catholic Church joined his fight.

Recognizing the pervasiveness and effectiveness of Hague's work only at the last minute, the leaders of the constitutional revision movement struck back several days before the election. "This 11th hour attack is the final gasp of Boss Hague in an effort to perpetuate his corrupt Jersey City dynasty," Governor Edge predicted. Edison denounced the mayor as a "dictator," a "bully," and a "coward." And Vanderbilt analyzed the opposition to the new constitution as small groups "marshaled under the whip of Mayor Hague, whose personal interest in defeating revision must be obvious to all."[36]

Their efforts came much too late. Those who were not actually opposed to the new constitution were confused by the heated campaign of distortion and abstained from voting. On November 7, 1944, the new constitution was soundly defeated by 126,000 votes.

On eighteen occasions between 1880 and 1930, and, after the

organization of the New Jersey Judicial Council, yearly from 1930 to 1940, court reform had been the object of amendments that had never passed both houses of the legislature. Commissions had been established in 1854, 1881, 1894, 1905, and 1941 as another means of examining the state judicial system and preparing amendments for its modernization. But like each of its predecessors, the Commission on Revision of the New Jersey Constitution proved unsuccessful in bringing about constitutional change.

THE DEAN

For Newark lawyer Arthur T. Vanderbilt, 1943 was a year of converging responsibilities. Nine of his sixteen associates had been drafted, and the rest worked long hours to keep up, often, when important litigation was pending, ending the working day late at night and beginning again at 6:00 A.M. the next day.[37] As a member of the Commission on Revision of the New Jersey Constitution, Vanderbilt had spent much of 1942 helping draft a model constitution for the state and much of 1943 gathering political support for its passage. Vice-chairman of Thomas E. Dewey's council of advisors and campaign committee since 1940, he was participating in the organization of the 1944 presidential campaign of the New York governor.[38] Chairman of the advisory committee to the United States Supreme Court to prepare the Federal Rules of Criminal Procedure, he had been traveling to Washington each month for several years to scrutinize and refine successive drafts of the proposed rules. And two evenings each week, he taught at the New York University School of Law.

At the start of the year he was debating whether to accept another major responsibility. "Very confidentially," he wrote to one of his sons on January 23, "the Chancellor of New York University has put it up to me to become Dean of the Law School starting next fall and to hold it for the duration of the War, Dean Sommer having reached the retirement age. Quite frankly, I wish it had never been suggested because it is going to be a difficult thing for me to attempt it at best. . . . Nevertheless, there are obligations that must be met. Fortunately, I have time to give it the fullest consideration."[39] On March 9, after Chancellor Harry W. Chase had met his request of obtaining the consent of the New York University Council, the Law School faculty, and the officers of the Alumni Association, Vanderbilt at the age of fifty-five accepted, in addition to his other activities, the position of dean of the School of Law. "We need some fundamental changes made in legal education," he wrote to a friend on the faculty of Wesleyan University, "and I hope I shall be able to bring them about in at least one law school."[40]

Although from its founding in 1838 by Benjamin F. Butler, a leader of the New York bar and attorney general in President Jackson's and President Van Buren's administrations, the School of Law at New York University was guided by a succession of deans as prominent in public service as they were distinguished in legal scholarship, the development of the school had been plagued for a century by persistent financial problems and severe competition from other law schools in the metropolitan district of New York.[41]

When during a period of modernization in legal education in the early twentieth century the school clung to some of its older traditions, its reputation was further weakened. Recognizing the benefits of part-time legal education in metropolitan areas, Dean Clarence D. Ashley and his colleagues had refused to abide by the requirement of the Association of American Law Schools that all member schools eliminate their evening divisions. They therefore withdrew from the Association in 1914. The Association later agreed with the position advanced by Ashley, but it was not until 1932 that the School of Law resumed its standing.

Similarly, against the recommendations of the American Bar Association, it maintained its tradition of a faculty composed primarily of lawyers and judges rather than professional teachers, and of keeping its doors open to high school graduates rather than insisting that applicants have two years of college education as a minimum requirement for admission. Each of these stands damaged the reputation of the School of Law and placed its graduates at a competitive disadvantage with the graduates of other law schools.

Dean Frank H. Sommer had taken steps to revive the law school's flagging reputation by hiring more professors, initiating a law review, and raising the standards of admission; and by 1930 the school was approved by the American Bar Association's Council on Legal Education. Sommer's efforts at modernization, however, were carried out during a period of adversity. The enrollment of 2,000 in 1930 dropped steadily because of the rising standards of admission, the increasing competition from other law schools, and the Depression. The school was not getting its first pick of law students, no new full-time professors could be employed, most of the well-known law professors had retired, and the faculty was depleted to sixteen men. The school itself, located on the top two floors of the American Book

Building in Washington Square, was old and deteriorating. Classrooms were inadequately furnished and poorly ventilated; elevators jammed; the small library of 40,000 volumes was overcrowded and almost completely uncatalogued. There were insufficient faculty offices, few seminar rooms, no auditorium, and no student quarters or recreational facilities.[42]

By the outbreak of World War II, the reputation of the School of Law had fallen to a low ebb among college students, law professors, and law firms. Because of the war, the number of students plunged from an enrollment of 1,000 in 1938 to 175 in 1942. It was estimated that by the fall of 1943 the enrollment would not exceed 100 students. In light of these problems, there was serious consideration whether the School of Law should be discontinued. It was at this time that Vanderbilt had agreed to Chancellor Chase's proposition to attempt a salvaging operation for the duration of the war and to make an effort to lay the foundation for a stronger institution once the hostilities ceased.

From his twenty-nine years as a professor at the School of Law's night school and from his examination of law schools during his travels in 1937 and 1938 as president of the American Bar Association, Vanderbilt had become aware of the limitations of legal education not only at New York University but in every law school. As president of the A.B.A., he had spoken before the Association of American Law Schools, warning of the widening gap between law school curricula and the realities of the judicial process:

True, we taught our students the fundamental principles of pleading, true, we instructed them in the rules of evidence and their rationale, true, we acquainted them with the jurisdiction of the courts; but was there any law school in the country that attempted to bring to their attention before they graduated the fact that our judicial system was not operating effectively or that directed their minds to the obvious standards which must be striven for in every state if our courts were to keep pace with the needs of the time? Had there been such a course in every law school, we should not be confronting the chaotic conditions that characterize the whole field of the aministration of justice.[43]

With the war disrupting educational institutions, cutting the total enrollment of the 109 law schools approved by the American Bar Association from 28,174 in 1938 to 4,803 in the fall of 1943, Vanderbilt recognized the time as a rare opportunity to develop at N.Y.U. a new School of Law with new goals and priorities, a law school that could inculcate in its students an understanding of the problems facing the law, a conviction of their professional responsibility to do something about the problems, a practical knowledge of how the problems could best be tackled, and equally, a sense of their professional responsibility for molding public opinion, for party leadership, and for public officeholding.

Because of the war, special measures had to be taken to consolidate and coordinate the work of the school to adapt it to the unusual conditions. In his first year as dean, he began an accelerated program of three terms a year to make graduation possible in two years instead of three years. Yet the education of the students could not be compromised to the exigencies of war. His foremost aim was to individualize their education. Each student was assigned a faculty advisor with whom problems could be discussed informally at periodic conferences; each was given individual instruction in the use of law books and the law library; each was required to write two law notes, the best of which were published in the *New York University Law Quarterly Review* and the rest of which were published in an *Intramural Law Review* Vanderbilt had established for this purpose. In this way, every student was given the training which in many law schools was confined to the students who were selected to serve on the board of editors of the law review, and every student would have a sample of his work to show a prospective employer as evidence of his ability to prepare a legal memorandum. These innovations were designed to give each student an opportunity to work closely with several professors and an opportunity to improve his written English, just as the introduction of required participation in moot court trials and in the traditional moot court competition gave each student training in oral argument that in many law schools was limited to the best students.

He brought to the School of Law the benefits of the old preceptorial system of clerkship by having students attend a number of trials under the supervision of their professors and by starting special courses in the drafting of wills and trusts, in conveyancing, and in general office practice.

With Judge Richard Hartshorne of New Jersey he introduced a plan in Essex County that later became popular throughout the United States, a public defender program in which members of the Essex County Bar Association agreed to serve in rotation without compensation as counsel for indigent criminal defendants, with students from the School of Law serving as assistants. The students did the so-called leg work in the case, conferring with the defendant and defense counsel, managing the investigation, and researching the law, and received valuable clinical experience by sitting in on the trial and watching the lawyers bring out the facts that they had ascertained.[44]

A sponsor system was also begun whereby each student once a year assisted his sponsor, a member of the bar of New York or New Jersey, in preparing a case for trial or in some important business transaction in the sponsor's office.

As dean, Vanderbilt realized a program he had first proposed at a faculty meeting in 1923, the use of "honors courses" to make it possible for the best students during their summers to study a subject to a greater depth than was possible in the classroom. If successful in the examination given in September, the student would receive credit toward an advanced degree. Vanderbilt believed that if a law student could complete this type of work during three summers, he would not only receive considerable advanced credit but would also become better prepared to practice law upon graduation.

In most law schools, substantive subjects were stressed at the expense of procedure, judicial administration, administrative law, legislation, and criminal law. While there was a general awareness that the substantive law had to be adapted to the needs of the times, the outmoded procedure under which courts were struggling to decide current controversies met with indifference in the law schools, and, hence, the legal profession. The philosophy of legal education Vanderbilt had been advocating since his presidency of the American Bar Association was put into practice at N.Y.U. An emphasis on courses in procedure and administrative law to teach students how to take a case through the courts or administrative tribunals, the elevation of the traditional status of criminal law in the curriculum, the introduction of courses in the legislative process, and the reorientation of the curriculum to help present the law as a living system were some of the most important changes introduced in his first years as dean. To encourage students to view the interrelatedness of the law, orientation lectures were developed for the beginning of each semester, and comprehensive examinations cutting across course lines were administered.

Vanderbilt foresaw the impact of new tax laws on the postwar world and recruited a tax law faculty headed by Professors Harry Rudick and Gerald Wallace, who developed the most extensive tax law curriculum of any law school. To help guide the practicing lawyer through this expanding field of law, the school began to

sponsor advanced courses, refresher courses, and shorter conferences and institutes for the metropolitan lawyer.

As a modern law school was known by its publications, Vanderbilt
began to expand the School of Law's publication program. Perhaps
the most ambitious undertaking of any law school faculty was the
Annual Survey of American Law he originated in 1943, a yearly
volume of from 750 to 1,000 pages to set forth succinctly the significant changes in the important fields of law. "The *Annual Survey of
American Law* is designed to aid both lawyers and laymen faced
with the task of keeping abreast of the current developments in the
law," Vanderbilt wrote in a preface to the first volume which summarized the growing density of the law, the consequent need for such a
survey, and, ultimately, the need for an expansion of the traditional
functions of law schools and the legal profession:

The task at best is not an easy one. In 1942, for example, the decisions of
American courts as published in the National Reporter System filled 74
books of 76,362 pages. Although the legislatures of most of the states did not
meet that year, 8,939 pages of laws were enacted by eight of them in regular
session, by ten in special session, and by the Congress. The volume of the
legislative and quasi-legislative rules and regulations promulgated by the
administrative agencies of the several states cannot even be calculated, since
many of them are not published. The 11,134 pages of the 1942 Federal
Register, however, bespeaks the activity of the regulatory bodies of the
national government. Nor can we hazard a guess as to the extent of the
judicial and quasi-judicial output of the federal and state administrative
agencies, for much of it, too, was not published. That it vastly exceeds the
volume of court decisions may be stated with confidence. When to this
plethora of official legal publications are added the digests, the encyclope-
dias, the annotated cases, the loose leaf series, the law reviews, the perennial
crop of law books, it becomes manifest that it is beyond the capacity of the
most devoted student of the law to read, much less digest and absorb, all of
the legal literature that is being made available to him currently.

[These] volumes [of the *Annual Survey*] covering the war period should
be of especial value to the many returning lawyers and law students whose
legal careers have been interrupted by military service. The hope is entertained that the *Survey* may also be of service to the specialist who feels the
necessity of keeping in touch with the broader fields of the law, as well as to
the editor, the statesman, and the publicist, all of whom frequently have
occasion to inquire as to the state of the law.[45]

A year later the *Tax Law Review* came into existence to present
authoritative articles in the field, to serve as a guide to the scattered

looseleaf and ephemeral materials, and to act as a vehicle for examining the need for improvement in both substantive and procedural tax law. Within a year, its circulation exceeded that of any other law review in the country. The *Annual Survey of New York Law,* the Judicial Administration Series sponsored by the National Conference of Judicial Councils, and a host of institute proceedings soon followed. Within several years, no other law school had a publication program comparable to that of the School of Law at New York University.[46]

Thus during his first year as dean, Vanderbilt consolidated and expanded the work of the School of Law. In March of 1944, he reported with pleasure to one of his daughters: "Even at the risk of your thinking that in my old age I am getting a bit conceited, I am going to risk it to quote a sentence from a letter just received this morning from the Chancellor of the University: 'I think you have gone farther in making progress in the Law School in the last six months than has been done in the last six years.' This in the face of some of the difficulties that I have been encountering is very much on the encouraging side."[47] And a year later, in May of 1945, he could report to his family that although the war was taking from the Law School the total attention of both students and professors, and though, in the midst of the far-reaching conflict, teaching, research, publications, and extracurricular activities had fallen under increasing stress, measures were being initiated to organize a strong law school to prepare for the end of the war and the return of the veterans:

Classes ended at the Law School last week. The year has been hectic but one of very great progress. I think I have got the jump on most other schools in assembling a very notable group of new faculty members. Tom Atkinson from Missouri is being honored today by the Missouri Supreme Court for the work he did in drafting the new court rules. Gerry Wallace comes to us from Yale where he taught several years after leaving Northwestern. Hans Kalsen is deemed by Dean Pound the outstanding authority in the country on International Law and Jurisprudence. He is now at California. Miguel de Capriles, one of our own graduates, is presently Chief of the Bureau of Latin American Republics in the Department of Justice and he is not only an authority on Civil Law, but tops in Economics and Accounting. J. Walter McKenna has done outstanding work in the Criminal Law Institute at Marquette and is one of the ablest men in Criminal Law, a field where it is very difficult to get a first-rate man. Tomorrow I am having lunch with Leonard Saxe who has taught New York Practice at Harvard for the last twelve years, and I hope to conclude arrangements with him. In addition to

all these, I have half a dozen new part-time instructors in Taxation, Labor
Law etc. all of whom are men known throughout the country.

If everything goes right, I think we are assured of one of the best faculties
in the country and if they work as well together as they promise I think we
can leave out "one of the" for after all one of the most important things is to
keep the group working together.[48]

THE IDEA OF A LAW CENTER

What the School of Law had been suffering from during the last
decade, Vanderbilt was convinced, was what he termed an inferior-
ity complex. He assumed the deanship in 1943 with a plan for
developing the school into a leading law school of the nation, a plan
to be realized both by strengthening it internally and by the establishment there of an institution that had long been germinating in his
thoughts—a national law center. His vision of a law center would be
his key to attracting students, professors, and funds to the School of
Law while creating a force for the systematic and continuous revision of the law.

The idea of a law center was so novel that it took a considerable
period of time and a great deal of explanation for the students,
faculty, administration, and alumni to grasp the significance and
scope of the concept. Essentially, a law school that lifted its sights
beyond the traditional role of training practitioners, that faced also
the problems of law reform, and that served as an intellectual meeting place for mobilizing, coordinating, and directing the constructive
forces of the profession to meet the great problems of the law,
especially the simplification and modernization of the law, was a law
center.

In an age of transition in which the velocity of economic, political, and
social change is utterly unprecedented, there is a demand that must be met if
we would safeguard our kind of civilization. The law must be simplified,
cleared of its barnacles of technicalities, and it must be modernized and
streamlined to meet the demands of the times.

In an earlier age when the tyranny of the Stuarts threatened the fundamental rights of Englishmen, in an age when the world was throbbing with
the excitement of far flung exploration and colonization, the common law
was saved by Lord Coke and a few judges and parliamentary leaders who
received their inspiration in the Inns of Court. A century and a half later on
the eve of the American Revolution, the French Revolution, and the English
Industrial Revolution, Hardwicke and Mansfield and Eldon, Burke and

Bentham and Blackstone in England, Madison and Hamilton, Jefferson and Marshall, Kent and Story in the United States, were adapting the common law to the needs of the new business and social order.

Again a century and a half later we are confronted with a similar but far more difficult problem, because we not only deal with a far more complicated society than they, but with a law of 49 jurisdictions in an era as truly revolutionary as either of those I have referred to. We cannot turn to any single man or small group of men for the task is too great. But we have not lost our initiative or our ingenuity. Fortunately we have learned the art of cooperation in the Restatement of the Law by the American Law Institute, in the work of the Advisory Committees of the Supreme Court on Federal Rules of Civil Procedure and Federal Rules of Criminal Procedure, and the American Bar Association is about to apply it to its projected Survey of the Legal Profession.

Where and by whom must the task be done? Obviously not by busy judges on the bench, nor by harassed legislators in Congress or at the state capitol, nor by overburdened chief executives or department heads, nor by the captains of industry or labor, nor by law school professors alone, but by leaders of each of these groups working together and submitting their product to the frank criticism of the rank and file.

This is my vision of a Law Center. That it may be one center of a nationwide movement that will mold our law to the needs of the time, assuring to our people for another century and a half the supremacy of law, a government of law and not of men, and above all individual liberty.[49]

The core of the law center was to be the law school, which would equip its students to be effective counsellors and advocates and awaken in them an awareness of their responsibility for improving the legal profession, the courts, and the law, and of their responsibility to be leaders of public opinion and leaders in public affairs.

Because no law school could hope to teach a student in three years all he had to know to be a valuable member of the legal profession or even to be a competent practitioner in a rapidly changing legal world, a second function of the law center was to provide a forum for postgraduate instruction, conducting courses and conferences in specialized fields of law and on topics of contemporary legal importance and publishing the proceedings of these conferences for the benefit of the entire profession.

A third function of the law center would be to explore the field of comparative law—to acquaint American and foreign law students with different legal systems in order to develop acceptable solutions to problems with an international aspect.

The overarching function of the law center would be to act as a stimulus and force in the improvement of the administration of justice and the resynthesis and modernization of the law.

Although the work envisioned could never be accomplished by one group of individuals or by one law center, the proposed Law Center at the New York University School of Law would be the start. The task of developing some of the functions of the Law Center began immediately.

Its program of continuing education was successful from the outset. In the spring of 1944 there were 164 practicing lawyers, graduates of 18 different law schools, taking 10 courses at the School of Law. In the spring of 1948, there were 456 from 69 law schools taking 55 different courses. These 456 lawyers represented almost half of the total of 1,017 graduate students in approved law schools in the nation. By 1951, of the total of 1,600 graduate students in law throughout the United States, over 700 of them from over 70 different law schools were taking over 80 courses at the School of Law ranging from specialized subjects like tax law, labor law, and advanced business law to general background courses in comparative law and jurisprudence. From 1943 to 1948, eighteen conferences were held at the School of Law, all dealing with new legal developments of national importance such as the Administrative Procedure Act, the Federal Rules of Criminal Procedure, war contracts, pension funds, a unified transportation system, and an accession tax. The proceedings of each conference were published by the School of Law and widely circulated.

The Inter-American Law Institute was founded in 1946 to bring yearly, on full fellowships, twelve to fifteen outstanding students from Central and South America to study civil and common law at the same time as lawyers studied Latin American law in the graduate division of the School of Law. The Institute was to be a training ground to pave the way for better business relations between Latin America and the United States and to contribute to an improved understanding between the United States and the Latin American countries. The Comparative Law Institute was thereafter developed to serve the same purposes with Europe and the Middle East. As the legal systems of the United States and of foreign countries were structured on essentially different concepts, the aim of education in foreign law was not to qualify the student to practice in another country but rather to foster in the student a flexibility to sense the differences in concepts between two bodies of law to qualify him to cooperate with his foreign colleagues in the flow of commercial and intellectual exchange and in formulating solutions to international problems. The establishment of these institutions was in preparation for the growing inter-American and international economic trade that was anticipated for the postwar years.

Two other programs at the Law Center grew out of a political trend that dismayed Vanderbilt: the majority of the electorate's lack of knowledge about the most rudimentary aspects of the political process coupled with the growing number of citizens who eschewed anything connected with "the dirty game of politics." "We are planning, it would seem, to train our young men and women for almost every profession in the world except for the most important and most difficult of all—public leadership."[50]

Vanderbilt took steps to help overcome this lack of knowledge of and interest in public affairs by establishing a Root-Tilden Scholarship program[51] for college graduates showing unusual potential for public service and service to the legal profession. In each state, the chief justice, the president of the state bar association, and an editor or publisher voted as a committee of selection for state candidates for the $2,100 annual scholarship. In each federal circuit, the chief judge of the United States Court of Appeals, the chairman of the federal reserve bank, and a college or university president chose twenty Root-Tilden Scholars from this group of candidates on the basis of their scholarship, their extracurricular activities, and their promise for civic leadership.

The second program, the Citizenship Clearing House, was established at the Law Center in 1947 with the support of the American Political Science Association and the American Bar Association. It was designed to encourage college men and women to actively participate in political affairs through the local, state, or national party organization of their choice.

Government was safe, Vanderbilt was persuaded, as long as its citizens remained awake; and the responsibility for wakefulness rested with its leadership. "I am convinced that our college men and women whose education has provided them a solid background for their activity, can supply the strongest possible constructive force in the politics of this country by working with their party organization in their home communities. It was with these thoughts in mind that I encouraged the establishment of the Citizenship Clearing House at the Law School of New York University. Its great objective is to put outstanding young college men and women in touch with opportunities for participation in politics on a self-respecting basis."[52]

Under the slogan "Better Minds for Better Politics," the program of the Citizenship Clearing House included: sponsoring a nation-wide series of conferences on training for politics; organizing workshops for politically inexperienced college professors of political science; aiding young people in starting discussion groups to debate local, state, national, and international issues of current interest; promoting conferences to bring groups of college students into direct contact with political leaders; and providing fellowships to students for practical service with the staffs of their mayor, governor, or state political party. The hopeful by-products of the Citizenship Clearing House would be the strengthening of the American two-party system through the infusion of new leadership into the political parties and the growth of an awareness of the roles of public opinion and active citizen participation in a democratic society.[53]

In 1952 the Institute of Judicial Administration was established to provide a special agency for the coordination of the movement to improve the administration of justice. Its purpose was to provide a national institute for the study of the structure, operation, and manpower of the state and federal courts, to assemble and supply information and data on subjects concerning judicial procedures, organization, and administration, and to hold summer training and refresher programs for state and federal appellate judges. The Institute served as a nonprofit advisory and consultative organization equipped to make surveys and studies for judicial councils, bar associations, civic organizations, and state and local governmental agencies interested in improving the operation of the courts. Within its first four years, it had provided such assistance to the federal government, to professional and civic organizations in a number of states, as well as to lawyers and judges representing forty-two foreign countries, among them Germany and Japan, which sought its aid after World War II in the reconstruction of their judicial systems along modern and efficient lines.[54]

The Law Center would embody these programs and institutions, but before they all could be organized, it was necessary both to sell the idea of a law center and to procure the money for its operation. Deciding that a logical first step would be to renovate the old law school building, Vanderbilt hired a professional fund raiser to raise $200,000 from the alumni. By the end of the year the response had been so meager that it was obvious that a drive to repaint and plaster an old building in New York City inspired no one. A new building, a new school was needed.

The architectural firm of Eggers and Higgins and the director of the Philadelphia Museum of Art were retained to design for Washington Square a neo-Georgian building whose exterior would be reminiscent of the Inns of Court in London and Independence Hall and whose entire structure would be suitable both for the traditional academic functions of a law school and for the professional and public activities of a law center.

To construct this building for the School of Law and Law Center, Dean Vanderbilt between 1945 and 1947 applied himself as completely to the task of raising money as he had to developing the Law School and the concept of a law center. He dismissed the professional fund raiser, increased the amount to be raised to $3 million, and took over the campaign.

"It is only because I believe almost as a religion," he wrote to one of the law school alumni, "that we must get the law in shape if the democratic representative type of government is going to survive, and that we can't do a good job at the Law School until we have a new building in which to promote the law, that I have nerved myself up to become a professional beggar. I can't imagine any other cause for which I would be doing it because quite frankly soliciting funds, or any other type of sales work, is not to my liking."[55]

The endowment of the School of Law in 1945 was only $250,000. It was clear that great sums would be needed to construct the new Law School and Law Center, to rebuild the neglected law library, to build up the faculty and staff, and to meet the needs of scholarships, research projects, publication programs, and the institutes. Vanderbilt decided that the best way to draw support for his idea was to present it directly to the alumni.

In the autumn of 1945, class dinners were held at the faculty club and at the Hotel Brevoort. Three or four classes met each evening, beginning with the class of 1945 on October 15, and ending with the class of 1882 on November 27. The dean attended and addressed each, explaining the need for a law center and why New York University was the school to pioneer in the field.

When these dinners were completed, he started visiting alumni throughout Connecticut, New York, and New Jersey. "If all of our alumni will put their shoulders to the wheel, the success of our campaign is assured. We can make this a Law School second to none."[56] Former Governor Herbert H. Lehman of New York agreed to serve as chairman of the campaign committee. County chairmen from each of the counties of New York, New Jersey, and Connecticut were selected from among the alumni who were judges. And the 7,336 alumni of the School of Law were asked to become responsible for a sufficient sum to initiate construction of the new building no later than the fall of 1947.

To further build the resources that would be necessary, the School of Law, together with the College of Medicine, acquired the Ramsey Accessories Manufacturing Corporation of Saint Louis, Missouri—a manufacturer of piston rings—and incorporated it under the name of Ramsey Corporation. The company was purchased with $3 million borrowed from the Prudential Insurance Company. The amortization of the purchase price was to be taken out of the earnings of the company over a period of not more than twenty years, while under the tax law Vanderbilt utilized, which allowed charities to enjoy tax free income from nonrelated activities, the School of Law and College of Medicine would annually receive from 30 to 70 percent of the profits of the corporation after provisions were made for the payment of creditors. Thereafter, all profits would be available to the two institutions.

Similarly, Vanderbilt acquired for the School of Law a half interest in the Howe Leather Company of Boston and the American Limoges China Company of Trenton, and complete interest in the C. F. Mueller Company of Jersey City. The leather concern and china company proved to be unsuccessful, and after five years the Ramsey Corporation had to be sold because changes in the tax laws made the combination unprofitable. But by then these companies had provided $400,000 to the Law Center drive, and the sale of the Ramsey Corporation produced a million dollar profit. The C. F. Mueller Company proved a major success, contributing $75,000 to the school in 1948 and $100,000 more a year later, eventually eliminating the mortgage on the Law Center and providing a steady flow of funds for its institutes.[57]

Although the acquisition of these corporations gave a substantial boost to the fund-raising campaign, the main support still had to come from the alumni before major foundation grants could be expected. The official opening of the campaign was held at the Waldorf-Astoria Hotel on June 6, 1946. It was announced that, of the $3 million to be raised, $500,000 was to be pledged by December 31. Dean Vanderbilt began his plea for support:

Mr. Toastmaster, Vice Chancellor Kimball, Governor Lehman, your Honours, and friends of the Law School:

As I followed the course of the toastmaster's remarks I rather gathered that he thinks that the Dean of the Law School is quite a fellow, and I must say as

I listened to the accumulation of evidence, I was somewhat impressed myself. And yet I know there are two undergraduates here who will probably fail to recognize their father from the toastmaster's description of him, as will divers politicians back in New Jersey. Mr. Toastmaster, I am indebted to you for the buildup with my family, and I am grateful to you for the loyalty which you have exhibited over the years to the School.

After discussing the advances at the School of Law and the plans for the Law Center, he focused on the central subject:

Now, I should not talk about money. That should be somebody else's job. But I can't resist. I never begged for money before September of last year and I have done little else since.

I want to submit a proposition or two to you. I submit that the very least that any alumni can do is to subscribe one hundred dollars over three years. The thought struck me last night that the Law School should mean at least as much to any lawyer as the cost of his newspaper. How much does a man spend for a morning and afternoon and Sunday newspaper? Well, if he is in the city it is $30.34 a year. If he lives in the suburbs it costs a penny more for the morning paper, $33.37. I am suggesting to every alumnus that for three years the least we have a right to expect is the equivalent of the cost of your daily and Sunday newspaper. Hearing of the campaign just a day or two before their examinations, 127 of our undergraduates have pledged $100 each. Surely no alumnus will want to be outdone by the younger generation. . . .

He read a letter from a father who had lost his son in the war, a son who had recently graduated from the School of Law and had sensed the promise of the new Law Center.

I am going to ask you as you go home and think over what you will personally contribute to this drive and how you are going to approach your fellow alumni under the direction of our judges, and when you are trying to think of the name of some foundation or wealthy client or friend who would be glad to contribute to what we are doing here if he knew about it—I am going to ask you when you think of these things to remember the spirit reflected in this letter. I am going to ask you to think of Washington Square not as one of the delightful spots of New York City but as the old training ground where men of an earlier period prepared to do their military duty for this country. I am going to ask you to think of the Washington Arch not as a beautiful monument but as reflecting the spirit of the Father of our country who found his peacetime duties far more onerous than his responsibilities as a general.

I am going to ask you to look through that Arch across the Square to envision the new building, strong, encasing its framework of steel, symbolic of the sturdiness of the common law, warm and human with the rosy colonial brick, faced with limestone columns, reflecting the humaneness of the spirit of justice. And I am going to ask you, as you think of that building, to say to yourself, "This is my law school. There men are toiling to improve the science and the art of the law. There young men and young women are being trained to be great leaders, great citizens, great in public service." We at the Law School, faculty and students, will not fail you and I know that our alumni will not fail in their loyalty to the School. With your loyal cooperation, victory is assured.[58]

Contributions began to arrive from class groups, alumni chapters, faculty, foundations, and corporations.

New York University School of Law had never drawn many students from well-to-do families. Many of the alumni had achieved professional success, but few had accumulated large personal fortunes. Yet as the campaign proceeded, sixteen contributed over $5,000, 150 between $1,000 and $5,000, over seven hundred between $500 and $1,000, and over four thousand contributed lesser sums, while many obtained contributions from clients and friends. By the end of the year, $521,000 had been raised.

The largest single contribution came from one of Vanderbilt's clients. Vanderbilt had won a suit in 1946 which ensured the continued existence of the Davella Mills Foundation of Montclair, New Jersey. Instead of submitting his fee, he sought a contribution for the Law Center drive. Before Vanderbilt made the request formally to the board of trustees of the foundation, he talked to some of the trustees personally. Each was receptive to the idea, but warned him that one member of the board would prove difficult to convince because he disliked all lawyers. Saving this man for last, Vanderbilt approached him with the suggestion that what the country needed badly was a drastic improvement in the caliber of lawyers. The gentleman agreed heartily.

On New Year's morning, 1947, Mr. Paul Hudson, president of the Davella Mills Foundation, called the dean at home "to say that they wanted me to have a fine holiday so they were advising me informally that on the 8th they would officially make us a grant of $500,000 conditional on our raising another $500,000 and letting the contract for the building before December 31, 1947. It begins to look as if what was considered a dream by many is on its way to becoming a reality."[59]

The twin conditions on the grant proved to be almost as valuable as the half million dollars itself for they allowed Vanderbilt to put spurs on the entire campaign.

[T]he significance of our program as well as the plight of the profession in a war-worn and weary world was sufficient to drive me day in and day out for well over two years to do something which I do not mind confessing now that I loathe and hate (and I mean this literally)—soliciting funds. There is no logic about it; I am simply allergic to it. Nor was my task made easier by the solemn warnings of men high in the general Alumni Federation—I forbear mentioning any names in view of subsequent events—that it was foolhardy to expect to raise more than $100,000 at most from our law school alumni. And while the University authorities and some of my associates on the faculty—yes, and some of our own alumni officers—were more tactful in their treatment of an overenthusiastic dean and not openly lugubrious, still I could not have been a trial lawyer for a third of a century without detecting their secret doubts. There were many set-backs, but much to encourage me. I still remember as if it were yesterday the first $500 gift, the first $5,000 gift, the first alumnus who really made an effort to interest his clients, the first substantial contribution from one of the foundations through the aid of Governor Lehman, and then the unparalleled good fortune of the remarkable New Year's gift from my friends of the Davella Mills Foundation of a conditional pledge of half a million dollars. When Paul Hudson read the terms of their grant to me over the telephone New Year's morning, I had no doubt that the hand of Providence was guiding our efforts. Three months later Chancellor Chase gave me assurance that the University would meet one of the terms of the grant by providing an acceptable site on Washington Square.[60]

PROMISE OF VICTORY, MIRAGE OF DEFEAT

After the defeat of the proposed constitution at the polls in 1944, the flame of enthusiasm for constitutional revision seemed to have burned itself out. Vanderbilt summarized the situation: "The opponents of court reform thought that constitutional revision was dead. All of the judges in the state except one or two were opposed to it. Most of the leaders of the bar were in opposition. Every county bar association and the State Bar Association likewise were opposed. . . ."[61]

Discouraged by the failure of the Commission on Revision of the New Jersey Constitution to put its new constitution successfully through the gauntlet of constitutional change, Vanderbilt nevertheless resolved that, as he had pushed for revision since 1930, he would try once more before giving up. "For the first time it dawned on me that we had not been pursuing the best methods in appealing to judges and lawyers and legislators and governors. After fourteen years of struggle, we decided to do what had been done in England almost a century before—to carry the battle to the people and ignore the judges, the lawyers, and the politicians."[62]

By 1945 he had begun to speak to every conceivable kind of committee and organization to spark once more the drive for a new constitution. Research and educational programs were launched by the Constitutional Revision Committee, and the Constitution Revision Foundation was established by a handful of proponents of revision including James Kerney, Jr., active member of the League of Women Voters Mrs. Gene Miller, New Jersey attorney Joseph Harrison, prominent businessman Winston Paul, and State Highway Commissioner Spencer Miller, Jr. The purpose of the committee and foundation was to demonstrate the need for extensive revisions of the constitution and to show how simple in conception such reforms were.

With annual budgets of about $35,000 raised through contributions, and with the volunteer assistance of civic groups like the League of Women Voters, the committee and foundation produced handbills, leaflets, cartoons, radio broadcasts, newspaper articles, and editorials, initiated legislative studies, and contacted for speaking time every organization in the state from the Chamber of Commerce, the A.F.L. and C.I.O., to the New Jersey Chess Club and the New Jersey Beekeepers Association, every service club, P.T.A., fraternal group, church, and library, always with the plea, "give the courts back to the people." So carefully organized was this educational-propaganda campaign that it was joked that if three men stopped for a traffic light, someone would run up and make a speech for a new constitution. It was the same pattern of grass roots action that Vanderbilt had found successful in Essex County and that he later hoped the Citizenship Clearing House could foster—the type of local action that would involve many citizens who had felt their legal rights were too distant, too confusing, or too boring to bother about.

In 1946 when Governor Edge's term in office was concluding, he began looking for a man to fight Hague as he and Edison had and who would use his position to bring about a constitutional convention. Alfred E. Driscoll, a lawyer and state senator from Camden County and an advocate of revision, was deemed to be the man for the job, but he told Edge that he was not particularly interested in being governor, that he had never really wanted to get into politics, and that his first love was the law. Edge reported this to Vanderbilt and asked him to see what he could do. The next day Vanderbilt invited forty-four-year-old Driscoll to lunch at the Down Town Club in Newark and told him that, if he would run for governor, he would see to it that Essex County came out solidly for him. Driscoll was quite certain that Vanderbilt had not consulted with anyone and was surprised that he could be so sure he could deliver the backing of Clean Government, but at last Driscoll accepted.

In the primary campaign against former governor Harold Hoffman and then in the general election campaign against Hague candidate Lewis Hansen of Hudson County, the Essex Clean Government group provided much of the money and manpower to promote Driscoll's candidacy. As in the Clee gubernatorial campaign of 1937, Vanderbilt spent every evening personally persuading county committee members of the importance of the election and of the necessity for success at the polls.

Hague, anxious to elect a governor loyal to him after five years of Edison and Edge, worked with equal vigor through his Hudson County machine, completing his campaign with the impassioned plea that "Hudson County cannot survive if Alfred E. Driscoll is elected tomorrow."[63]

New Jersey politics, however, were not what they once were. Voting machines had taken much of the old mystery and magic out of the Hudson County electoral process. In the November election, Driscoll carried nineteen of New Jersey's twenty-one counties and won the election by well over 200,000 votes.

On January 21, 1947, in his inaugural address, Governor Driscoll called for a constitutional convention and immediately began to organize the convention machinery. He proposed to the legislature that the convention consist of sixty delegates with each county having the same number of delegates as it had members in the assembly, in accordance with the composition of every other state constitutional convention.

He had no difficulty in pushing through the assembly bills authorizing a convention and the election of delegates, but when the bills got to the senate, many demands were made for amendments. Driscoll rejected every one. On February 10 he was advised by Majority Leader John M. Summerill, Jr., that he had a majority of one to get the bills through, and shortly after Summerill left Driscoll's office, Senator David Van Alstyne of Bergen County reported, "You are going to get your bills through, but you will never get a new Constitution—the division is too deep."[64] Driscoll reviewed each demand for amendments and decided conditionally to accept the one supported by Atlantic County Senator "Hap" Farley and the senators from smaller counties: that the number of delegates to the convention from each county equal the total number of assemblymen *and* senators from that county, thus increasing the number of delegates from sixty to eighty-one.

Governor Driscoll sent word that he would accept this amendment provided the bills passed the senate unanimously and that the bill authorizing a constitutional convention receive unanimous approval in the house. After an afternoon and evening of deliberation and negotiation, the package was passed by the senate on February 10, 1947, at 10 P.M. and by an exhausted assembly at 1 A.M. that morning.

Despite the fact that Driscoll had given his assurances to Vanderbilt, Edge, and others in the spring of 1946 that the convention would consist of only sixty delegates, repeating this number again after his election, at his inauguration, and after the bill was introduced providing for a convention of sixty delegates, he felt forced to increase the number of delegates to secure enough votes to bring about a convention. Whereas in a convention composed of sixty delegates, Essex County would have controlled 20 percent of the convention votes, the proposed change in the number of delegates would increase the per capita representation of the smaller counties in comparison with the larger counties so that, for instance, each citizen of a small county like Cape May would receive four times the representation of a citizen of a large county like Essex. The percentage of the total represented by the Clean Government delegates from Essex that Vanderbilt was counting on to assure the success of the convention would thereby be substantially reduced.

It was so late at night when Driscoll asked his counsel to telephone Vanderbilt to advise him of the compromise he had made and of the necessity for this change that the counsel waited until early the next morning to call. By that time, Vanderbilt had learned the news from Clean Government assemblymen.

When the counsel called, Vanderbilt was enraged. With the increase in the number of delegates and with Governor Driscoll's efforts to organize a bipartisan convention which necessitated winning the confidence of Mayor Hague—a move Driscoll had begun by halting the five-year campaign against the mayor and by appointing common pleas judges in Camden County and Hudson County who were acceptable to Hague[65]—Vanderbilt was certain that the Hague delegates and rural county delegates—traditionally allies of Hague against constitutional revision because of their fear of legislative reapportionment—would unite to exercise a veto power over the convention proceedings and block any constructive work. He was convinced that Driscoll had entered into a deal with Hague and assured the counsel that "the beaches strewn with the bleached bones of Republican politicians who had listened to the siren voice of Mayor Hague"[66] would soon see Driscoll's. In what appeared to be "one midnight change of policy,"[67] the new constitution for which Vanderbilt had fought seemed once more to have slipped through his fingers, blocked again by Hague's maneuvers.

The flustered counsel remarked, "Well, you will probably be in Maine this summer anyway," [and therefore not at the convention].

"That's exactly where I will be," Vanderbilt replied.[68]

Although he feared that the convention would lead to the same frustrations and failures of the past seventeen years at the hands of "devious distinguished gentlemen of both parties"[69] intent on preventing constitutional revision and judicial reform, Vanderbilt urged the Clean Government leaders to press forward, though warily, toward a new constitution. Whereas Governor Driscoll had hoped to make the convention bipartisan and had even persuaded Hague to assign three of Hudson County's ten delegation seats to Republicans, Vanderbilt, despite pressure from the governor, the county bar association, and a number of civic groups, selected a slate of thirteen Republicans from Essex to solidify the influence of Clean Government in the convention and counteract the opposition he expected. "I shall not deny that I have my misgivings as to the possibilities of the new convention, but I personally intend to work for a new constitution as insistently as I have in the past, reserving, however, my right as a citizen, as I hope the delegates will, to oppose the new constitution in November if it does not measure up to reasonable expectations."[70]

Vanderbilt's juggling act—performing his multiple responsibilities as lawyer, political leader, law professor, dean, fund raiser, chairman of the War Department's advisory committee on military justice, and spearhead of the drive for a constitutional convention— finally came tumbling down in the spring of 1947. All at once in April and May, when he had "more on my hands than I can possibly do,"[71] he was faced with what seemed like four insurmountable obstacles. His hope of finally achieving a new constitution for New Jersey seemed to have drifted away because of what he perceived as "the grand double-cross of Governor Driscoll."[72] He had been elected chairman of the board of trustees of Wesleyan University in 1946 and was finding himself, because of the personalities involved in the

group that composed the board's executive committee, quite powerless to bring about what he felt were imperative changes in the
curriculum. He was involved in an important case in Trenton, where
the

trial judge was on the verge of nervous prostration and had to be handled for
six weeks like a psychopathic case in a trial which should not have lasted
over two. I succeeded in getting the solvent individual defendant non-
suited, but the corporate defendant of limited liability suffered a resounding
judgment of $360,000. I sensed that there was something very foul, and by
some real sleuthing, we discovered that certain papers had been used by the
jury in reaching their verdict which had never been offered in evidence and
which were not submitted to them by the Clerk of the Court nor returned to
him by the jury—dirty work at the cross roads which will result eventually in
a new trial.[73]

Finally, at a time when over $200,000 had to be raised in a month to
meet one of the conditions of the Davella Mills grant, the administration of the School of Law seemed to be falling down in supporting
his drive for a new School and Law Center.

As he was tired each evening when he left court in Newark to
catch the train to the School of Law for the fund-raising activities and
exhausted by the time each night's program was over—this combination of obstacles, his effort in trying to surmount them, and perhaps
his sudden intuition that they might be insuperable, proved too
much even for the man of fifty-eight who joked to his friends that he
had "iron in his veins" and "fire in his belly." After taking a night off
from the Law Center drive to speak in Montclair, New Jersey, in
support of the constitutional convention, he awoke the next morning,
May 22, 1947, having suffered a stroke which paralyzed his left arm
and leg. "As I fell to sleep that night I am afraid my will was not on
guard. My old loathing of the raising of money must have asserted
itself in my subconscious mind. At any rate, the next morning I was
unable to carry on."[74]

He was confined to his bed at home in Short Hills even after he
regained the use of his arm in three days and the use of his leg a
week later. The only activity he was allowed was to see his secretary
for a half hour of dictation each day and to receive one phone call
from his office.

For days he was not seen, and no explanation was given for his
sudden withdrawal from his numerous activities. The days dragged
into weeks, and in the middle of June he was taken to Maine to

recuperate from what he told his friends was a "severe physical crack-up."[75]

"I am still sleeping ten to eleven hours a night as well as an hour or two in the afternoon," he wrote on June 23 to a member of the Wesleyan board of trustees. "I have been a bit worried about this because it may get me in bad habits, but my doctors at home and my doctor up here as well, merely laugh at me."[76] "They tell me that if I will take it easy this summer, I have twenty years of real 'go' in me— and believe me, I am all for those twenty years."[77]

When news of his retreat to Maine became public, rumors that he was a helpless invalid circulated among the delegates to the constitutional convention and throughout New Jersey. There was speculation that he would never again be a political power in New Jersey; that the Clean Government party and Essex delegation to the convention, without his leadership, would soon break apart; and that the Law Center drive would fail. To determine the nature of his illness and the truth of these stories, the editor of the Newark Star-Ledger and a photographer went to Maine in July to visit him.

"Yes," Vanderbilt said to Mr. Hammerslag with a broad smile when the reason for their visit was explained, "I've heard the rumors that I'm flat on my back and out of the pictures. Well, as you can see for yourself, they're about as true as that story of Mark Twain's death."[78]

Although far from well, Vanderbilt convinced the newspapermen that he was merely taking his customary summer vacation. Walking through the woods and swimming with him in the pool, they were told that his only complaint was a twinge in one leg—arthritis, he said, for which he carried a cane as a precaution if his muscles suddenly got tired. Besides keeping busy with his mail and telephone calls from New Jersey in following the progress of the constitutional convention, he was preparing a series of lectures to be given the following spring at the University of Michigan for the Cook Foundation Lectureship on American institutions. "Send my regards to all my friends in New Jersey," he told the reporters, "and tell them I'll be back in September to take up where I left off last month."[79]

By the end of the summer he was his old self again. In a letter to a colleague at the School of Law, he reported: "I am glad to be able to tell you that I am improving constantly. . . . I have never felt quite so rested since my high school days. This time I am going to try to take advantage of the warning and not get in trouble again. While my evening appearances may be more restricted, I am sure that week in and week out I will be able to do better work than ever before."[80]

FIRST FRUITS OF AUTUMN

Perhaps his rapid recovery was partially a result of the progress that was made that summer with the Law Center campaign and in the New Jersey Constitutional Convention.

At the time of his stroke, there had been only forty days remaining to reach the goal of $1,500,000 to meet one of the conditions of the Davella Mills grant. Calling an emergency meeting of the campaign's executive committee on May 24, Governor Herbert Lehman of New York had agreed to increase his previous contributions by another gift of $10,000 if the committee could find nineteen other individuals or groups who would each contribute $10,000 so that the balance of $200,000 could be raised at once. "[P]aradoxically as it may seem," Vanderbilt wrote on June 16, "I think my illness may turn that project into a real success—at least that is my hope."[81] By the deadline at the end of June, the immediate goal had been reached.

At the same time, the constitutional convention was snowballing forward.

In addition to the issue of the size of the convention, Vanderbilt had also disagreed with Governor Driscoll over its political composition. "When I say that the shift from a convention of 60 to one of 81 took me by surprise," Vanderbilt had told the Clean Government leaders in April of 1947, "I have no words left to characterize my state of mind over the development of the idea of a bipartisan or nonpartisan convention."[82] Although Vanderbilt was not suggesting that Democrats be excluded from the important committees of the convention as they had been excluded from the legislative committees when the general assembly sat as a convention in 1944, he believed that there would be Democratic delegates from Hudson, Middlesex, and Warren counties who could be counted on to effectively represent their party, and that, given Hague's domination of the state, any attempt to achieve a perfect political balance would be a mere sham. "In one Republican county after another we have been treated to the spectacle of the Republican County Committeemen accepting the recommendations of the Democratic County Chairmen, in each case the direct representative of the Hague machine, which fought constitution revision in 1944 and may be confidently expected to do so again."[83]

Governor Driscoll, on the other hand, believed that with a Republican governor and Republican legislature, a Republican-dominated convention would no more be able to put across a politically acceptable constitution than had the Republican legislature in 1944. For this reason he was willing to risk the possibility that a bipartisan convention would be torn apart by party warfare and be unable to produce a coherent document to ensure a marketable final product. He therefore set forth to win the favor of Mayor Hague.

Early in 1947 Driscoll had invited to the State House Senator Edward O'Mara of Hudson County and former United States Senator John Milton, two of Hague's principal advisors. Driscoll opened the meeting by pulling at his cuffs like a magician to indicate that he had nothing up his sleeves. He explained the importance of a nonpartisan approach to a constitutional convention and emphasized that a new constitution would not be designed to harm either party or to be of assistance to either party. Driscoll expressed his hope that each county would send its best Democrats and Republicans to the convention. When asked how the Democrats would be treated, he responded that they would be treated better than the Republicans would be if their positions were reversed.[84]

Mayor Hague's response to this peace overture was one of the most uncharacteristic of his career. Immediately after his strenuous efforts had scuttled the constitution of 1944, he had stated that he would support a constitutional convention if the convention was postponed until after the war and if it would be bipartisan. At the time, there were few who believed the sincerity of his statement. Former Governor Edison's incredulity was typical: "There can be no constitutional convention worthy of the name with Frank Hague in it. The obvious conclusion is that there can be no constitutional convention unless we first get rid of Hague."[85]

Three years later, after the meeting with O'Mara and Milton, word got back to the governor that Mayor Hague would support a constitutional convention. Although the reasons behind this decision have remained clouded, it was speculated that Hague felt any new constitution would strengthen the governor's office, which the Democrats in future elections could capture, and also that, as constitutional revision seemed inevitable and Hague's power to resist it lessening, it would be the least of all evils to have a convention at which his representatives could fight for the Democratic interests and, with the smaller counties, have a veto power over the convention proceedings. If Hague didn't like the final product, he could always bring out the Hudson hordes and attempt to vote it down in November.

On June 3, 1947, with the backing of both parties, Governor Driscoll submitted the referendum for a constitutional convention to the vote of the people. The referendum passed by a majority of five to one, with Hudson County even turning in a plurality of 55,937 in favor of the convention.

The next day, June 4, 1947, another unexpected event occurred in the unpredictable world of New Jersey politics: seventy-one-year-old Frank Hague resigned as mayor of Jersey City and handed the office over to his nephew, Frank Hague Eggers, the commissioner of Jersey City parks. This move, which was thought to be a strategy to avoid a political war in Jersey City with the increasingly powerful forces of John V. Kenny, had an unexpected ramification. Hague, though still controlling Jersey City through his nephew, left for California for the summer.

With Hague on the West coast and with Vanderbilt recuperating, the two major political powers of the state were off stage. The potential for an explosive confrontation at the convention was reduced. The stage was set for an orderly convention.

On the morning of June 12, 1947, Governor Driscoll opened the first session of the convention at Rutgers University in New Brunswick. Dr. Robert C. Clothier, the president of Rutgers and a delegate from Middlesex County, was elected president of the convention and he in turn appointed nine committees, five of which—(1) committee on the executive; (2) committee on the legislative; (3) committee on the judiciary; (4) committee on rights, privileges, and amendments; and (5) committee on taxation and finance—were to consider the substantive provisions of the constitution and four of which would conduct the business of the convention. The convention was composed of 54 Republicans, 23 Democrats, and 4 independents. Senator O'Mara was appointed by Clothier as chairman of the committee on the legislative. The four other substantive committees were chaired by Republicans, but important Hudson County Democrats sat on each committee, including Frank Hague Eggers and Lewis G. Hansen on the committee on the executive, John Milton on the committee on taxation and finance, and former Chief Justice Thomas J. Brogan on the committee on the judiciary.

With one exception, there was little grumbling that party or county interests had not been fairly distributed among the committees. The exception was the committee on the judiciary, which some felt had been stacked by Clothier and Driscoll to guarantee sweeping reforms.

Although the central aims of the delegates were to define more clearly the powers and limitations of each of the three branches of the government, to provide for the more efficient operation of each branch, and to strengthen the executive branch, the primary reason for the persistent demands for constitutional revision had been to reorganize the state court system. The attention of the convention and the public was focused on the committee on the judiciary. It was there that the most drastic changes would be wrought.

Late in May, Governor Driscoll had sent James Kerney, Jr., and Robert Hendrickson, two members of the 1941 Commission on Revision of the New Jersey Constitution, to visit Vanderbilt to ask his advice about the best person to be appointed chairman of the judiciary committee. Upon his recommendation, the seat was filled by seventy-five-year-old Frank H. Sommer, who, despite illness and age, characteristically accepted this call to public service. Vanderbilt commented, "[T]hough in none too good health, I think he will be able to do more for me in the cause that I have given so much time to than I could have done myself if I had been in attendance."[86] Although there was always a nurse and physician at hand for Sommer on the humid summer days when the delegates were soaked with sweat by early morning, his tact, humor, and diplomatic skill played a significant part in holding together the committee, in soothing the shortening tempers of August, and in preventing the dissension that had marred revision attempts in the past.

Nathan L. Jacobs, an Essex County lawyer and professor of law at Rutgers who had been an associate in Vanderbilt's law firm and an active advocate of judicial reform, was named vice-chairman of the committee. There were six members of the legal profession on the committee: Sommer, Jacobs, Lester A. Drenk, and Edward A. Mc-Grath, who were proponents of revision, and former Chief Justice Brogan and Walter G. Winne, who were known to be sympathetic to the existing court system. Surprisingly, there were five laymen members of the committee, several of whom, such as Mrs. Gene Miller and Wayne D. McMurray, editor of the *Asbury Park Press*, had expressed their sentiments for judicial reform. As it was generally believed that laymen would be more receptive to arguments for judicial reorganization than would lawyers, there was some feeling that the members of this committee had been carefully chosen as a concession to Vanderbilt, just as certain appointments seemed to have been made to please Hague.

But any criticism of the composition of the committees soon dissolved as the delegates worked in the gymnasium at Rutgers from June 12 to September 10 to turn the antiquated state constitution into a document that would modernize the state government.

The committee on the judiciary worked to achieve three goals for the state court system, goals that had been set forth by Roscoe Pound in his famous address of 1906 and which had been contended for, fruitlessly, in academic and legal circles since then: the unification of the court system; the centralized administration of the court system; and the flexibility of the court system to meet changing conditions. In a hearing before the committee on July 1, seventy-seven-year-old Dean Pound of the Harvard Law School explained these basic requirements of a modern judicial system that he, Judge Parker, and Vanderbilt had long been advocating:

> In this process of making over and simplifying the organization of courts, the controlling ideas should be unification, flexibility, concentration of judicial power and responsibility.
>
> Unification is called for in order to concentrate the machinery of justice upon its tasks. Flexibility is called for to enable it to meet speedily and efficiently, the continually varying demands made upon it. Responsibility is called for in order that some one may always be held and clearly stand out as the official to be held if the judicial organization is not functioning the most efficiently the law and the nature of its tasks permits. Concentration of judicial power is a *sine qua non* of efficiency under the circumstances of the time. There are so many demands pressing upon our state governments for expenditures of public money that so costly a mechanism as the system of courts cannot justify needless and expensive duplications and archaic business methods.[87]

The changes the committee on the judiciary proposed in Article VI, the judicial article of the new constitution, were radical departures from the system existing in 1947. Decentralization of the judiciary had been carried so far that no one person or agency was charged with supervision of the work of the courts. It was no one's business to find how to make their operation more effective or how to relieve waste and expense and eliminate delay. With the changes the committee proposed, the new court system—from the standpoint of administration—could be compared to a large business concern, with the justices of the supreme court as a board of directors, the chief justice as the chairman of the board and president, and an administrative director as the manager.

Article VI would vest the judicial power of the state in a supreme court, a superior court, county courts, and such courts of limited jurisdiction as provided by the legislature.

The supreme court would consist of a chief justice and six associate justices and exercise appellate jurisdiction in the last resort in all causes, thus superseding the sixteen-member court of errors and appeals. A superior court, with "original general jurisdiction throughout the State in all causes," would consist of such number of judges as authorized by law, but not less than twenty-four, and be divided into an appellate division, a law division, and a chancery division,[88] each to "exercise the powers and functions of the other division when the ends of justice so require." The superior court would merge within its jurisdiction civil and criminal law, and law and equity, eliminating the chancery courts, the former supreme court, the prerogative courts, and the civil courts. A county court in each county would be granted jurisdiction previously exercised by the court of common pleas, orphans' courts, court of oyer and terminer, court of quarter sessions, and court of special sessions.

By these measures designed to concentrate the machinery of justice into three major levels of courts with a single court at the trial level with power to grant legal and equitable relief, the old conglomeration of seventeen different types of courts and the distinct systems of law and equity would be eliminated. The court system would be unified and simplified to make it susceptible of efficient and economical administration. Jurisdictional controversies unrelated to the merits of cases, which delayed justice and wasted the time and money of litigants and courts, would be abolished. The emphasis could be upon the dispensation of justice, not upon where or by what tribunal it would be dispensed.

Through the judicial exercise of the rule-making power, the supreme court would be granted control over the operation of the courts, their administration, and their rules of practice and procedure. It was hoped that a uniform set of rules to be drafted by the supreme court, with the aid of committees of experts, would eliminate the conflicting rules in various courts and the technicalities on which too many cases were being decided.

It was proposed that "the Chief Justice of the Supreme Court shall be the administrative head of all the courts in the State," centralizing control and placing the responsibility for the effective operation of the entire court system with one man. With statistics kept to date weekly, the chief justice would learn the case load of each court and each judge and the time consumed in each case, in general, all information needed for the strategic deployment of judicial personnel for the most efficient operation of the court machinery. By assigning judges to those courts where they were most needed, the court system could be managed so that some judges were not overworked while others sat by half idle. Judges could thus be assigned according to their ability and according to the volume of business in each court, and judicial business could be apportioned among the courts, divisions, and parts according to the volume and type of cases.

Never before had changes in court administration, organization, and procedure been initiated at one time in such a complete sweep of an existing judicial system. The work of the committee on the judiciary was an unusual experiment in the progress of judicial modernization, for at the same time as the court system was freed from the burden of legislative regulation by granting all rule-making power to the supreme court, the court system underwent a complete structural reorganization and an administrative hierarchy was installed. Together, these changes promised a centralized, flexible system with which the courts could handle with a maximum efficiency and expedition and minimum expense to litigants and the public any volume of litigation that arose with the changing social and economic order. Such an integrated court system, however, had never proved politically acceptable in any state and had therefore never been tested in practice.

The committee was aware that the proposed judicial article bucked the vested interests of many lawyers and judges and clashed with the comfortable familiarity of the profession with the existing courts and even with its sense of the historical importance of the courts. "To preserve the time-honored and historical structure and jurisdiction of these courts, it seems to me, is and ought to be a matter of pride, and may I add duty, of the members of the bar of this state," Chancellor Edwin Robert Walker had declared to the state bar association in 1912 in words that matched the sentiment of some of the bench and bar in 1947. "Is it not better to cherish the courts we have than fly to others we know not of? We do know about our present courts. They have existed about two centuries. Their jurisdiction, power and limitations are known and defined. Is it not a waste of energy to plan and consider a change in the structure of courts, which, after all, practically changes nothing?"[89]

Similar feelings concerning the court of chancery in particular were especially strong because of the high quality of the decisions of the court and of the theoretical advantages of the specialization of courts.[90] To reflect his own views concerning the chancery court—and the views of Hague, who did not want to let go of his control of a court that had so much discretionary jurisdiction—former Chief Justice Thomas J. Brogan, one of two Democratic members of the committee on the judiciary, and a group of fifteen lawyer delegates who wished to retain a separate court of chancery drafted a substitute judicial article which would preserve those ancient English courts of equity.

To prevent the formation of a bloc of delegates supporting Brogan's article, a spirited offense on the convention floor was led by vice-chairman Nathan L. Jacobs and three lay members of the committee. They condemned the Brogan article as emasculating the basic principles of a flexible, integrated court system and criticized Brogan's efforts as an attempt to substitute for the committee's article a complicated proposal whose main purpose seemed to be to ensure seats in the new court system for all sitting judges. Their presentation was concluded with a summary statement by Frank Sommer, whose remarks—even though interrupted by a recess after he suffered a faint spell—drew a round of applause from the convention's delegates:

As far back as 1892 I took a modest part in proposing judicial reform, and I had a modest part in connection with every movement or judicial report since that time. . . . I have no fear of the dire results that are prophesied from the proposed changes in the judicial structure. In every step that I have taken in judicial reform, I have found the same dire prophesies coming from certain members of the bar, and those prophesies have not proved verities. . . .

You symbolize justice as a fair lady holding the scales of justice even. You symbolize that lady as blindfolded. I want that lady to continue to hold the scales of justice even . . . but I want to take . . . that blinding band from off her eyes so she can clearly see the end to her objective. At the present time the lady must tread a maze, a maze in which she sometimes becomes lost, a maze in which at least she has difficulty in finding her way out. . . . The committee proposal destroys that maze and lays out at the feet of this lady of justice a broad and plain highway. It avoids the detours . . . she is required to take under our present judicial system—detours that she will be continued to be required to make under the proposed [Brogan article]. I submit that this [article] should be defeated.[91]

After the delegates to the convention had repulsed the Brogan assault by a vote of 63 to 15, an amendment from his article was introduced: that the county courts remain as constitutional tribunals. This proposal met with the vigorous objections of Sommers, Jacobs, and the other ardent reform members of the committee, who believed that as the county courts would have jurisdiction which overlapped that of the superior court, a truly unified court system would be compromised and the realization of full judicial efficiency would be impeded. Nevertheless, because of the general belief that the superior court could not handle all the trial work of the state, of the reasoning of the rural counties that a superior court which sat in the major cities would not be responsive to their needs, and of the desire of the county political leaders to keep their power over the county courts, the Brogan amendment passed and remained in the final draft of the judicial article as the only major concession that had to be made to the ideal of a modern court system as proposed by Dean Pound.[92]

On Tuesday, August 26, 1947, the constitutional convention approved the judicial article by a vote of 67 to 7. "On the whole, the article seems to me as good as could reasonably be expected," Pound wrote. "I agree that the County Court provisions are the least satisfactory but it is always necessary to make compromises in such matters. . . . It is never possible to get a one hundred percent ideal political constitution. The important thing is to get a workable one, the best that may be had under the circumstances, and make the best of it."[93]

The opposition that had always existed to any plan for judicial modernization was not easy to dispel. Even at the end of the summer a disturbing majority of the state's legal profession objected to the new constitution because of the reorganization of the judicial system proposed in the judicial article. When called to New Jersey along with Professor Edmund M. Morgan of the Harvard Law School to address a gathering of lawyers and judges in Newark to explain the new judicial article, Harold R. Medina, a law professor at Columbia and a practicing lawyer in New York, sensed a hostility in his audience and recalled how it always seemed that "whenever any much needed reform in judicial procedure was under consideration, the judges made up the tail end of the procession, liberally sprinkling sand in the machinery in an endeavor to continue in the old ways however archaic or outmoded they might be." He later commented: "I shall never forget the way in which some of the judges heckled me after my little speech was over. They had the greatest collection of quibbles you ever heard to demonstrate that the administration of justice in New Jersey would be in a bad way if the separate and autonomous Court of Chancery were abolished."[94]

Most of the judges in the state were against the new constitution. The chancellor and chief justice had both appeared before the delegates that summer to speak in opposition to it. No bar association in the state declared in its favor. But unlike the efforts of the legislature in 1944, the proposed constitution, even at the end of a stifling summer, retained the support of both parties. Having put together a bipartisan convention, Governor Driscoll, with the help of Dr. Clothier, worked constantly behind the scenes throughout the summer to maintain the stability and order of the convention. They emphasized the historic significance of the work of the delegates, strove to inspire a mood of civic dedication that rose above partisan politics, discouraged the formation of coalitions along party and regional lines, and fought the influence of pressure groups and political leaders on committee deliberations. Ultimately, their conciliatory tactics and willingness to compromise proved more effective than the all-or-nothing attitude of Edison, Edge, and Vanderbilt in 1944.

Having been in frequent telephone contact throughout the summer with Sommer, Jacobs, and other members of the committee on the judiciary and with the members of the Essex delegation, and having met with Governor Driscoll in the middle of the summer when he flew to Maine and spent the day at "At Ease," Vanderbilt was well satisfied with the new judicial article, which was based on the model article of the 1941 Commission on Revision of the New Jersey Constitution and which incorporated all the major proposals that the New Jersey Judicial Council had advanced between 1930 and 1940. In September, he urged the Clean Government forces to work with total commitment for the adoption of the constitution.

Hague also had reason to be happy with the new constitution. His nephew had been able to excise from the draft of the committee on the legislative the provision giving the legislature the right to investigate the conduct of local officials. Through the work of Brogan and John Drewen, a Republican delegate from Hudson County, the county courts were to be retained and given constitutional status, thus leaving with each county political leader some degree of control over the judiciary. Perhaps most important of all, the committee on taxation and finances, in order to win the support of the Hudson County delegation, was forced to include a provision that second-class railroad property be taxed at local rates, a provision which meant an increase of $5 million in the annual revenues of Jersey City. Hague had no complaints. "With this new constitution, we forgive everyone—because we won."[95] On October 20, 1947, in his first public appearance since retiring, Hague, at a Jersey City pro-constitution rally, urged a "yes" vote in the coming election.[96]

Just as the convention delegates had made the right number of compromises to win the support of both political parties, so they had drafted into their document all the measures and provisions necessary to modernize New Jersey's government and to win the approval of the many citizen groups that had called for the convention. The *Newark Evening News* wrote two days before the election, "Hundreds of organized bodies of all shades of activities and public interest have endorsed the new charter in recent weeks in an unparalleled example of unity on a public referendum."[97]

One provision of the new constitution was of special interest: all sitting judges would be carried over to the new court system and the supreme court would be composed of judges who had served on the higher courts before the adoption of the constitution. There was speculation whether the chancellor or the chief justice would be chief justice in the new court system. All summer, politicians had been expressing their delight to Governor Driscoll that he had had differences of opinion with Vanderbilt and thus would not appoint him chief justice. "Don't be too sure," was his only reply.[98]

On Thursday, October 30, 1947, six days before the election, Governor Driscoll announced the appointment of Arthur T. Vanderbilt to the New Jersey Circuit Court "in order that a man of his extraordinary experience as a lawyer, student of jurisprudence, judicial procedure, and judicial structure, may be available" for the office of chief justice if the new constitution was ratified.[99]

The morning after this announcement, as Vanderbilt left his house to start for the train station, there stood an important client, fidgeting nervously with his hat.

"I'd like to drive you to the station," the client explained. "I have something I want to ask you about right away."

"Sure, George," Vanderbilt answered, climbing into the car. "What's on your mind?"

"I understand that you are going to become Chief Justice of the new State Supreme Court?"

"That's what the Governor tells me."

"What are they going to pay you?"

"The salary is twenty-five thousand a year, and my first appointment is for seven years. Why?"

"I'll write you a check for two hundred and fifty thousand today, if you'll stay in practice and continue to be my lawyer."[100]

Although leaving his law practice, giving up the long-anticipated experience of practicing law with his two sons who would soon be graduating from the School of Law, leaving the political arena completely, ending his teaching career, and handing over the deanship of the School of Law when the campaign drive for the Law Center was nearly complete and construction of the new building about to begin was not easy and caused him "very real regret, more than you can possibly know because I am not at all a good one at expressing what is going on inside my being," nevertheless, "the work of translating one of the most conservative judicial systems in the country into something modern and effective is a challenge, one which I could not turn down without being accused of refusing to practice what I have been preaching."[101]

On the morning of November 3, Vanderbilt was sworn in as a circuit judge by Frank H. Sommer, his choice of the man to conduct the ceremony.

The next day, Tuesday, November 4, 1947, the seventeen-year siege for judicial reform broke through the bulwark of apathy, ignorance, and opposition, storming, as it was said, practically over the dead bodies of most lawyers and judges. The constitution was ratified by a popular referendum vote of three and a half to one—633,096 to 184,632, the highest majority ever cast for a public question or a candidate for state office.

"[T]he people of New Jersey will exchange America's worst court system for America's best," stated an editorial in the *Journal of the American Judicature Society*. "It is only three years since the last proposal to overhaul the New Jersey Constitution was rejected at the polls. The 1947 triumph was fashioned from the ashes of the 1944 defeat. Leaders of the bench and bar of Florida, Louisiana, Arkansas, Michigan, California, Ohio, and other states where court organization projects are pending or constitutional revision is in prospect, should gain renewed faith that in spite of setbacks both past and future, there as well as in New Jersey, *it can be done!*"[102]

On December 8, 1947, Governor Driscoll appointed Vanderbilt chief justice of the new supreme court, and on December 15 the New Jersey Senate confirmed his appointment. The associate justices were to be former Chancellor A. Dayton Oliphant, former Chief Justice Clarence E. Case, Justice Harry Heher, Justice William Wachenfeld, Justice Albert Burling, and Circuit Judge Henry E. Ackerson. Their appointments would become effective on September 15, 1948, when the new judicial article became operative.

In spite of the warning of his doctors, that "if I were to resume my previous pace, they would not assume responsibility for a single month,"[103] Vanderbilt plunged into his new duties with all his former vigor. The job at hand was to prepare before September 15 a set of rules for each of the courts, supplanting the existing legislative rules pertaining to court practice, procedure, and administration. As chief justice-designate, Vanderbilt was excused from his responsibilities on the circuit court in order to devote all his time to formulating these rules.

In one respect, the channeling of his energy to a single purpose was a welcome relief; " . . . while I have to keep working consistently, the old-time pressures of being hauled in half a dozen different directions all at once is happily quite lacking."[104] In another respect, he knew from experience that the work ahead was the hardest he had ever attempted, both inherently—for as he remarked later "the drafting of rules is the most difficult work that a judge can be called upon to do. . . . It is easier to write half a dozen opinions than it is to draft a single adequate rule . . . ,"[105]—and also because of the professional opposition he knew he would encounter and have to overcome. From his experience with the 1912 Practice Act as Sommer's clerk, to his years of frustration as chairman of the New Jersey Judicial Council and of the National Conference of Judicial Councils, to the defeat of the efforts of the Commission on Revision of the New Jersey Constitution, he had no illusions about the difficulty of legal change. To Dean E. Blythe Stason he confided, "The job ahead of me of drafting rules for all the courts is the toughest I have ever undertaken. Not only intrinsically, but because I should have to carry along with me the dead weight of the conservatism of our bench and bar. The question at every turn would not be merely what is best but how big a dose I can get them to swallow without gagging. . . . Fortunately, the Junior Bar and a minority of the judges are vociferously for me, as are the newspapers generally."[106]

As rules of practice, procedure, and administration differed between the various courts and divisions of the courts of the old system, the new supreme court would be faced at the outset with the decision as to whether to content itself with a general rule continuing the existing rules while awaiting the study and report of judicial commissions, or to discard immediately the old rules and establish a uniform administration and practice for all the courts.

Although less than a year was provided for the process of reorganization, the justices-designate concluded that a single book of rules governing the courts was necessary from the start. In December, Vanderbilt announced the timetable to be followed in promulgating the rules: recommendations relating to the new supreme court were to be submitted by January 15; those concerning other courts by January 31; a tentative draft of the rules would be prepared and distributed for public criticism by April 1, and criticisms and suggestions would be received until May 15; the final draft was to be completed by the end of June, allowing the summer for the members of the bench and bar to familiarize themselves with the new rules before the beginning of the court year.

The preparation of the rules followed the pattern Vanderbilt had found successful in his work on the various committees to draft model bills for the federal judicial system. Suggestions were solicited from every judge, lawyer, and interested citizen in the state. The New Jersey State Bar Association and every county bar association were asked to submit recommendations. The aid of the American Judicature Society, the National Conference of Judicial Councils, and the Administrative Office of the United States Courts was sought. Vanderbilt wrote to the chief justices of each of the states to ask what rules they had found essential in their own state and what they would do if they could reorganize their court system. To promote understanding and acceptance of the new court system and to elicit suggestions and recommendations, he toured the state explaining the structure of the courts and the nature of the rules to bar association meetings and civic groups.

The tentative draft of the rules produced by committees of draftsmen, each expert in various fields of law, drew hundreds of suggestions. Each suggestion was considered by the appropriate draftsman, who made recommendations concerning the suggestion. Each suggestion and recommendation was then studied by each justice of the supreme court, first individually and then as a group. The final New Jersey Court Rules, closely patterned after the Federal Rules of Civil Procedure and the Federal Rules of Criminal Procedure, reflected the enlightened opinion of the New Jersey legal profession as to what was best in state and federal practice.

At the same time, a task force was preparing to launch the new court system. Judicial statistics from 1900 to 1948 were assembled to forecast the prospective work of the new courts. The personnel of the courts were selected, modernized office systems were planned, and the records and accounts of the existing courts were transferred to the new courts, all while the existing judicial system continued operating. An administrative office of the courts was created by the legislature. Plans were made for the use of pretrial conferences. Annual judicial conferences were proposed to provide a continual means of examining the problems confronting the court system. A uniform body of rules of procedure for traffice courts was adopted. High standards of punctuality were agreed upon by the supreme court to set an example for every other court.

Any of these measures would have been a major achievement in itself in the old court system. The fact that all were attained in one year was indicative of the course of the new court system and the promise it held for restoring "Jersey justice" as a slogan for justice speedily and impartially administered.[107]

On Monday, September 13, 1948, two days before the inauguration of the new judicial system, the changes in the administration of the New Jersey courts were outlined by the chief justice-designate at the first judicial conference. Stating his intention to clear the dockets as rapidly as possible of the 7,000 cases that had piled up in recent years, Vanderbilt gave every indication that he planned to make New Jersey judges among the hardest working in the country:

> Some of the cases pending in these courts [the supreme court and the circuit court] and in the Court of Common Pleas in the Fall of 1947 were started many years ago, one in 1934, three in 1935, seven in 1937, 13 in 1938, 21 in 1939, 50 in 1940, 86 in 1941, 135 in 1942, 126 in 1943, 208 in 1944, 468 in 1945, 2,055 in 1946 and 2,125 in 1947, with no date of summons issued being designated on the notice of trial, as required by law, in the case of 2,727 of the total. A number of these cases may have been disposed of without being marked off the list.
>
> While the number of all kinds of cases in Chancery shows a marked falling off from the peak of 26,300 in 1932 to 13,900 in 1947, we are still far from the goal of a trial or final hearing within one month after the pleadings are complete and the pretrial procedures are finished. . . .
>
> I am stating now for the record, that any such overdue decisions will be specified with the name of the judge and the name of the case in quarterly statistical reports which will be compiled as of December 31, April 1, July 1, and September 1 of each year hereafter.
>
> Justice delayed is justice denied and cannot be tolerated in this state. It is my hope and expectation that there will be no such arrearages to report in the future.[108]

On Wednesday morning, September 15, 1948, in the former court of errors and appeals in the State House at Trenton, Mr. Justice Case as the senior associate justice administered to Chief Justice-Designate Vanderbilt the oath to support the Constitution of the United States and the Constitution of the State of New Jersey, the oath of allegiance, and the oath of office. Chief Justice Vanderbilt then administered the oaths to Justices Case, Heher, Oliphant, Wachenfeld, Burling, and Ackerson.

In a short address, Vanderbilt stated: "I do not need to tell you that each and every one of us has entered whole-heartedly into the spirit of the new Constitution. It is our ambition to be known as an independent court, an efficient court, a just court, and I hope, a friendly court. We of the Supreme Court are determined to a man to give the State the finest judicial organization and administration within our power."[109]

That morning, the old eighteenth-century judicial system of New Jersey came creaking to a halt, replaced by the judicial structure blueprinted in the Constitution of 1947. At 1:30 P.M., oral argument began in the first case on the list of appeals.

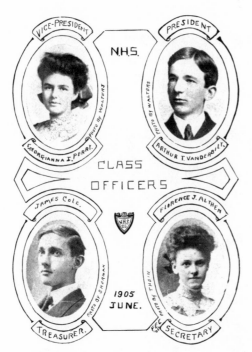

Class officers of Newark High School—
1905

"Art Van" as a senior at Wesleyan University—1910

Frank H. Sommer by Emile Alexay (*courtesy of New York University School of Law Collection*)

The American Book Building in Washington Square. The top two floors were occupied by the New York University School of Law until 1951.

Arthur and "Floss" with Jean, Betty, and Lois—circa 1925

The Vanderbilt home in Short Hills, New Jersey

And Every So Often She Needs It!

Hal Donahey's cartoon comment of July 26, 1938, on the work of the American Bar Association during Vanderbilt's presidency (*courtesy of The Plain Dealer* [*Cleveland*])

"What's going on here?" (*courtesy of* Kansas City Star)

Hague's actions as seen by the nation's press

"The banner with a strange device!" (*courtesy of* The Pittsburgh Press)

Frank Hague, Mayor of Jersey City, 1917–1947 (*from Dayton David McKean,* The Boss: The Hague Machine in Action [1940], *courtesy of Houghton Mifflin Company*)

Norman Thomas being deported from Jersey City—April 30, 1938

Vanderbilt being sworn in by Frank Sommer as a circuit court judge under the old constitution—November 3, 1947 (*courtesy of* The Newark Evening News)

First Fruit

Lute Pease's cartoon of September 14, 1948, on the inauguration of the new judicial system (*courtesy of* The Newark Evening News)

Outside Vanderbilt Hall at its dedication on September 15, 1951, are Dean Roscoe Pound of Harvard Law School, Governor Alfred E. Driscoll of New Jersey, and Chief Justice Vanderbilt (*courtesy of* New York University Law Center Bulletin)

Arthur T. Vanderbilt Hall: the Law Center at New York University (*courtesy of* New York University Law Review)

The New Jersey Supreme Court in conference—1952. Left to right: Justice Heher, Justice Burling, Justice Oliphant, Justice Vanderbilt, Justice Brennan, Justice Jacobs, Justice Wachenfeld

VI The Chief Justice, 1948–1957

"TO PRACTICE WHAT I HAVE BEEN PREACHING"

Shortly after Vanderbilt assumed his new duties, a Short Hills neighbor remarked to the local ticket agent what a great honor it was for the township to have the chief justice living there.

"That can't be much of a job," the agent observed. "I see he still takes the 7:23 every morning."[1]

Each Monday morning for forty weeks every year, Vanderbilt took the train to Trenton, where he was met by a state trooper and driven with two of his colleagues to the State House Annex. The old court schedule of meeting three times a year for two-week terms to hear sixty to seventy appeals, without prior examination of briefs or records, had been abandoned in favor of oral argument each Monday and a conference of the seven justices each Thursday. "I have never been able to understand how our judges could be expected to hear arguments day after day for two or three weeks and really remember what counsel had said in every case," Vanderbilt remarked, "especially if they have not read the briefs in advance. Frankly, I doubt whether I could do it and perhaps I may be pardoned for doubting whether many other judges can do it. . . . We in New Jersey, out of deference either to my limited mentality or my unwillingness to do useless work, hear arguments only on Mondays."[2]

At 9:30 on Monday morning administrative director of the courts Willard G. Woelper would meet with the justices of the supreme court to discuss the administrative problems of the state judicial system. Then a half hour later—by a new rule of court and by the example set by the supreme court—the first cause of judicial delay was eliminated: the delay of the judges in getting on the bench in the morning. More than any single judicial fault save lack of integrity, this cause of delay created a bad impression of the courts for it indicated the judge's lack of interest in his judicial work, his own unwillingness to conform to rules of court while insisting that others conform, and his failure to appreciate the value of others' time. Under the old judicial system the courts were to convene at 10:30, but in practice it was often much later before the judges made their way to the bench. The justices of the new supreme court concluded that if they, having traveled to Trenton from various parts of the state, could start court at ten o'clock, every judge could be on the bench at ten o'clock in his own county.

Hence at ten o'clock a door would open behind the bench in the spacious and high-ceilinged courtroom on the fourth floor of the State House Annex. The people in the courtroom would rise and the seven black-robed justices would walk briskly to their high-backed leather chairs in inverse order of seniority, the two newest members taking seats at the ends of the bench, at the center the chief justice. Chief Justice Arthur T. Vanderbilt would rap his gavel once, and the Supreme Court of New Jersey would be in session. For five hours, with an adjournment for lunch from one to two o'clock, a procession of counsellors would present their arguments why decisions of the lower courts or administrative agencies must be affirmed or reversed. At four o'clock, having heard five or six appeals, the court would adjourn, and the justices retire from public view until the next Monday.

Vanderbilt's goal for the supreme court was to have the maximum participation of each justice in each decision as contrasted with the practice of the old court system, where often one judge handled one decision by himself. In the former court of errors and appeals, where decision assignments were made before a case was argued, some suspected that only the judge responsible for the opinion would listen carefully to the argument; it was in fact possible to determine which judge had been assigned a particular case because, as the case was called for argument, a court attendant deposited before him two large bundles tied in their original wrappings, still uncut, containing the record and the briefs. Practiced counsel learned to address the judge with the bundles.

"Letting one judge do all the thinking on a case is not only an insult to the litigant and lawyer but a fraud on the taxpayer," Vanderbilt believed. "It is just as bad as letting one member of a jury hear all the evidence and bring in a decision while the eleven other members stay home. Judges have a perfectly natural human tendency to coast, and if they know in advance they are not going to have to write an opinion, they can let themselves go completely. But if they think some mean chief justice may assign them that opinion, they have to stay awake."[3] New practices were designed and perfected during the first year to guarantee the participation of the entire court in each decision.

Two and a half weeks before an appeal was scheduled to be heard before the supreme court, the court clerks would distribute the briefs and appendixes to each of the justices. Each justice would read each brief and prepare a typewritten memorandum setting forth his tentative views concerning the counsellor's points and the questions he wished the counsellor to answer during oral argument.[4]

On Thursday the justices would return to the State House Annex to the large oak-paneled conference room behind the courtroom and sit at the table built to accommodate the sixteen members of the court of errors and appeals. There they would discuss the cases to be heard the following Monday to determine, without discussing the merits, what they believed were the critical issues of each case. Thus when the cases were argued before them several days later, they would already be familiar both with the facts and the law involved and be in a position to reap the greatest benefit from oral argument. At the outset of the argument, counsel could be advised by the chief justice which points were of most interest or concern to the court and therefore could allocate the allotted forty-five minutes to their best advantage. Quite often Vanderbilt would say something like "'We are interested in your first and third points. Your second point seems to us to be somewhat trivial, but you may, of course, argue it as you see fit. Your time is yours to employ in whatever manner seems wise.' Then counsel will mutter something about his second point being a transition point on which he does not rely too heavily, which in turn leads me to ask him if he formally waives it so that we find we are getting down quickly to the meat of the case."[5]

No counsellor was excused from appearing in court to support the argument in his brief, a rule devised to discourage the shading of truth in the briefs and to discourage appeals that never would have been perfected had counsel realized that he must ultimately present the matter orally in open court.

The fact that the justices read the briefs in advance of trial, a practice followed only in several federal circuits and in no other state court, served the same purpose. It prevented lawyers from appearing before the court

to present in their oral arguments an idealized state of facts as being involved in the appeal before us, instead ... of the facts as they actually were. . . . How often we have all done that or tried to do it, taking the one black fact that will simply put us out of court and patiently painting it gray and then dusting it with powder until it almost looks white to the unsuspecting judges who have never read the briefs or looked at the records in advance of the argument. . . .

Having read the briefs beforehand, all the presiding judge had to do was to say, "Mr. Jones, at what page of the record do you find that remarkable fact?" and Mr. Jones would know from the use of the word "remarkable" that the game was up. After two or three weeks of this, every appellate lawyer in the state learned to stick to the facts of the case and to distinguish certain facts and his inferences from the facts.[6]

The practice of mandatory oral argument led to better preparation of cases for trial, to appeals on more meritorious grounds, and to a diminution in the number of appeals. In addition, in a large number of cases, the justices were forced to change their views obtained from their initial study of the briefs and to agree on a result that would not have been reached had they relied on the briefs alone.

The reading of briefs and the oral arguments helped cure another traditional delay in the judicial process: the length of time it took to decide a case after it had been argued. Reading the briefs not only helped judges readily comprehend the essentials of the case and lawyers clarify their cases in argument, but also, for these two reasons, helped judges write their opinions immediately after trial. Vanderbilt firmly believed that a judge was never better able or better equipped to decide a case than directly after it had been tried. The longer he delayed his opinion, the more his memory would be blurred by other cases and the harder would be the task. And so a rule of court stated: "As a matter of routine, all motions heard by the trial courts in any week shall be decided at or before the opening of the court the next week. As a matter of routine, all cases submitted to trial courts shall be decided within four weeks after submission." The supreme court abided by the same rule.

At the noon recess and again at the conclusion of the afternoon session, a tentative vote on two questions concerning each case that had been argued would be taken in writing without prior consultation: Should there be an affirmance, a reversal, or a modification?

And on what point of law raised in the briefs? If there was agreement, the case would then be assigned for the writing of an opinion.

If there was any disagreement, either as to the decision or the ground of decision, the case would be taken up at the conference on Thursday, which would give the justices an opportunity in the intervening days to restudy the briefs and appendixes in light of oral argument. These cases could then be discussed at length, the justices debating the various issues in informal fashion, each presenting his own views. At the conclusion of the discussion, a vote would be taken and Vanderbilt would assign the case to one of the justices voting in the majority for the preparation of an opinion. Each of the other justices would then give the writer a copy of the preliminary memorandum he had prepared prior to oral argument, with any changes in his thinking resulting from the argument or conference discussion noted. In these ways, both orally and in writing, the views of each member of the court would be made available to the opinion writer.

Also at the Thursday conference, drafts of opinions were distributed for discussion and criticism, not only of conclusions, but also of facts, law, and style. The writer would make the final decision of which suggestions he would accept while the other justices could decide whether they would vote to support his opinion as written. The writer could then revise his draft, a process that continued until general agreement was reached that the opinion reflected as nearly as possible the views of those in the majority. Concurring and dissenting opinions were distributed and discussed in the same way.

By this process, a reflection of the views of all the justices who had joined in voting for a particular decision was incorporated into the opinion. Gone were the days of one-man opinions when one justice spoke for the court with the others remaining in varying states of ignorance about the case. "After a considerable study of appellate methods elsewhere," Vanderbilt concluded, "I can truthfully say that I think there is no state in the Union in which each judge makes a greater contribution to every decision than in the appellate courts in New Jersey."[7]

Tuesday, Wednesday, and Friday each of the justices would work alone in his chambers. A familiar figure to early morning commuters, Vanderbilt left his home at seven o'clock, drove his 1939 Cadillac coupe to the Short Hills station, and walked from the parking lot to the station platform with a bulging briefcase to catch the 7:23 Lackawanna to Newark. On clear days, he walked from the Newark station to his chambers in the National Newark and Essex Building at 744 Broad Street; in bad weather he took the bus from Broad Street. He would spend the early part of the morning answering correspondence, much of it from individuals or organizations asking advice on the proposed reforms of their own state constitutions or court systems, and from judges and lawyers concerned with the improvement of the judicial machinery in their states or countries. The rest of the day would be a solid period to study briefs, examine drafts of opinions, prepare drafts of his own opinions, study motion papers and petitions for certification, prepare for the Thursday conferences, and manage the administrative affairs of the courts. It was this last category of work that was the most trying, that in the first year under the new constitution consumed almost two-thirds of his time, and that had the most far-reaching consequences in giving New Jersey the first modern state judicial system in the United States.

Despite the importance both of the structure of the state court system set forth in the 1947 Constitution and of the organization of that system through the rules of practice and procedure promulgated by the supreme court, a third major change sparked the entire judicial establishment into operation and made possible the advances that were brought about in New Jersey in the 1950's. That catalyst was the unorthodox clause in Article VI of the constitution: "the Chief Justice of the Supreme Court shall be the administrative head of all the courts in the state."

Beyond legal and judicial qualifications, a chief justice needed the executive and administrative ability to run a business as large as many of the contemporary corporations and commercial giants, for the New Jersey court system was truly a big business. It consisted of over 500 judges, 1,500 clerks, secretaries, court reporters, and courts attendants, and 7,500 practicing lawyers. The cost to the taxpayer of staffing and maintaining the courts was more than $10 million a year. The revenues received from filing fees exceeded $5 million, additional millions were paid into the public treasury in fines, penalties, and forfeitures, and one could only speculate as to the total value of money and property that changed hands each year by reason of decisions of the courts. In an average year, the appellate courts heard over 600 appeals and even more motions and applications. The courts of general jurisdiction heard 50,000 civil and criminal cases. The juvenile and domestic relations courts heard 29,000 matters. The courts of limited civil jurisdiction disposed of 137,000 cases. And the 487 municipal courts heard 70,000 minor criminal cases and processed over 1,144,000 complaints for traffic violations. Courts had been the only type of agency or business that had ever attempted to function without any administrative machinery, without supervision, without work records or statistics, without the power to assign personnel—a surprising situation when contrasted with the high degree of efficiency in the administration of most large business corporations, many of them with lawyers as chief executives. The New Jersey Constitution of 1947 gave free rein to the introduction of a businesslike administrative organization in the state courts through the person of the chief justice.

Having advocated a modern judicial system since 1930 both in New Jersey and across the United States, and having been an early draftsman of the framework of such a system for New Jersey, Vanderbilt was, as chief justice, in a position to put his theories into practice. Never before had a state court system been reorganized and simplified to the extent that Roscoe Pound had proposed. Never before had the minimum standards of judicial administration first recommended by Judge Parker's committee of the American Bar Association been implemented together in one court system in a full-scale program to improve the administration of justice. New Jersey was to be the testing ground for the proposals of Pound, Parker, and Vanderbilt. "To be Chief Justice of New Jersey under the new set-up would be one of the greatest honors that could come to any man," wrote Judge Parker, "and I know that in that position you will make the legal system of your state a model for the other states of the Union."[8]

At first the administrative principles Vanderbilt introduced resulted in varying degrees of consternation in the judicial and legal ranks and required the full use of his official position and persuasive powers to institute. It was only after these measures had proved effective in creating a streamlined and efficient court system that most of the judges recognized their value and became ardent supporters of the methods. Convinced from the start of the efficacy of the principles, Vanderbilt found it necessary to sell them to his judicial colleagues and to work constantly to ensure their success, a continual and wearing process. His attitude toward his administrative duties was

very much that of the hired hand who picked potatoes so well that his boss rewarded him with a new job, that of sitting on a box and sorting the potatoes into three heaps, large, middle-sized, and small. At noon the boss asked the hired hand how he liked his new job and was surprised to hear him say he was going to quit: the physical work wasn't hard, but the business of making decisions every minute was wearing him down.

My administrative duties take a full third of my time. There are moments when I rebel inwardly at the unceasing daily problems. When I do I recall the story which Chief Justice Weygandt of Ohio told me some years ago about his expressing similar thoughts to Chief Justice Hughes of the United States Supreme Court. Said the great Chief Justice, "You are quite mistaken. What I have accomplished in the Federal Courts will live for decades after my opinions are forgotten, and so will it be with you."[9]

The first applied administrative technique that caused considerable grumbling in the robing rooms across New Jersey was the requirement that each judge every Friday afternoon fill out a one-page report on which he listed how many hours he had sat on the bench during the preceding five working days, how many cases he had presided over and their outcome, what motions he had heard and disposed of, and any other business attended to. At the bottom of the page he was to state the number of cases still pending in his court and the date of the oldest case heard but not yet decided. The original copy of the weekly reports was sent to the administrative director who, having analyzed and summarized them, gave them to the chief justice every Tuesday morning; a copy of the reports went to the assignment judge of the county where the particular judge was sitting. A week later, compilations of these reports were sent to every judge in the state. The weekly reports were then compiled by the administrative office into monthly reports, quarterly reports, and annual reports, providing a running source of statistics for the judges, the press, and the public to examine the state of the New Jersey judiciary.

In the few states where any judicial statistics were employed, they were gathered only at the end of the year and for the most part proved useless in affecting the continuing work of the judicial establishment. After working with his "live statistics" for several years, Vanderbilt was so impressed with their importance that he could not understand how a judicial system could function effectively without them any more than a business could be run without current reports from the accounting department.

Such a simple technique as the filing of these weekly reports had wide-ranging effects on the New Jersey court system. They provided a convenient means for each judge to review his week's activity and served to remind him of matters needing further action. They gave the assignment judges of the counties specific information about how the judges they had assigned cases had utilized their time. They permitted each judge to see what his colleagues were doing and, if one was lagging, others would remind him that he must bear his burden. The effect on indolent judges when their laziness was thus exposed was, as Vanderbilt commented, "truly remarkable." Although the chief justice and the administrative director couldn't hope to make a lazy judge work, nor could they be expected to be policemen, it was found that when the weekly reports were circulated among the judges, the relatively few laggards began to mend their ways rather than incur the silent or occasionally vocal censure of their colleagues. In addition, the weekly reports revealed those courts in which congestion problems were being encountered and gave the chief justice an overview of the work load of each judge to help him in the most effective use of his assignment power.

If from these reports it was found that a case ran over the four-week deadline for decisions, the judge received a letter from the administrative director asking for an explanation. The administrative director found that, after an initial period of adjustment, he had to write only three or four such letters a year. The judges learned that it was generally easier to write an opinion than to invent a reason why the opinion was being delayed. "Judges are like other human beings," Vanderbilt said. "They don't like to fall behind in their work. But there are always some whose temperament runs toward delay and cogitation. The system we have in New Jersey does one very simple but all important thing—it makes the judges make up their minds."[10]

How often have you and I known judges burdened with so many undecided matters that they were exhausting their intellectual effort in determining which case to dispose of first and devoting what little strength they had left to telling all and sundry how overworked they were?

I submit that a trial judge will never know as much about the case he is trying as he does after he has read the trial briefs, after he has heard the evidence, and after he has listened to the argument of counsel. Then, if ever, the moment of decision has arrived. If he lets it go until the next day, he is going to start off on a new case, and then another case and then still another case, and each case he tries will render the facts of the initial case still dimmer in his mind.[11]

When over a period of time a judge was unable to meet the general deadlines in a large number of his cases, his failure suggested that he was not well qualified for the work to which he was assigned.

Experience demonstrated that, for example, many trial judges on the law side were relatively poor in performance in appellate or chancery work, and that there were good trial judges who shuddered at the thought of opinion writing just as there were good equity judges who shrank from working with a jury. A judge who was equally proficient and equally interested in appellate, criminal, civil, equity, and matrimonial work was indeed a rarity. Effective judicial administration demanded that the judges be assigned to the work they most enjoyed and for which they were most suited—another responsibility of the chief justice.

To many of the judges of the state who had long cherished their judicial independence, the filling out of a time sheet was the ultimate degradation. The fact that the chief justice knew what each judge was doing all the time added to their resentment. At first some of the judges treated these reports as a mere formality. One judge in Essex County made the mistake of having his secretary mail a completed week's report to the administrative director on Thursday. It arrived in Trenton Friday morning, listing in detail what he had done that entire day. The judge was summoned to see the chief justice to explain how he could have filled out the details for Friday when Friday was not yet over. Gradually the judges came to see the value of the weekly reports, and those who had resented Vanderbilt's use of them became admirers who "described him with the profane yet begrudgingly respectful language a Marine might use about an exacting battle commander."[12]

It would have been impossible for the chief justice alone to have handled the administrative affairs of the court system and still attend to his other judicial duties; therefore the legislature, supplementing the constitutional provision for an administrative director, had provided for an administrative office of the courts, making New Jersey the first state to follow the federal example set by the establishment of the Administrative Office of the United States Courts in 1939.

The administrative office consisted of a director appointed by the chief justice, three other lawyers, four secretaries, two clerks, and one bookkeeper, cutting by 20 percent the number of clerical and administrative employees in the state judicial system despite the increase in the volume of work of the courts. The function of the office was to relieve the chief justice of the mass of administrative details of running a great statewide business with branches in every county and community. It collected and published statistics on the work of all the courts and all the judges; handled the fiscal affairs of the court system and prepared a master budget; assisted the several committees appointed by the supreme court in studying specific aspects of the judicial process; served as an office to investigate citizen complaints about judicial shortcomings and about individual judges; and acted as the public relations office of the courts in the distribution of press releases and, on occasion, in meeting unwarranted criticism leveled at the courts that the judges were not in a position to answer.

The most important function of the administrative office was to keep a watchful surveillance over the administrative machinery of the court system and the performance of the judges in order to aid the chief justice in the exercise of his assignment power. For example, during the 1957 court year, Vanderbilt and the administrative director

were able to tell in late September that by early November there would only be enough ready appeals to keep one part of the Appellate Division fully occupied. Plans were accordingly made to disband one part of the Appellate Division and to assign its judges to other work commencing the second week of November. By the end of October it was reported that this condition would prevail until the end of January at which time there would be sufficient ready appeals again to occupy the time of two parts of the Appellate Division. Accordingly plans were made to terminate the trial assignments and reconstitute the second part of the Appellate Division commencing the first week in February. While the number of appeals being filed during the winter months were running heavier than usual, the projective report previously described showed that by the middle of April, although a large number of appeals would be pending, few would be maturing and so plans were again made to utilize three appellate judges in the trial courts for four weeks, re-assigning them to the Appellate Division in the middle of May at which time the number of appeals would again be sufficient to fill the calendar of two parts of the Appellate Division.[13]

Although, for example, the total number of appeals taken to the appellate division of the superior court could vary as widely as from 30 to 100 a month, from 400 to 700 a year, the appellate division was never behind in its calendar, and the average time for the passage of a case from argument to decision remained at about a month.

The second result from the power to assign judges is that—and this is something you will have to take on faith because it doesn't sound possible until you see it tried—if you have Judge A sitting in Courthouse A and Judge B sitting in Courthouse B, each operating from a separate list of cases, they will try a certain number of cases. Yet if you put Judge A and Judge B in the same courthouse and let them operate from a common list, they will try half again as many cases as they did sitting alone in different courthouses. You can continue the process up to the limit of trial judges available, the number of courtrooms available, and the number of trial lawyers available. There is something about having a lot of judges working together on an active integrated list that makes for the rapid disposition of cases. Don't ask me why it is so for I don't know, but I do know that it is so. It works that way.[14]

In the assignment of judges an effort was made to arrange temporary assignments with a minimum of personal inconvenience. Under ordinary circumstances, the administrative director would advise the judge in question that the chief justice was contemplating assigning him to temporary duty in another court or county for one or two weeks of the forthcoming month. The judge would then be in a position to report that, for instance, he was not readily available during the first week because of a scheduled full-week murder trial in his own county, but that the second week could be made available by minor calendar adjustments. On the other hand, the administrative director might be advised as late as 8:30 Monday morning that one of the regular judges of the appellate division would not be able to sit that day due to illness, a situation which would mean that the two other judges of the division and the lawyers scheduled to argue cases would be seriously inconvenienced. After telephone conferences with the chief justice and other judges, an immediate temporary assignment order would be prepared and issued.

For each county of the state a judge of the superior court was selected by the chief justice, on the basis of his potential for dealing aggressively with administrative problems, as the assignment judge responsible for the administration of the civil and criminal calendars in every court in that county. These assignment judges were, to continue the business corporation analogy, the vice-presidents of the system. In addition, in each county court and municipal court, one judge was designated as the presiding judge responsible for the administrative affairs of that court: the branch manager.

A management team was thereby established consisting of the chief justice, the justices of the supreme court, the administrative director, nine assignment judges who had control over the assignment of judges in the twenty-one counties, and the presiding judges, a clear chain of command to translate the administrative policies of the judicial system into action in every court in every county of the state. The full use of the assignment of judges and of this administrative hierarchy proved a major solution in eliminating unnecessary delays in moving cases on to trial.

The most controversial measure that Vanderbilt introduced into the court system, a measure that well illustrated that efficient judicial administration and the conduct of trials as systematic searches for the truth were complementary and not contradictory goals, was the use of pretrial discovery procedures and pretrial conferences.

On March 13, 1948, at the invitation of the New Jersey Supreme Court, Chief Judge Bolitha J. Laws of the United States District Court for the District of Columbia and six leaders of the Washington bar presented a skit of a pretrial conference at a New Jersey State Bar Association meeting. Though well-accepted and widely used in the federal court system after the provision for their discretionary use in the Federal Rules of Civil Procedure, pretrial conferences aroused little enthusiasm from the bench and bar of New Jersey. Judge Harold R. Medina of the United States Court of Appeals for the Second Circuit recalled how even during the presentation of this pretrial skit, "a considerable number of the trial judges, seated here and there in the middle and rear of the hall, got up and walked out, right in the middle of the demonstration."[15] Even convincing the judges to conduct pretrial conferences in their courts for a short experimental period required salesmanship of the highest order, and throughout his years as chief justice it was a cause Vanderbilt could never neglect without losing ground.

Believing that pretrial conferences were an important step in obtaining a trial on the merits of a case, in making a trial an orderly proceeding concentrated on the issues, and in reducing the length of trial time spent on nonessentials, Vanderbilt wished to fully implement their compulsory use in the courts. He placed great reliance on them to eliminate weak cases and so to ease congested dockets.

One week each month was reserved for pretrial conferences of pending cases during which week all trials were discontinued and every judge except those assigned to the trial of criminal cases conducted twelve to fifteen pretrial conferences a day. In a pretrial conference, the opposing lawyers—having consulted with each other about the issues of law and fact involved in the case, having questioned each other's clients and witnesses through such means as interrogatories to the parties, depositions, physical and mental examinations, production and inspection of documents, and requests for admissions, and having each prepared for the judge a memorandum of the issues they agreed upon as well as their factual and legal contentions—met in open court with a judge who had read the pleadings and memoranda. The conference served to focus the later trial of the case by providing an opportunity for the judge and lawyers to review and simplify pleadings, to restate issues, to determine what facts could be stipulated and what documents could be admitted, and to agree to limit the number of expert witnesses to be called by each side.

In the process, those elements of surprise and technicality that could make a trial more of a sporting event for spectators than an orderly search for truth were revealed. Often for the first time, as Vanderbilt observed, the plaintiff's lawyer understood the plaintiff's case and achieved a proper perspective on the defendant's case, as did opposing counsel. "Suddenly it dawns on each of them that instead of this being a case that the plaintiff can't lose or the defendant can't lose, it begins to be one that has a monetary value in terms of settlement. But this is not the most important result of a pretrial conference, for month in and month out, in every county in our state—metropolitan, suburban, and rural—three quarters of the cases are settled between the date of the pretrial conference and the date when the case gets to trial two weeks later without the judge saying a word about settlement."[16]

Neither the settlement of cases that should never have gone to trial, the reduction of the economic waste that resulted from engaging in lengthy and expensive preparations to present legally sufficient proof on formal issues which were not really in dispute, the savings in public and private time and money arising out of a final disposition of the cause at the pretrial stage, nor the fact that pretrial procedures shortened the length of trials by a third to a half were the primary advantages of pretrial conferences, although they were certainly valuable by-products. Of central importance was the fact that the judge would begin to gain a familiarity with the case and could review the law involved before the trial. Rather than being obliged to fumble through the pleadings and guess in the maze of language that only counsel could invent what the real issues were that he had to try, he could better follow the course of the trial as it unfolded and better guide its direction. The objective of a pretrial conference was therefore to prepare the trial judge and counsel for the best possible trial of a particular case, just as at the appellate level the reading of briefs in advance of trial and the preparation of written memorandum of tentative conclusions prepared the judges for oral argument and led counsel to improve their briefs and argument.

Previously, neither lawyer in a lawsuit had known until the day of trial what the other would present in witnesses, or facts, the object being that in keeping one's case closely guarded the elements of surprise or maneuver could so confound the opposing lawyer, or the jury, as to win the day. Now the nature of the whole case was laid bare, and each lawyer's position became clear. With the exact issues of the case, the actions taken, and the agreements reached formulated in a succinct pretrial order dictated in open court by the judge and signed by the judge and the lawyers, the course of the subsequent trial was already charted. The pretrial conference helped speed the judicial process by ensuring that each lawyer's brief would be ready before the trial, by producing documents that would be necessary in the trial which, unless they were controverted, were immediately marked as evidence to avoid the necessity of formal proof and production of attesting witnesses at the trial, by increasing the understanding of the lawyers and judge about the case, by decreasing errors of law on the part of the judge, thereby minimizing appeals, and by putting the judge in a better position to write his opinion directly after the trial.

Many lawyers rebelled at the thought of a pretrial hearing that would disclose anything about the strengths or weaknesses of their case before trial. These discovery methods were contrary to their tradition of concealing facts until the last possible moment, the foundation of the ancient but lasting conception of a lawsuit as a trial by battle with the victor and justice emerging together from the fray and the judge's decision awarded to the most skillful fighter. Although mandatory pretrial procedures did not abolish the adversary system of justice, they did act as a handicapping device to equalize the relative experience and skill of the counsellors to guarantee a fairer contest in the judicial arena.

Judges were equally adamant in their opposition to the procedures because of the extra work the conferences entailed if they were conducted properly. "Strangely enough," Vanderbilt noted, "no opposition arose from either judges or lawyers who practiced on the equity side of courts—for discovery has always been the essence of equity. It was with causes on the law side that resistance arose." At the outset, fear was expressed that these pretrial procedures, especially the discovery process by deposition, would be abused. "At every judicial conference, at almost every bar association meeting I have addressed, and without exception at each general meeting of judges I have asked to be informed of any instance of abuse of pretrial procedures, but in a period of five years I have yet to hear of a single complaint."[17]

Over the centuries in the development of judicial freedom from royal prerogative, the total independence of judges from any control had become a universally accepted principle. In addition, some of the New Jersey judges carried over from the days of Mayor Hague considered their judicial positions more as a reward for past services than as an active job. To some, therefore, Vanderbilt's insistence on a tight organization and control of the court system was "sheer judicial autocracy" and quite intolerable. To Vanderbilt, the reluctance of the judges to try modern methods of judicial management, each of which had been employed elsewhere and found helpful in improving the quantity and quality of justice administered in the courts, was equally intolerable and a constant obstacle to overcome. Having often observed the antipathy of the legal profession to change, he had come to believe that complacency and lack of will were all that stopped most reforms. "Professional apathy, I may say from experience, is merely a euphemism for judicial and professional unwillingness to learn anything new, however simple it may be. To be blunt, it is unadulterated selfishness and gross disregard of the public welfare in an area which we are charged with primary responsibility."[18] "I know that there are judges and lawyers [in New Jersey] who will sigh for the good old days which in some respects were not so good if one looks at the facts of life squarely and objectively, just as there were many who sighed and thought the world was coming to an end when the Practice Act of 1912 and the Chancery Act of 1915 were enacted. . . . There is not the slightest doubt that the new system will work, if there is the will to make it work."[19]

It was Vanderbilt's purpose in the application of sound principles of administration to the new court system to improve the quality of justice rendered in the courts by working to eliminate from trials delay, obfuscation, technicalities, and surprise—the allies of the sporting theory of justice. Each of the changes initiated in the courts was developed to further the realization of this purpose.

RESULTS

More visible and more dramatic than the improvements in the quality of New Jersey justice were the quantitative improvements that did much to win the support of the bench and bar of the state and to arouse the curiosity of the legal profession of the nation, making further advances possible. At the judicial conference on September 8, 1949, Chief Justice Vanderbilt issued the first official report describing the year's operation of the courts:

This, the first Judicial Conference under the new Constitution, meets in quite a different atmosphere from the conference held last year on the eve of the organization of our new judicial system. Then, despite the strenuous efforts of every branch of the profession through many months of rule-making and despite the fact that we had drawn largely on Federal experience and the best practices in forty-eight states, there were misgivings on the part of some as to how the new system would work. Now, however, we convene in an atmosphere of genuine confidence, engendered by the substantial accomplishments of every court of the State over the past year. In mentioning our achievements I do not refer primarily to the quantitative results reflected statistically in the Administrative Director's reports for the first three-quarters of the year, spectacular though they are. Rather I desire to emphasize something that cannot yet be demonstrated statistically, but which is, nevertheless, very real. I refer to the improved judicial methods in use in every court and the consequent improvement in the quality of our work throughout the State. We may take credit for a very good beginning, while frankly conceding that there is much still remaining to be done before we can truthfully express full satisfaction with the judicial establishment as a whole.

Over the past year the Supreme Court has disposed of 203 appeals, 221 motions, 15 petitions for certification and 12 disciplinary matters—50% more appeals than in the previous comparable year—and it has disposed of them in 74% less time from the date of argument to the date of decision. Parts A and B of the Appellate Division of the Superior Court heard 239 cases and 197 motions by June 30th—70% more than in the previous comparable year—and in 73% less time.

When our appellate courts adjourned on June 30th there was quite literally not a single case left on the dockets of either court ready for argument.

During the past year the Law Division, with one less judge most of the year, has disposed of 98% more cases than its predecessor courts, and the county courts have disposed of 77% more cases. With this record of accomplishment and with ten more county judges giving their full time to these judicial duties under the act passed last winter, we have every reason to expect to achieve by the end of June, 1950, our objective of clearing the dockets as we have in the appellate courts and thus to eliminate the first kind of delay that had been a blight in our trial courts.

The Chancery Division with seven judges, and for part of the year only six, instead of ten vice-chancellors as formerly, disposed of 126% more matters per judge than in the previous year and ended on June 30 with an average of only 64 cases per judge on the docket in contrast with the 384 cases per judge pending in the Law Division.

The new Municipal Courts, which went into operation on January 1st, 1949, have given general satisfaction. In six months they have disposed of the staggering total of 209,630 cases of which 83.7% were traffic cases.[20]

These results were more than mere figures. For example, according to statistics gathered by the Institute of Judicial Administration in

1954, if a person was injured in an automobile accident and sued for damages, he would wait, on the average, 39 months for his case to come to trial if he lived in Boston; he would wait 40 months if he lived in Chicago; he would wait 49 months if he lived in Queens County, New York; he would wait 45 months if he lived in Kings County, New York; he would wait 53 months, almost four and a half years, if he lived in Brooklyn, New York; he would wait 31 months if he lived in Fairfield County, Connecticut; he would wait 21 months if he lived in Allegheny County, Pennsylvania.[21] The situation was even worse than some of these statistics indicated for in many instances they related, not to the date of the filing of the complaint, but to the time when the case came to issue and was put on the trial calendar after all preliminary motions had been disposed of. A sad commentary on American urban justice, these figures revealed the plight of families deprived of their breadwinner, of accident victims suffering incapacitating injuries, oppressed with medical expenses, their earnings cut off or curtailed, all denied recourse to the courts for several years as witnesses disappeared and memories dimmed, as reputations were tarnished and jobs lost, if indeed the victims were not forced by need to settle out of court for whatever they could get despite the merits of their case. Justice delayed was indeed justice denied. In New Jersey, a similar accident victim could have a trial six to seven weeks after suit was filed and a decision a month or less later.

Most remarkable in surveying the quantitative results of the first year was the fact that the New Jersey court system was operating with the same judges as under the old system but with a smaller number. In addition, with the population growing and commercial and industrial activity increasing, there was a steadily rising volume of litigation. The advances in the courts made in view of these circumstances furnished convincing proof of the value of administrative practices consistently applied to a streamlined judicial system.

In each succeeding year the results continued to improve. All of the old chancery cases were cleared during the first year. On the law side, all arrearages were eliminated in two years in sixteen of the twenty-one counties so that decisions could be handed down within three to four months after pretrial procedures were started, the remaining five counties attaining a similar state of currency in the third court year. By 1950, every case remaining from the days of the old system, some of which had been pending for twenty years, had been cleared. The average time from the filing of the last brief to the date of trial was a week or ten days. The average time from appeal to decision in the supreme court was reduced to a month from the average of 105 days in the court of errors and appeals. All courts continued to keep abreast of their work. And the supreme court and appellate division of the superior court maintained an unbroken record of deciding every ready case before rising for summer recess. "The most flattering thing that happened," remarked the administrative director, "was when a labor lawyer sent a telegram complaining of a 10 day delay on a decision. Imagine anyone noticing 10 days in the New Jersey courts!"[22]

Although the ancient problem of judicial delay had been alleviated, Vanderbilt and all the judges were aware that it had not been eliminated. The increasing litigation in the wake of the postwar economic and population boom constantly challenged the ingenuity of the bench in keeping abreast of its work. The important consideration was that, while the steps in litigation necessarily took time, any unnecessary delay in the numerous stages of the process had to be remedied.

The supreme court recognized that the rules of court it had promulgated and the administrative techniques it was implementing were continually becoming outmoded, that the search for ways to improve the administration of justice in the state courts was a dynamic, never-ending process. "[T]hrough such a continuous process," wrote Vanderbilt, "and through this process only, may we hope for a system of procedure that will be at all times adapted to its purpose and that will at all times be subordinate to establishing the substantive rights of the litigants."[23]

To this end a plan originated by Judge Parker in 1931 in his Fourth Circuit—a yearly judicial conference—was adopted in New Jersey and developed into a conference of lawyers, judges, representatives of the legislature, the attorney general, the county prosecutors, the president and directors of the state bar association, the president of each of the county bar associations, delegates appointed by the president of each of the county bar associations, and several selected laymen. The purpose of the annual conference was to review the work of the courts, to review amendments to the New Jersey Rules and propose new rules to meet the changing demands of litigation, the courts, and the state,[24] and to provide a forum for the discussion of the common problems of every branch of the profession, particularly as these problems related to the administration of justice.

The annual judicial conference served as a convenient force for receiving, evaluating, and recommending new ideas for improving the courts. For example, soon after the judicial system went into effect, the conference received a letter from a woman juror asking why, since all the courts commenced work at the same time, the jurors in the county courts had to report for duty at 9:30 A.M. when the jurors serving on the superior court did not have to report until 9:45 A.M. Vanderbilt inquired into the reasons for the difference only to receive the stock reply that it had always been that way. Thereafter, every juror was permitted to report at 9:45 A.M. to avoid the irritating experience of having to report early and then wait for the courts to get started.

On another occasion, an active trial lawyer pointed out to the judicial conference that every two weeks when a new panel of jurors was being indoctrinated at the start of its period of service, an hour was lost while the judges and lawyers waited for a jury. The lawyer suggested that this time could be utilized by scheduling a pretrial conference for every judge. This was done, and the time was put to productive use. It was the constant receptiveness to simple, commonsensical suggestions such as these that made the judicial conference an important agency in ensuring the continued effectiveness and growth of the New Jersey judicial system. Many of the suggestions made might have seemed insignificant and trivial in themselves; collectively they marked the difference between a good judicial establishment and a merely tolerable one. "We all realize that in this field we must either move forward systematically or we will inevitably drift backward," Vanderbilt stated. "There is no room for complacency in the administration of justice."[25]

Committees of the judicial conference, created to examine problems in court operations and often headed by a supreme court justice, proved a success in furthering the progress toward the day when procedure would be as simple as possible and the administration of the courts as efficient as possible consistent with protecting the rights both of the individual and of society. For instance, during the period between 1951 and 1955—as more cases were started each year, as the average case became more complicated, as the miscellaneous work of the judges increased, and as conflicts between the governor and legislature resulted in long delays in filling judicial vacancies—such trends, which could have led to a deterioration of the court calendars, were neutralized by the application of the recommendations of Justice Ackerson's committee on Pretrial Conferences and Calendar Control. Part-time judges were placed on a full-time status; pretrial procedures and calendar practices were reexamined to make them more effective; legislation was secured permitting the transfer of minor cases from the courts of general jurisdiction to the courts of limited jurisdiction, where they could be tried more expeditiously; and the court day was lengthened in eight larger counties where the cases were accumulating fastest.

The changing scope of the responsibility of the courts led to the formation of other committees to examine the role of the judicial system in dealing with modern social problems. A committee on divorce and custody of children headed by Justice Vanderbilt and a committee on reconciliation headed by Judge John Francis reported on the close relationship between crime and the breakdown of the family and stressed the need for the courts to be equipped to deal realistically with the problems of the family. As a result of the recommendations of these committees, municipal juvenile conference committees of laymen were organized in several counties to handle informally minor cases of juvenile delinquency that otherwise, not dealt with for lack of sufficient court personnel, might have led to more serious offenses.

Similarly, other committees were organized to deal with other problems. In 1950 Judge Richard Hartshorne was chairman of a committee on providing counsel for indigent defendants, Judge Milton Conford was chairman of a committee on uniformity of sentences, Justice Burling was chairman of a committee on marital desertion, Justice Oliphant was chairman of a committee on jurors, James Kerney was chairman of a committee on traffic rules, Justice Wachenfeld was chairman of a committee on improving the administration of criminal justice, and Justice Heher was chairman of a committee on probation. These committees, not content merely with sponsoring a few technical amendments to the New Jersey Rules, attempted to find real solutions to the particular problems that had been brought to their attention through the judicial conference. Thus it was recognized that a modern judicial system must deem it part of its responsibility to possess a social conscience and to probe into realities not before regarded as being within the formal ambit of judicial function. It was hoped that the courts could make available their substantial preventive and corrective resources in meeting problems that cut across legislative, executive, and judicial lines.

In addition to these activities of the judicial conferences, a secondary benefit was that judges who had never been personally acquainted with many of their colleagues on the bench had an opportunity to meet on common ground and to begin to understand the workings of the different courts. Although the rules of court called for only one two-day judicial conference each year, Vanderbilt called special sessions of the conference to consider immediate problems and held frequent informal conferences with different groups of judges to consider the problems they were encountering in their own courts. These were often dinner meetings attended also by the administrative director and one or more associate justices. They provided a chance to discuss in depth the specific problems of the courts while leading to a spirit of cooperation which was in itself a necessary ingredient to achieve a truly integrated and effective state judicial system.

Because the municipal courts in New Jersey presented special problems by reason of their number and the volume of matters they handled, the supreme court also called an annual conference of municipal magistrates which provided a similar forum for an exchange of ideas among the magistrates and between the magistrates and representatives of other branches of the state government.

Despite his interest in finding new methods for improving the efficiency of the administration of justice, Vanderbilt always emphasized that each case that came to court was a problem of supreme importance to one or more individuals, not merely a statistic to be added to the court records. "We want speedy justice. We don't want hasty justice."[26] The emphasis of the new court system was not merely on promptness. It was no improvement to be wrong quickly. Mass production methods and assembly-line techniques were incompatible with a sound judicial system. Every case was entitled to all the time and effort necessary for a fair trial, but not to one minute of delaying tactics. The emphasis of the New Jersey courts was on a well-prepared case and on the elimination of any unnecessary delay after the case was prepared and awaiting trial, and after it had been tried and was awaiting decision.

Vanderbilt believed that improving the efficiency of the judicial machinery served to improve the quality of justice rendered by the courts. Criticized as a worshipper of promptness for its own sake, he replied that he would prefer slower decisions if they resulted in better serving the ends of justice, but that he believed a prompt decision was a better decision. The mere passage of time did not assure that a case was receiving the careful, undivided attention that it deserved, as example after example from the old court system had demonstrated. The importance of improving the administration of justice was that the quality of trials and appeals and decisions be improved at the same time. The goals were inextricably united. A valuable result of pretrial conferences was the settlement of cases out of court. An equally important result was that a case could be pared down to its essential elements, revealed clearly to the lawyers and judge, and organized for a more effective trial. The reading of briefs before trial, not only facilitated decisions, but sharpened the judge's questions during oral argument, improved oral argument by discouraging flights of fancy both as to facts and to law, and permitted a more detailed exploration of the merits of the case. The oral argument of every appeal discouraged frivolous appeals as delaying tactics while improving the judge's understanding of a case. The pressure put on the judges to decide a case immediately after trial allowed them to consider it when it was still sharpest in their minds.

The simplified, integrated judicial system, the uniform rules of practice, procedure, and administration prepared and promulgated by the supreme court, the responsibility for the effective administration of the courts vested in the chief justice, the use of live judicial statistics, the establishment of the administrative office to oversee the affairs of the judicial system and to aid in the assigning of judges, the introduction of pretrial procedures, the calling of judicial conferences, and the new cooperative spirit of the judges together ushered in changes that swept away the infirmities of the former judicial system and began to restore the public's confidence in the courts. Concluded Vanderbilt:

> . . . in curing court congestion in New Jersey we have had a revolution in judicial and professional practice, a minor revolution which nevertheless has done much to increase public respect for law in our state. No longer is the successful litigant unnecessarily delayed. No longer do cases lie around law offices bringing in no income and serving no useful purpose. No longer does the trial judge needlessly carry a heavy pack of troubles on his back. The bench and the bar have won the respect of the public for industry and efficiency. And what has been accomplished in New Jersey may be accomplished anywhere.[27]

The example of the New Jersey judiciary, organized and empowered to administer justice speedily, efficiently, and at no more than reasonable expense in a complex urban industrial state, could be followed in any state without additional judges, without increased court fees, and without resorting to irregular or improper court practices.

THE COURTS OF FIRST INSTANCE

An important step in constructing the type of modern judicial system blueprinted in the New Jersey Constitution of 1947 involved engendering in the judges—all carried over from the old system—a new sense of responsibility for their courts' performance. Nowhere was this more necessary than in the courts of first instance, and nowhere was Chief Justice Vanderbilt more successful.

In addition to the supreme court, the superior court, and the county courts, the Constitution had provided for such other courts of limited jurisdiction as the legislature might create. Following the advice of the delegates to the constitutional convention, the legislature in 1948 replaced the complicated growth of local courts— consisting of juvenile and domestic relations courts, surrogate courts, justice of the peace courts, county traffic courts, recorder courts, police courts, small cause courts, city district courts, criminal judicial district courts, and family courts—with a unified system of county district courts with civil jurisdiction up to $1,000 and municipal courts with local criminal jurisdiction. These new courts became effective on January 1, 1949.

The courts most frequented by the people were, in Vanderbilt's judgment, the most important courts in the entire judicial establishment. One year he asked the sergeant-at-arms to keep a record of attendance at the supreme court. Aside from lawyers involved in appeals and groups of school children who came in and stayed several minutes on a tour of the State House, exactly 248 people came to the court in the course of a year. In contrast, by 1955, one citizen out of every five annually appeared before the municipal courts for traffic violations in addition to countless others involved in a wide variety of criminal cases, disorderly conduct offenses, and violations of local ordinances. It was in these courts of first instance that most citizens, particularly young people and the foreign born, received their first and perhaps only direct impression of American justice. In most cases, these courts of first instance were also the courts of last resort. Therefore the degree of respect for the law gained by the people through their contact with the courts—a respect Vanderbilt considered the foundation of a democratic society—depended largely on their encounters with the municipal magistrates.

Vanderbilt frequently cited a national public opinion poll that had indicated that 28 percent of the American people believed their local and municipal judges were dishonest. "Leaving aside the question of whether this large group of people is right or wrong, the fact remains that too many judges have behaved in a way which creates a widespread impression of dishonesty."[28] As chief justice, he took action to bring new respect to the New Jersey municipal courts by integrating them into the judicial system of the state and thereby elevating them to the dignity of the other courts in the eyes of the citizens.

Joint municipal courts serving two or more neighboring municipalities were established by the legislature to make it financially possible for rural areas to avail themselves of the advantages of a well-run local court.

The supreme court exercised its rule-making power to promulgate uniform rules regulating the practice, procedure, and administration of the municipal courts.

Like all judges, municipal magistrates were subject to the Canons of Judicial Ethics, but for the first time a strict adherence to the Canons was demanded. All political activities of the judges were forbidden, from belonging to political clubs to giving political speeches, attending victory dinners or celebrations, or making campaign contributions.

At first there was discontent when the supreme court imposed a rule that magistrates who were members of the bar were to wear robes, both to remind all concerned that the judge represented the law and also to act as a constant reminder to the judge that he did not have the freedom of the private individual but was bound to submerge his personal feelings in the impartial administration of the law. Within the year, a request came from the lay magistrates that the rule be amended so that they too could wear robes, a privilege that was granted.

While previously New Jersey magistrates had not been required to have a law school training or even a college education, as magistrates retired only qualified members of the bar were eligible to fill their positions.

Fixed salaries were established to replace the treacherous system whereby compensation depended on the costs the judges assessed against defendants found guilty of some offense. A uniform system of fines and penalties was initiated.

Vanderbilt brought to the attention of the individual magistrate every citizen's charge of discourtesy or bad manners by sending him a copy of the complaint and asking for his version of the facts. Sometimes the judicial alibis were almost transparent, and they were often accompanied by a considerable show of indignation, but it was noticeable that, following such correspondence, complaints ceased.

Several years after the introduction of these simple measures, there was so much public confidence in the municipal courts that the legislature in 1951 downgraded fifty-six offenses from indictable crimes to disorderly conduct offenses and gave the municipal magistrates jurisdiction over them, thus freeing the grand juries from considering many minor cases.

The greatest progress in raising the prestige of these courts was brought about by the adoption of a rule of court creating a uniform "nonfixable" traffic ticket to eliminate the special privileges and forms of unequal treatment that had marred the reputation of the local courts and done more than any other abuse of the judicial system to breed disrespect for the law. Having been chairman of the National Committee on Traffic Law Enforcement since 1938[29] and a member of the President's Highway Safety Conference since 1945, Vanderbilt was familiar with the problems of traffic court justice and the remedies available. The system of nonfixable tickets he introduced in New Jersey had been tried in several cities in Michigan and had proved simple and effective. It consisted of a ticket made up in quadruplicate. One copy went to the offender, one to the court, one to the police chief, and one to the police officer who made it out. To quash a ticket, three public officials had to be persuaded to violate their sworn duty. The tickets were numbered consecutively, each had to be accounted for, and the penalty for attempting to fix or dispose of a traffic summons was a citation for criminal contempt. The nonfixable traffic violation ticket was put into use on January 1, 1949.

Public reaction to this new system of traffic tickets was shrill. For several days Vanderbilt worked full time "keeping the hands and feet of some of my colleagues from becoming too chilled"[30] as the beneficiaries of the old order bewailed their loss. He had not been a trial lawyer for several decades, however, without learning how to handle the confrontation that ensued.

When the no-fix ticket was introduced, . . . a storm broke loose such as had never before been known in New Jersey judicial history. The executive secretary of the State Police Chiefs Association condemned it in two words, "It stinks." Some of our newspapers disliking such vulgar language, softened his condemnation to "It smells," which sounds just as bad to me. Much to my surprise the police chiefs and the directors of public safety throughout the state succeeded in convincing a certain number of newspapers that a gigantic fraud was about to be perpetrated upon an unsuspecting public. For a week the hurricane continued without abatement. Finally we decided to call a conference of the directors of public safety and the police chiefs so that they might air their grievances and explain to us the defects, if any, of the new ticket.

I shall never forget the session. Three or four hundred men with lowered brows and tight-set lips were there to greet us. Now, ours is a very simple court; for well over two centuries it has opened without fanfare. The justices merely enter in single file, everyone rises, the chief justice taps his gavel lightly once and everyone sits down. This particular audience apparently had determined not to rise when we entered, but there were twenty or thirty lawyers in the group whose better instincts prevailed. It took the rest of the audience, however, as I watched the clock in the rear of the room, well over two minutes to struggle to their feet before I could tap my gavel.

For forty-five minutes I addressed this sullen audience on the problem at hand, stressing the fact that respect for law meant even more to them out on the highways and byways than it did to us in court. Statistically, they were much more likely to be run over than the judges. I concluded my remarks, however, by stating that I had not invited them down to listen to a speech, but to give them an opportunity to state their objections which I would be glad to answer one by one.

The first question was from a well-known director of public safety: "How can a traffic officer direct traffic, if every time he gives out a ticket he has to look up a notary public before whom to swear to the complaint?" I asked him to repeat his question and then I repeated it. Repetition is a wonderful weapon. I then proceeded to answer his question by asking whether there was anyone else in the audience who was afflicted with the same doubt, indicating by my manner that if there were, he too should be considered as a candidate for speedy admission to the hospital for mental diseases. There was no one else in the audience who had that particular doubt or at least was willing to voice it. I then proceeded to give my friend the answer slowly, plainly, just as I would to a five-year-old and when I was through I asked him if he understood. Reluctantly he said, "Yes."

The next question from a burly police chief was intended to be a "Big-Bertha." He wound up much like the greatest exhibitionist you have ever seen on the baseball mound, but essentially his question was "How can you make out this very complicated ticket on a very cold rainy night with the wind blowing a gale and your fingers numb?" I had him repeat the question, and then I repeated it. Finally, I answered it by asking another question, "Is there anyone in this room who has ever known a police officer who could not find a warm, dry spot in which to make out a ticket on a very cold night when it was raining very hard and the wind is blowing a gale?" Laughter ensued. The question had answered itself, and the tension was broken.

A police chief from a small municipality then arose to object to our request that no police officer, for obvious reasons, should be permitted to receive fines. Every public official in his town except himself, he said, also had private employment and there was no one around other than himself to whom a motorist might pay his fine. I probed his statements of the activities of his colleagues rather thoroughly. I then remarked very quietly, "Up till now I had thought that there was only one indispensable man." The audience roared with laughter and the police chief cried, "But I am a Republican, sir." "That helps a lot," I said, "it evens things up."

I was about to adjourn the meeting when a distinguished-looking gentle-man in the rear of the room requested to be heard. He remarked that all of the people in the room were either directors of public safety or police chiefs, but he, however, represented 12,000 policemen throughout the state. He was the executive secretary of the Patrolmen's Benevolent Association. He characterized the new nonfixable traffic violation ticket as a Declaration of Independence, yes, as an Emancipation Proclamation for the ordinary policeman, who resented the fact that his chief had all too often killed the traffic tickets he had issued. He carried the new ticket for a touchdown and then he kicked the goal to a round of applause that I should have deemed utterly impossible an hour and a half before.

Let me give you the sequel. In the first quarter of 1949 with the new ticket in operation there were 607 tickets unanswered in court in the largest city in the state and almost all of them were issued to nonresidents passing through the state and not intending to return. Compare this figure with the same quarter of 1948 with the old ticket and the old fix in operation when there were 14,529 tickets not responded to in court. These figures tell their own story. Municipal magistrates, policemen, police chiefs, and directors of public safety have achieved respectability in the public eye. There have been no complaints about the new ticket. On the contrary, a few days after the incident in court which I have been describing a man stopped me outside the State House, remarking that I didn't know who he was but he felt very much indebted to me for saving him an hour or two a day of disagreeable work. When I asked him how, he said by sparing him all of the time that he had had to spend every day in killing tickets for his friends and acquaintances. He told me he was one of the Democratic leaders in Trenton. When I asked him why he had to do it, he frankly said that if he didn't his Republican rivals would and that he might lose those votes. Please do not misunderstand me; we have not reached the millennium, even in the traffic courts, but we have eliminated the greatest single cause of disrespect for law—"the fix."[31]

With the introduction of the no-fix system, New Jersey was the only state in which traffic ticket fixing had been rendered an impossibility. Overnight the influence of local politicians on the magistrate courts was greatly weakened. In 1955 the nonfixable ticket resulted in over one million cases in the traffic courts and fines of over $6,500,000. "We would not be so brash as to suggest that it is solely because of this fine record of the municipal courts for law enforcement that New Jersey is the third lowest state in the Union in the number of fatalities per miles travelled," Vanderbilt commented, "but we do venture to assert that without this type of law enforcement New Jersey could never have achieved its present high standing. One has but to consider the number of defendants who appear in the traffic courts and to estimate the number of witnesses in addition thereto in order to appreciate the unique opportunity of traffic judges to increase or decrease the average citizen's respect for law."[32]

One traffic judge who kept careful records of his cases for a year discovered that over 80 percent of the defendants who had appeared before him thanked him for the way he had conducted their cases while at the same time he had increased the amount of fines collected by 50 percent from the preceding year. This was because he had taken the time to tell each defendant the reason for his sentence, a practice Vanderbilt subsequently urged all the magistrates to follow to neutralize the bare statement, "Ten dollars and costs. Next case."

During an intermission of a statewide conference of municipal magistrates at Trenton, a suburban judge told Vanderbilt that he had spent over two hours the previous evening in the trial of a case. At the end he fined the defendant $100 and committed him to jail for lack of money to pay the fine. The defendant then asked the judge if he could say a word to him at the bench. Granted permission, the defendant stepped forward, shook hands with the judge, and thanked him for the fair and impartial trial that he had been accorded.

These were the kinds of results that made the difference in the new court system.

VANDERBILT, C.J.

Vanderbilt considered the constitutional, procedural, and administrative innovations to overhaul the New Jersey judicial system as the necessary prelude to an even greater task, the simplification and modernization of the state's substantive law. Before the New Jersey Supreme Court was reconstituted in 1947, "there were those who were mean enough to say that it hadn't moved in a quarter of a century," Vanderbilt remarked. "We were behind the procession in many fields of the contemporary juristic thinking in the United States."[33]

Through his opinions during his years as chief justice, Vanderbilt began to remold aspects of the substantive law brought before the court in specific cases: ". . . After I have studied the briefs and prepared my memorandum on each case and listened to the oral argument, I find that my work has just begun. In every case I find myself seeking light from the lessons of the past and the best experience from other jurisdictions struggling to ascertain what is the best rule not only for the pending case but for the future of our jurisprudence. . . . Having always in mind the necessity of adapting the law to the needs of our rapidly changing society, it is our task to seek out and apply the best rule. . . . Even seemingly insignificant cases become important as they are woven into the fabric of our law."[34]

Occasionally asked what his philosophy of judicial decisions was, Vanderbilt responded: " . . . I have been so busy deciding individual cases and trying to find the reasons for them which will stand up that I have not had any chance to acquire a philosophy. I am trying to state them in as clear language as I can, so that after a month or two even the losing party will be able to understand them and say, 'Well, if I have to lose, I was glad I lost for these reasons.'"[35] "I think of myself as a very moderate progressor," Vanderbilt added, "but every so often my colleagues look at me as if they thought I were quite a radical."[36]

A common thread woven through many of his 211 opinions was an attempt to make the substantive law of New Jersey suitable to contemporary conditions by pushing aside procedural or technical intricacies and discarding legal doctrines, no matter how ancient or revered, that were no longer compatible with a modern court system or with the economic and social realities of the age. In his opinions he sought to clarify the law and demonstrate its compelling logic and authority while avoiding slavish adherence to precedent that produced "slot-machine justice" at odds with contemporary needs.

Other justices on the court were at times less enthusiastic about blazing new trails through the common law. Although there had never seemed to be static voting blocs, some of Vanderbilt's efforts at changing the law were stymied when a majority felt that precedent was too strong or too important to be tampered with. Their position in such cases was based on the countervailing theory that courts should be reluctant to overthrow established rules, especially involving property rights, because people had relied on the rules in arranging their affairs. To abandon them could result in greater disruption than to abide by them, even if the justification for their being had disappeared in the mists of history. The question of whether the doctrine of *stare decisis* should be adhered to in such cases was always a choice between relative evils.

Recognizing that there should not be such a sense of velocity in the change of the law as to alarm either the trial bench or the public, Vanderbilt strove to alter the law gradually; but even a moderate pace was too fast for some of his colleagues on the supreme court. After a year of Vanderbilt's efforts, his predecessor as chief justice, Justice Clarence Case, stopped Justice Henry Ackerson one day to talk about the new directions of the court. "Henry, you were the most really able trial judge we ever had. So skillful were you in protecting the thought and learning of this court that you handed down some fifty opinions, which we adopted, and never were you reversed. We are busy in reversing case after case now, with this new man, and, if I can be very frank with you, as an old man, I think you have been seduced by the new Chief Justice." Justice Ackerson pulled out a little notebook which listed the cases he wanted to overrule. "I haven't had much luck yet," he said. "I have only overruled eight and have to overrule 250 more within the next two years before I retire."[37]

Vanderbilt did not feel bound by history and tradition when it could be shown that a legal principle was not only outworn but deleterious. The courts, he believed, were under as great an obligation to revise an outmoded rule of the common law as the legislatures were to abolish or modernize an archaic statute. In his dissent in *Reimann v. Monmouth Consolidated Water Co.*, 9 N.J. 134, 149, 150 (1952), urging that tort liability be extended to public utility water companies with respect to the furnishing of water in sufficient quantity and at sufficient pressure to fight ordinary fires, he wrote:

The common law is not merely a conglomeration of rules to be gleaned from decisions of the ancient past, it is a living and growing body of legal principles. It derives its life and growth from judicial decisions which alter an existing rule or abandon an old rule and substitute in its place a new one in order to meet new conditions. It is because of this gradual but continuous process of change that the body of our common law today is as different from that of mediaeval England as our physical surroundings are from those of that era. And it is absolutely essential that this be so, for it would be an impossible situation indeed if we attempted to determine 20th century disputes by means of rules of law applicable to 15th century facts.

These thoughts were expanded in another dissent, in *Fox v. Snow*, 6 N.J. 12 (1950), in which he was also unable to persuade the court to ignore precedent and alter the law according to the dictates of public policy and sound principles of justice.[38] In this case, involving a technical rule of property law, the testatrix bequeathed to her husband all the money she had in a specified bank and provided that whatever was in the account at the time of the husband's death should go to her niece. The majority of the court held that the testatrix's husband took the entire deposit and that the gift to the niece was void. Vanderbilt dissented in a long opinion that not only assembled materials attacking the rule as an unwarranted frustration of testamentary intent but also grappled with the doctrine of *stare decisis* in a live and thriving common law. The opening and concluding paragraphs of the dissent gave the nub of the philosophy developed in the opinion, and also, as clearly as anywhere, his philosophy of law:

I am constrained to dissent from the views of the majority of the court, first, because they apply to the case a technical rule of law to defeat the plain intent of the testatrix without serving any public policy whatever in so doing and, secondly,—and this seems to me to be even more important—because their opinion involves a view of the judicial process, which, if it had been followed consistently in the past, would have checked irrevocably centuries ago the growth of the common law to meet changing conditions and which if pursued now, will spell the ultimate ossification and death of the common law by depriving it of one of its most essential attributes—its inherent capacity constantly to renew its vitality and usefulness by adapting itself gradually and piecemeal to meeting the demonstrated needs of the times.

... We should not permit the dead hand of the past to weigh so heavily upon the law that it perpetuates rules of law without reason. Unless rules of law are created, revised or rejected as conditions change and as past errors become apparent, the common law will soon become antiquated and inefficient in an age of rapid economic and social change. It will be on its way to the grave.

Vanderbilt's use of the courts to deal with contemporary problems was exemplified by his opinions in several zoning cases, opinions that helped preserve some of New Jersey's rural areas from the sprawling housing developments and industrial congeries that were blighting major portions of the small state.

The 1927 Zoning Amendment to the New Jersey Constitution of 1844 had always been narrowly construed by the New Jersey courts. Subsequent to the adoption of the Constitution of 1947, which incorporated the terms of the old zoning amendment, the new court in a series of opinions by the chief justice liberally construed the zoning provisions to give them vitality and modern effectiveness. "Sound social, economic and governmental policy dictates a separation, where possible, of residential areas and industrial areas," wrote Vanderbilt for a unanimous court in *Duffcon Concrete Products v. Cresskill*, 1 N.J. 509, 515 (1949). "In the case of . . . fully developed communities, it is now too late to do more than preserve such beneficial features as may have survived the period of spontaneous and uncontrolled growth, and by such costly measures as slum clearance and low-cost housing to attempt to rectify the unwholesome conditions caused by our earlier lack of foresight. Proper zoning today, however, can do much in our newly developing communities to provide and to maintain safer and more healthy living conditions." This decision saved the farming country rolling down from the west of the Palisades to the Hackensack River Valley from being mutilated by an unnecessary industrial development which could well be accommodated in the nearby flats of the Hackensack Valley, which were unsuitable for residential development.

In *Cresskill v. Dumont*, 15 N.J. 238, 247 (1954), the court held that in four adjoining municipalities in Bergen County, all of the same suburban character, one municipality could not zone a piece of property at its boundary so as to change the neighborhood character of the zone to a business district to the detriment of the other municipalities. Zoning power and responsibility did not stop at borough boundaries, Vanderbilt wrote: "At the very least [there is a] duty to hear any residents and taxpayers of adjoining municipalities who may be adversely affected by proposed zoning changes. . . . To do less would be to make a fetish out of invisible municipal boundary lines and a mockery of the principles of zoning." This decision did away with the weakness that had previously existed of regarding zoning as purely a local municipal affair. These and several other zoning decisions[39] formed the basis of later attempts to preserve all of New Jersey beyond the coastal plans from undesirable overdevelopment, and were often cited with approval by other state courts intent on maintaining the character of their own suburbs and farmlands.

Vanderbilt's philosophy of law was evident in the most controversial and perhaps the most important opinion he delivered: *Winberry v. Salisbury*, 5 N.J. 240 (1950), cert. denied, 340 U.S. 877 (1950). The opinion split the state's legal profession into two camps: Critics were convinced that Vanderbilt had been swayed by impulse to find a way of reaching a desired result, that he had disregarded the clear language of the New Jersey Constitution, and that he had sought the first available opportunity to establish the primacy of the supreme court over the legislature; defenders were convinced that the decision was the linchpin that saved the new judicial establishment from collapse and made possible the reforms that placed the New Jersey courts at the forefront of the nation's state judicial systems.

The facts of the case were both intricate and relatively insignificant. Winberry had brought suit in the superior court to expunge an alleged libel on him from a report of a grand jury which had commented on his work as special prosecutor. Salisbury, the grand jury foreman, was joined as defendant. Salisbury moved for a summary judgment, a motion that was granted. Thereafter, Winberry served notice of appeal to the appellate division of the superior court, and Salisbury moved to dismiss the appeal.

Brought into conflict at this stage were the rule promulgated by the supreme court requiring an appeal from a final judgment of the trial division of the superior court within forty-five days and the statute permitting an appeal within one year after judgment. Winberry had waited more than forty-five days to appeal.

The appellate division held that, in the absence of legislative action, the rule of court prevailed over the statute. The court added, however, that by the phrase "subject to law" (in Article VI, section II, paragraph 3 of the Constitution of 1947, which directed that "The Supreme Court shall make rules governing the administration of all courts in the State and, subject to law, the practice and procedure in all such courts,") "the Legislature is given the final word in matters of procedure; it may expressly or by implication nullify or modify a procedural rule promulgated by the Supreme Court or it may take the initiative in a matter of procedure when it deems that course wise" (5 N.J. Super. 30, 34 [App. Div. 1949]). According to this dictum, a rule of court could be altered or abolished by legislative action.

At issue was whether the supreme court or the legislature had the upper hand in regulating court procedure.

The legislature had not previously sought to alter the court rule involved in the *Winberry* case. The jurisdictional question of the meaning of the phrase "subject to law" was therefore not directly raised and in one sense need not have been tackled by the supreme court. The importance of the rule-making power in superseding old statutes concerning court procedure and in establishing a modern judicial system without encountering legislative interference necessitated, however, that any ambiguity concerning that power be resolved. This necessity was rendered pressing by previous legislative action which was interpreted as an attempt to scuttle the new court rules.

In August of 1948, one month before the court system became operative, a bill had been introduced in the legislature which stated that the rules promulgated by the supreme court "shall regulate practice and procedure in the courts established by the Constitution until modified, altered or abrogated by law."[40] This bill, which amounted to a legislative evisceration of the supreme court's rule-making power, had unanimously passed both the general assembly and the senate in what must have been a record of nine days. Governor Driscoll vetoed the bill stating that "it would, if effective, completely deprive the Supreme Court of any further rule-making authority."[41] The fact that it had been only through the veto of a governor who was unusually knowledgeable about the courts that the most important method of instituting a modern judicial system had been preserved was not lost on the new justices.

Nor was the mood of the legislature in doubt. The record of the legislature thereafter continued to indicate a desire on the part of that body to usurp the rule-making power. Bills which passed both houses in 1950 but which were vetoed by the governor included: Senate Bill No. 237 to restore the former method of allowing counsel fees which the supreme court had restricted; Senate Bill No. 273, which attempted to establish the chancery division of the superior court as a court of separate jurisdiction comparable to the former court of chancery abolished by the constitution; and Assembly Bill No. 87, which would have given a litigant in the municipal courts the right to appeal directly to the appellate division of the superior court without first appealing to the county court. Moreover, a legislative advisory committee had been created on June 2, 1950, to prepare a revision of statutes "relating to practice and procedure in the courts in order to reconcile and make more consistent the respective provisions of said statutes with each other and with the Rules of Practice and Procedure promulgated by the Supreme Court, to correct errors, to cause to be omitted redundant provisions and provisions which, in the committee's judgment, are more properly includible in said Rules of Court, and to aid the Legislature in making the same into a more compact and consistent body of law."[42]

In light of the record of achievement of the new court system, the great concern of the legislature with curtailing the court's power to make rules of practice and procedure by making the rule-making power subject to legislative review was surprising. But it would have been unusual, if not impossible, to have brought about such drastic changes to a branch of government without generating a considerable amount of opposition and resentment. The opposition to the judicial system was being expressed, not by the press or by the people of the state, but by the legislators.

The actions taken by the legislature in the various bills manifested none of the alleged concern of that body to protect the people of the state from arbitrary action by the supreme court; on the contrary, every rule of the supreme court which the legislature sought to supersede was a rule designed to raise the standards of conduct of the bench and bar and to improve the administration of justice. The legislature's efforts to control the rule-making power were therefore less surprising to the politically astute, who recognized the dissatisfaction with which many of the court's reforms were being viewed.

The rule creating the uniform nonfixable traffic ticket was regarded as a source of embarrassment by some politicians, who were no longer able to help out friends and constituents. The rules prohibiting all employees of the courts, including judges, from practicing in the courts, the rule prohibiting prosecutors and their assistants from appearing on behalf of defendants in criminal causes, and the rule prohibiting sheriffs and deputies from arguing before the courts—rules designed to prevent possible abuses—were not universally welcomed. The court rules making all lawyers and judges subject to the standards set in the Canons of Professional Ethics and Canons of Judicial Ethics were considered burdensome by some. The rules concerning pretrial procedures, designed to avoid surprise testimony and maneuverings of counsel at trial, were thought to unduly restrict counsel's prerogatives. The rule imposing limitations on the allowance of counsel fees disgruntled some lawyers. In particular, the rule preventing magistrates from engaging in political activity was criticized although the rule was intended to keep the courts free from politics.

The temper of the legislature was even more threatening because of the importance of judicial rule-making in a progressive court system. The justices of the supreme court were in a position to observe at all times the operation of the rules in practice. With the aid of the administrative staff, the judicial conference, the bar associations and their committees, and other judges and lawyers, the justices were in a position to discover quickly procedures requiring alteration. As soon as the evil and the remedy were apparent, the court could act without delay.

The legislature, on the other hand, was made up of men who were only engaged part time in their duties as legislators. Moreover, it met only at stated intervals and could only act in accordance with relatively cumbersome procedures. Bills introduced had to be printed, referred to committees, reported out, put through successive readings, sent to the other house for similar treatment, and eventually submitted to the governor for signature. If amendments or refinements of the bill were attempted on the floor, the process was even more difficult. More important was the fact that the legislators were in each session confronted with approximately one thousand proposed revisions of the substantive law. Even if each legislator was an experienced lawyer, the pressure of other business could prevent him from performing an adequate rule-making job. The almost inevitable result was that the legislature could only tinker occasionally with the rules without any complete comprehension of the entire picture. It was clear from the procedural histories of many states that, whenever the legislature had control over the details of judicial procedure, the rules became encumbered with measures urged by some member with a particular case or a special interest in mind, not always for the better as to the general administration of justice.

The most important single device for achieving the prompt and just disposition of cases on their merits was a uniform, simplified, flexible procedural system; without such a system the work of the courts, no matter what other reforms existed, would wallow in bogs of procedural technicalities. So apparent was it from history that only judicial rule-making could create and maintain this desirable system of procedure that the American Bar Association committees of 1938 headed by Judge John Parker had specified as the first Minimum Standard of Judicial Administration: "[P]ractice and procedure in the court should be regulated by rules of court, and . . . to this end the courts should be given full rule-making powers."[43]

It was against this political and theoretical backdrop that the case of *Winberry v. Salisbury* was brought before the New Jersey Supreme Court.

The phrase "subject to law," on which the meaning of the constitutional provision depended, was ambiguous and elliptical. More constraining was the convention history of the rule-making provision in the 1947 convention. Although there was no debate on the meaning of the phrase, the Report of the Committee on the Judiciary presented to the convention on August 28, 1947, clearly indicated that the draftsmen considered "subject to law" to mean subject to statute or legislation:

Administration, practice and procedure in all courts is to be governed by rules of the Supreme Court, subject to legislation in the case of practice and procedure. . . . Responsibility for administration, practice and procedure in all the courts of the State is vested in the Supreme Court, but the Legislature may revise or repeal the rules of practice and procedure, or initiate new provisions on the subject. . . .[44]

And on August 5, 1947, vice-chairman Jacobs, in presenting to the convention the final draft of the judicial article with the committee's recommendation for adoption, had said:

You will note that the Supreme Court is given comprehensive power to adopt rules of practice and procedure for all the courts in the State, a power analogous to that possessed now by the United States Supreme Court. However, the Legislature would have the power under the Committee proposal to alter those rules of practice analogous to the power now possessed by the Congress of the United States.[45]

What would prove most embarrassing of all was Vanderbilt's only official contribution to the work of the committee on the judiciary. In a letter of July 29, 1947, sent from Maine, where he was recovering from his stroke, he had listed twelve recommendations for changes in the draft of the judicial article. The first recommended:

1. The rule-making power by Section II, paragraph 3, is made subject to legislative control by the words "subject to law." The trend throughout the United States has been to confide the rule-making power to the highest court and to hold that court responsible for results. I therefore suggest the deletion of the phrase "subject to law."[46]

In 1950 as chief justice, in an opinion which won the support of the majority of the justices, Vanderbilt endeavored to ascertain the meaning of the phrase in light of the entire Constitution and of the intent of the people in adopting it. Rejecting the interpretation that "subject to law" meant subject to legislation—an interpretation that he demonstrated would have rendered the courts, in some of their essential judicial operations, subservient to the legislature instead of being one of three coordinate branches of the state government— Vanderbilt concluded that:

The only interpretation of "subject to law" that will not defeat the objective of the people to establish an integrated judicial system and which will at the same time give rational significance to the phrase is to construe it as the equivalent of substantive law as distinguished from pleading and practice. . . . The phrase "subject to law" . . . serves as a continuous reminder that the rule-making power as to practice and procedure must not invade the field of the substantive law as such. While the courts necessarily make new substantive law through the decisions of specific cases coming before them, they are not to make substantive law wholesale through the exercise of the rule-making power.[47]

In addition, in comparing the judicial article to the model constitution formulated by the 1941 Commission on Revision of the New
Jersey Constitution, which was the foundation of the work of the
1947 Constitutional Convention, he pointed out that the report of the
Commission made it clear that its use of the phrase "subject to law"
did not refer to legislation; rather, the supreme court was given
complete power and responsibility with respect to making rules as to
administration, pleading, and practice. Finally, the only official convention statement concerning the phrase, the statement contained in
the Report of the Committee on the Judiciary, had not been handed
to the convention delegates until two days after the judicial article
had been adopted by the Convention. "The report of the Judiciary
Committee therefore could not be deemed a part of the parliamentary history of the Constitution, for it was not known to and not acted
upon by members of the Constitutional Convention in voting in favor
of Article VI. . . ."[48]

An equally compelling opinion written by Justice Case concurred
in the holding of the majority but dissented concerning the Vanderbilt dictum on the rule-making power. It was Case's understanding,
after tracing the history of the phrase and examining its use in other
sections and articles of the Constitution, that "subject to law"
applied to rules regarding pleading and practice and meant subject
to general statutory law, whereas rules regarding the administration
of the courts were within the total control of the supreme court. Since
the founding of the nation, in every state and in the federal government, this field of enactment had been within the legislative province.

Constitutions are not made, and ought not to be construed, upon the hypoth-
esis that men presently or prospectively in office will continue indefinitely
to function in their particular capacities [concluded Justice Case in words
that seemed directed at the chief justice]. . . . It would be disastrous to build
or develop a constitution upon the assumption that the characteristics manifested at a given time in one or another of these governmental parts will
continue without variation. . . . If our Supreme Court exceeds its powers,
who shall impose the check? Therein lies the danger when the court
undertakes, not to construe law, but to *make* it. . . .[49]

The application of much of what I have been saying is to the wisdom of this
court in stretching words beyond their reasonable sense in order to hold a
subject matter within the court's unresponsible creation and control. A
constitutional mandate to take what has always been a legislative function
and place it both initially and finally in the hands of the court ought, as I have
said, to be very clear; particularly since it is the court which makes the

decision in its own favor. . . . There is greater danger to our democratic form of government in following the lure of expediency than in marking our course by the compass.[50]

Winberry v. Salisbury was decided on June 27, 1950. Several weeks later when the legislature next convened, the senators were so irritated by the opinion that they pushed aside all other business at hand to examine it. There was discussion about the advisability of introducing a constitutional amendment to restore to the legislature the power it had prior to the court's decision; but when study of the amending clause of the Constitution indicated that it would be impossible to initiate an amendment at that time of year and submit it to referendum at the general election, the idea was abandoned for the current session. Instead, a four-member bipartisan committee was appointed to study the opinion and to report to the 1951 session of the legislature.

On March 12, 1951, a resolution was introduced in the state senate[51] to overturn the *Winberry* decision by a constitutional amendment of the rule-making provision which would strike the words "subject to law" and substitute "subject to such laws as may be enacted by the Legislature." In the intervening months, however, almost every state newspaper and every county bar association, impressed with the record of the courts in comparison with the old system as well as with the role of the judicial rule-making power in achieving that record, came out in favor of the majority opinion. Although the sentiment in the senate was strongly in support of the spirit of the proposed amendment, the senators felt that such a referendum would be rejected by the voters because of the high esteem in which the courts were then held. The chairman of the senate judiciary committee, who was not friendly to the courts, reported that "[N]ow is not the proper time to move such a constitutional amendment, because the courts are too popular with the people."[52] "I really get an unholy satisfaction out of this grudging testimonial from the enemy camp," Vanderbilt confided to Roscoe Pound.[53]

Thereafter the legislature, by directing its advisory committee on the revision of statutes to delete all of the procedure from the remaining articles of the Revised Statutes, put its stamp of approval on the supreme court's exercise of the rule-making power; the governor took a similar position by approving this legislation. By their actions, all three of the departments of government had in effect agreed in the interpretation of the making of procedure as a judicial function.

The majority opinion in *Winberry v. Salisbury* could be considered a reaction to an obstreperous legislature, a reaction which in theory would be an insufficient and inadequate reason for a judicial determination of the proper vesting of ultimate controls. While it is debatable whether the decision was sound constitutionally, it is difficult in light of the political realities of the day to call it misguided. It might well be concluded that the opinion protected the advances of the new judicial establishment from a legislative attack that could have crippled further progress before the merits of the new system, promising though they seemed, could be fully and fairly assessed. In fact, three years after the *Winberry* decision, the man who had led the fight to have the state legislature take over the rule-making power—Democratic minority leader of the senate Robert B. Meyner—was elected governor of New Jersey. Had not the constitutional battle already been fought and won in the courts, another legislative salvo—this time unchecked by a veto from the governor's office—could have toppled the court's rule-making power in a matter of weeks. In addition, the use of the judicial conferences with regular meetings and with an opportunity to present findings and recommendations to the judiciary provided at least a partial check on an irresponsible or regressive supreme court.

As Pound concluded in an article in support of the *Winberry* decision: "[I]t must be borne in mind that rules of procedure are the work not of a single judge but of a bench of judges after submission in any important case to a conference of judges, state officers, representatives of bar associations, and lay representatives of the public. The chances of any high-handed infringement of substantive rights by judges proceeding in this way are too small to be taken seriously."[54]

The majority of the court, in refusing to reason in a vacuum, arrived at a practical solution to a difficult constitutional controversy: as the court was free to continue its rule-making responsibilities, there was reserved in the people of the state, if ever the court began to enact rules that were unsatisfactory to the bar and to the public, the right to pass a constitutional amendment to give the legislature the power to review, or to make, rules of judicial procedure.[55]

"FREEDOM AND JUSTICE THROUGH LAW"

When Vanderbilt resigned as dean of the New York University School of Law in September of 1948,[56] the Law Center drive had raised over $2,000,000. Foundation and corporate support was beginning to arrive. The Charles Hayden Foundation would give $1,250,-000 and the Arthur Curtis James Foundation $125,000 for the purchase of a residence hall for the School of Law. The Citizenship Clearing House was being financed by the Maurice and Laura Falk Foundation, the Davella Mills Foundation, and the Ford Foundation, and the Inter-American Law Institute by the Standard Oil Company (of New Jersey) and several other corporations; the Root-Tilden scholarship program would be financed by the Avalon Foundation, and the Institute of Judicial Administration by the Rockefeller Foundation.

In September of 1948, New York University had purchased a block of land adjoining Washington Square from Columbia University for $1,000,000 and had given it to the School of Law for the construction of the Law School and Law Center. A suit to settle title to the land and the difficult task of relocating the commercial and residential tenants continued until August 2, 1949, when demolition operations began on the cold-water tenements and bars. Thereafter, the days were filled with the sounds of steam shovels, pile drivers, pneumatic drills, and riveters.

On January 31, 1950, on a cold afternoon at Washington Square South and Sullivan Street, Chief Justice Vanderbilt laid the cornerstone of the Law Center. That evening at the joint sixty-second annual dinner of the New York University Law Alumni Association and the Cornerstone Celebration Dinner at the Grand Ballroom of the Waldorf-Astoria, Chancellor Harry W. Chase rose to speak:

Mr. Toastmaster, and Ladies and Gentlemen: I have a very simple and a very happy task to perform tonight.

I think that his Honor, Arthur T. Vanderbilt, ought to stand up for a moment. I want to read you something which is just confidential between you and me. This is a resolution adopted by the Governing Council of New York University at its last meeting:

"Whereas Chief Justice Arthur T. Vanderbilt while Dean of the School of Law conceived the idea of a Law Center of New York University and inaugurated the program, and whereas by resourceful and energetic leadership he inspired the alumni and friends of the University to contribute the funds to make possible the construction of the permanent home for the Law Center,

"And whereas as lawyer, teacher, Dean, civic leader, exponent of law reform and Judge, he has made contributions to legal education of national significance and has thereby brought honor and prestige to the University,

"Therefore, be it resolved that the building designed to accommodate the School of Law and the Law Center of New York University be named Arthur T. Vanderbilt Hall in recognition of his services to the University."[57]

Within a year, the steel, concrete, glass, Harvard brick, and gray limestone had been combined to form the five and a half story Law Center. On Saturday, September 15, 1951, after a day of ceremonies that included a symposium on the legal training of the lawyer, a luncheon at the Brevoort Hotel, and addresses by Dean Roscoe Pound, Chief Justice Vanderbilt, and Sir Francis Raymond Evershed, Master of Rolls of England, at a dinner attended by the chief justices of the forty-eight states, the chief judges of the eleven United States Courts of Appeals, the Board of Governors and the House of Delegates of the American Bar Association, many distinguished editors, the presidents of the forty-eight state bar associations, the presidents or other representatives of 294 colleges and universities, the deans or professors from 149 law schools, and the faculty and administration and many of the students and alumni of the School of Law, the Law Center was dedicated to FREEDOM AND JUSTICE THROUGH LAW.

In 1838, New York University had organized the intellectual framework of the first modern law school. A century and a decade later, it had developed the first law center, an institution for improving the law and the legal profession that was already serving as a model for twelve law centers in various stages of development across the United States.

A FORECLOSED SITUATION

Late in the night of September 7, 1953, Chief Justice of the United States Fred M. Vinson, having returned to Washington from an American Bar Association meeting in Boston, complained to his wife of indigestion. At one-thirty in the morning, Mrs. Vinson called the family doctor. Forty-five minutes later, sixty-three-year-old Chief Justice Vinson was dead of a massive heart attack.

On September 3, five days before Vinson's sudden death, Governor Earl Warren of California had announced that he would not run for a fourth term as governor. The following day, the *Los Angeles Times* quoted a "White House source" as saying that Warren could have the first vacant seat on the Supreme Court if he wanted it.[58] "I do not propose to answer rumors, surmises, and conjectures,"[59] Warren stated when asked if he expected to be appointed to the Supreme Court seat which many believed would soon be vacated by the aging Justice Felix Frankfurter.

The announcement of the assurance of a Supreme Court appointment for Governor Warren was widely assumed to be the revelation of a political commitment Dwight D. Eisenhower had made to Warren in the presidential campaign of 1952, when both men had been candidates for the Republican nomination for the presidency. "A few months prior to the death of Chief Justice Vinson," President Eisenhower wrote in his memoirs, "I had talked to Warren about his basic philosophy and been quite pleased that his views seemed to reflect high ideals and a great deal of common sense. During this conversation I told the governor that I was considering the possibility of appointing him to the Supreme Court and that I was definitely inclined to do so if, in the future, a vacancy should occur. However, neither he nor I was thinking of the special post of chief justice, nor was I definitely committed to any appointment."

The truth was that I owed Governor Warren nothing. The ridiculous character of these accusations was amply proved, I thought, by the history of the 1952 convention. Governor Warren would not take any action to throw his seventy California votes to me and thus assure my nomination after he realized that on the first ballot my nomination could be assured by a change of only nine votes. Minnesota supplied those votes, and even then Governor Warren's delegates refused to switch until after the motion was made to make the selection unanimous.[60]

Eisenhower neglected in his memoirs to mention Warren's initial support at the convention when he gave his California votes to Eisenhower on a question of the seating of over one hundred contested delegates. This support prevented a deadlock between the Eisenhower and Robert A. Taft forces which would have been to Taft's advantage, and, at the same time, ended a move to stop Eisenhower, thus eliminating any possibility of Taft's or Warren's nomination.[61] After Eisenhower's victory in November, Warren turned down an offer for the cabinet position of secretary of labor and mentioned again his hope to serve on the Supreme Court.

On August 15, 1953, the *Nation* described "a curious war of nerves" which had begun to dislodge Justice Frankfurter from the bench:

It has taken the form of inspired stories that his letter of resignation is on the President's desk, pointed inquiries about his health, a drum-beat insistence in the gossip columns that he is about to retire, and more recently direct questions from California political writers about when he intends to retire. Governor Warren would quickly relieve his own, and by this time nearly everyone else's, embarrassment if he would publicly repudiate this unseemly campaign.[62]

Whether or not they had any connection with this early campaign, it became known that, after Vinson's death, Vice-President Richard M. Nixon and Senate Majority Leader William Knowland, both from California, strongly urged on Eisenhower the appointment of Warren as a means of removing him from the California political scene so that Knowland could run for governor.[63]

President Eisenhower expected that during his term in office he would make a number of appointments to the Supreme Court, for six of the justices were over sixty and Justice Frankfurter, over seventy, was reported to be in poor health; but if Eisenhower had made a commitment to Warren, he had apparently never considered the possibility that the first vacancy on the Court would result from the death of the chief justice. For several weeks after Vinson's death, it appeared that Eisenhower was delaying appointing Warren, who had had no previous judicial experience. During those weeks the White House announced that Chief Justice Arthur T. Vanderbilt and Judge Orie Phillips of the Tenth United States Circuit Court of Appeals were under consideration for the appointment of chief justice.

On September 27 Attorney General Herbert Brownell flew to California to talk with Warren. Although his avowed purpose in making the trip was to inform Warren that he was being considered for chief justice—a purpose that could well have been accomplished by mail or telephone—an aide of the governor's later confirmed the rumors that Brownell was sent to urge Warren to accept the next appointment as associate justice. According to the aide, the governor had insisted that "it was to be the chief justice or nothing."[64]

On October 5, 1953, President Eisenhower announced his decision to appoint Earl Warren as the fourteenth chief justice of the United States, later stating that Vanderbilt and Phillips had been passed over because of their advanced age. It had been reported to Eisenhower that both Vanderbilt and Phillips were sixty-eight, although in fact Vanderbilt was sixty-five, only two years older than Warren.[65]

Since his term as president of the American Bar Association, Vanderbilt had been mentioned frequently as a possible appointment to the United States Supreme Court. There was considerable agreement among political reporters that, had Governor Thomas E. Dewey won the presidency in 1944 or 1948, Vanderbilt would have been appointed to the Court; and it was known that in May of 1946 former Chief Justice Charles Evans Hughes had recommended to President Truman that Vanderbilt be appointed to fill the vacancy created by the death of Chief Justice Harlan Fiske Stone.[66] In 1953, because there was only one Republican, Justice Harold Burton, on the Supreme Court and considerable dissatisfaction among the nation's legal profession that the men recently selected as the nation's highest jurists had little, if any, prior judicial experience, the possibility of Vanderbilt's appointment seemed reasonable.

As much as Vanderbilt might have desired the appointment, he had sensed immediately the impossibility of receiving it. "I had had enough political experience in bygone days to recognize when I read the story in the *New York Times* of September 4th, four days before Chief Justice Vinson's death, of Earl Warren's decision not to run again for the governorship and the statement in both the California and Washington parts of the article about his being regarded as available judicial material for the Supreme Court that the situation was foreclosed."[67]

To many of his friends who reported that they had recommended his appointment to President Eisenhower and who, after Warren's appointment was announced, wrote to express their regret that he had not been selected, Vanderbilt responded that, although he had declined to permit his friends to do anything on his behalf, "the many generous offers like yours by telephone and the fine letters which I have received and the numerous editorials have been a source of heartwarming encouragement to carry on the work that I am doing here on the theory that if anyone can develop a sound judicial system in such a conservative state as New Jersey on both the civil and criminal side it can be done anywhere. Personally I can think of no more useful job that I might be doing and so I can say to you in all sincerity that having had no expectations or grounds therefor I have likewise no regrets."[68] "I am happy where I am, especially because I have a consciousness that New Jersey is setting an example in judicial matters which other states are beginning to follow. I have never been given to chasing rainbows. Rather I prefer to cross each bridge as I come to it."[69]

But in a letter to his friend Raymond Moley, an editor of *Newsweek*, a glimpse of his personal disappointment emerged: "I must confess . . . that I have always had a very considerable bump of curiosity and I would like to know very much what went on behind the scenes. Everything is quite clear to me except Herbert Brownell's plane trip to Sacramento. Some day you are likely to learn what that was all about and if you do I wish you would tell me."[70]

Two other openings occurred on the Supreme Court with the death of Justice Robert H. Jackson in 1954 and the retirement of

Justice Sherman Minton in 1956, but because of Vanderbilt's age, his rapidly failing stamina, and his belief that in the last years of his life he could be of more service as chief justice of New Jersey than in beginning a new career as an associate justice of the United States, he declined to have his name considered. In answer to a letter from Judge Alexander Holtzoff of the United States District Court for the District of Columbia urging him to reconsider accepting the position available in 1954 as associate justice, Vanderbilt revealed not only his feelings about an appointment but much about his personality:

Your points, I must admit, are well taken, but up to the time I went on the bench I ran my own law office for 34 years with the help, of course, of some very good lawyers; I was county counsel for 25 years, and unlike other county counsels declined to have an associate because I knew he would be sure to get in the way; and for even a longer time I ran the Essex Republican Organization, with plenty of advice but with the ultimate decisions my own; and the same was equally true at the Law School. It was very hard for me to learn how to work in harness, but I think that all of my colleagues will grant that I have practiced the art of cooperation without deviation. I should doubt very much, however, my capacity to do so elsewhere.[71]

And in a confidential letter to the editor of the *Paterson Evening News*, he elaborated these thoughts:

One has to be practical in ordering one's life. If I were to go to Washington there is little that I would be able to accomplish in the few remaining years that I will in the normal course of events be able to work at full capacity, and the chances of frustration will be very great. Here, on the other hand, I think I can do something very much worthwhile for New Jersey in the four years remaining before I must retire, and in addition to that at the same time be setting an example to every other state of what a judicial system should be. . . . I do not think I should allow any mere matter of honor and distinction take me away from an unfinished job.[72]

With the opening on the Supreme Court in 1956, Vanderbilt again made it known that he had no personal aspirations for appointment.[73] He strongly recommended to Eisenhower the appointment of his colleague on the New Jersey Supreme Court, Justice William J. Brennan, Jr., a man of fifty who had proved himself an outstanding judge with, as Vanderbilt wrote to the President, the "finest judicial mind" that he had known in his experience.[74] His recommendation was supported by Secretary of Labor James Mitchell, a New Jersey Republican, by the two senators from New Jersey, Alexander H.

Smith and Clifford P. Case, and by Democratic Governor Robert B. Meyner. In March of 1956 Brennan's nomination to the Supreme Court was confirmed by the United States Senate.

"FOR FEAR OF DRYING UP"

In spite of his resolve after his stroke in 1947 to work only "eight hours four days, four hours two days, and nothing on the seventh, as distinguished from a seven day week with I hate to tell you how many hours,"[75] to set the new court system in motion Vanderbilt soon slipped into his customary seven-day week. The toll on his vitality and health was inevitable. In a personal memo written in December of 1954 during his yearly winter vacation at Montego Bay, Jamaica, the divergence between his will to get work done and his inability at the age of sixty-six to accomplish as much as he wanted first became apparent: "This entire quarter [from September to December] I was as unsuccessful in making my physical machinery behave the way I wanted it to as I was last summer, despite plenty of sleep except for three weeks in December.... All I needed was a couple of weeks no one else had (the perennial but fruitless wish) or the capacity to really get something done at home evenings.... All of this means that I must either cut down my outside activities, which I am reluctant to do for fear of drying up, or manage to get more out of my daytime hours; I think the latter possible by better management."[76]

In addition to his judicial work and his administrative responsibilities as chief justice, Vanderbilt was frequently asked to address judicial conferences and bar association meetings in other jurisdictions. During the 1951 court year, for example, he spoke in Connecticut, New York, Pennsylvania, the District of Columbia, Virginia, Kentucky, Georgia, Texas, and California. Each year he gave a major lecture—the William W. Cook Lectures at the Law School of the University of Michigan in 1948; the John Randolph Tucker Lecture at Washington and Lee Law School in 1950; the Knapp Lecture at the University of Wisconsin and the Pitcairn-Crabbe Lecture at the University of Pittsburgh in 1951; the Roscoe Pound Lectures at the University of Nebraska in 1952; the William H. White Lectures at the University of Virginia School of Law in 1954; the Gaspar G. Bacon Lecture at Boston University in 1955; the Tyrrell Williams Lecture at the School of Law at Washington University in 1956; and the Robert S. Marx Lectures at the University of Cincinnati College of Law in

1957. He also spoke at many other gatherings of the legal profession, both in New Jersey and in other states, to report on the record of the New Jersey courts and to encourage other states interested in judicial reorganization.[77]

The success of judicial modernization in New Jersey promoted or revived similar experiments in other states. Steps to amend the judicial article of their constitutions to simplify their court structure were initiated in Alaska, Arkansas, California, Colorado, Connecticut, Delaware, Florida, Illinois, Louisiana, Maryland, Massachusetts, Michigan, Minnesota, Missouri, New York, North Carolina, Pennsylvania, Texas, Vermont, and Wisconsin. In addition, these and other states were introducing into their court systems specific administrative techniques that had been tried in New Jersey. Almost daily Vanderbilt received inquiries about the New Jersey judicial system, inquiries that over the course of his nine-year term came from every state of the Union. Scarcely a month went by that he did not confer with a delegation of judges, lawyers, or bar association leaders from other states or foreign countries interested in the progress in New Jersey. Ideas gained from these visits were introduced in state judicial systems as well as in the judicial systems of Belgium, Norway, France, Israel, India, Peru, Ethiopia, Ceylon, Taiwan, Indonesia, Iran, Germany, Italy, Luxembourg, Japan, New Zealand, the Philippines, Canada, England, and Australia. "I am telling you nothing but the plain truth," Vanderbilt wrote in 1957 to Chester Barnard, president of the Rockefeller Foundation, "when I say that most of the advances over the last eight years in terms of actual day by day improvement in administration in the affairs of the courts have occurred in New Jersey, which has become the pilot plant of judicial administration for many states and even for nations as far away as Japan and Ceylon."[78]

As the architect and builder of the new New Jersey court system and as a result of his years of work to improve the administration of justice, Vanderbilt began to receive both national notice in the press and numerous awards: among them, thirty-two honorary degrees, the American Bar Association Gold Metal, the Columbia University Lion Award, the Harlan Fiske Stone Memorial Award, the Outstanding Citizen of New Jersey Award, the New Jersey State Bar Association Gold Medal, the New York State Bar Association Gold Medal, and the American Bar Foundation Award. Of these Vanderbilt commented: "For many years before I went on the bench I was quite active in politics and I was blamed for so many things I had never done, in fact, never had even contemplated, that when I went on the bench and occasionally had nice things said about me I concluded that I would accept them with demur, at face value, until the unkind things had averaged up with the kind things. My wife says that the balance was struck long ago, but I still continue to accept praise that I know I do not deserve, and let it go at that."[79]

But legal change, while easy to praise in the abstract, or from a distance, was rarely universally popular among those who had to abandon their habits and take up new ways. Elsewhere it seemed possible to speak of Vanderbilt only in superlatives. In New Jersey his detractors were neither few nor reticent. To bring about change was difficult enough. To see that new measures became institutionalized required constant pressure. At a breakfast meeting Vanderbilt leaned over to his colleague, Justice William Brennan, and in speaking of the obstacles he was encountering at every step in his attempt to introduce a modern court system in New Jersey remarked, "I now recognize that one has to be a complete son-of-a-bitch to get this job done. One man in this set-up has to be the son-of-a-bitch and I'm it."[80]

Praiseworthy in theory, the changes Vanderbilt wished to introduce in the judicial establishment usually required considerable additional effort on the part of judges or members of the bar and afforded no direct additional compensation. One example was the postgraduate legal instruction Vanderbilt insisted upon as a condition to appearing before the higher courts of the state.

Discovering, from a special study prepared by the judicial conference, that in many briefs questions were not properly stated, facts not presented in chronological order with proper references to the record, counsel were failing to distinguish when they were quoting from the record and when they were making an inference that they hoped the court would draw, and that in over 80 percent of the cases that came before the supreme court the briefs did not cite all the necessary precedents and the judges had to look them up themselves—with some briefs so bad that on over twenty-five occasions Vanderbilt had to have his law clerk write complete briefs on the cases—the supreme court established in 1955 a formal distinction in New Jersey between attorneys and counsellors. For a lawyer to reach the higher level—counsellor—and thus be able to argue in the New Jersey appellate courts, he had first to attend and satisfactorily pass a special course in legal research, brief writing, and appellate argument that was given at Rutgers University under the instruction of judges and law professors. To young lawyers who had already safely passed through the rigors of three years of a legal education and who would rather have been home with their wives and young children than attending a two-hour course at Rutgers Law School one evening each week for a year, this added requirement was the "essence of oppression" and met the heated opposition of the younger members of the bar intent on abolishing it.[81]

As annoying to the state's legal profession as were some of Vanderbilt's programs were his "imperious" methods of assuring their implementation. In 1955, as the court calendars became more difficult to maintain because of the rising population and business activity, a supreme court committee recommended to the legislature the compulsory transfer of accident cases from the superior court to the county courts whenever it appeared at the pretrial conference that the damages would be within the jurisdictional limits of the county court. Lawyers were strongly opposed to the enactment of the proposed legislative bill to accomplish this transfer because the bar was then waging a battle to make pretrial conferences voluntary rather than mandatory in automobile accident cases (despite overwhelming evidence that it was precisely in this field of litigation that the state was realizing the greatest benefits from pretrial procedures[82]).

When a participant at a judicial dinner meeting arrived late and reported to the chief justice that the state bar association and all but one or two of the county bar associations had just come out in opposition to the bill, Vanderbilt was reported to have smiled and said, "Morris, why didn't you persuade them to be unanimously against me? The slaughter would be so magnificent."[83] Thereafter a memo was sent to every judge announcing a change in court schedule.

... Notwithstanding the lack of appreciation of the problem [of court congestion], it continues to be increasingly acute and demands immediate attention. In the circumstances the Supreme Court has no alternative, if the interests of the litigants in the courts are to be protected by affording them a trial of their cases within a reasonable time, other than to resort to such administrative measures as will correct the situation, unpopular though they may be with some of the bar. Accordingly, commencing Monday, April 11, 1955, the trial divisions of the Superior and County Courts will sit 6 hours per day (9:30–12:30, 1:30–4:30), rather than 5 hours per day as at present, and motions instead of being heard on Fridays as at present will be heard on Saturday (commencing at 9:30) with Friday being a regular trial day.[84]

The threat of holding court on Saturday to clear the backlogs had an amazing effect on speeding the legislative process. Lawyers, weighing the alternatives, quickly opted for the first proposal of the supreme court and the once-reluctant legislators put through the bills calling for the transfer of cases to the county courts.

There were many well-circulated stories concerning Vanderbilt's efforts to keep the judges busily at work on their case lists. One true story concerned Judge Frederic R. Colie, who in 1951 was seriously ill and had to take a leave of several months. As they drove through Maine on their way home from a long rest in Canada, his wife convinced him that they should stop and thank the chief justice for having been so understanding during his illness. They found Vanderbilt in his side porch study with law books and papers strewn over every chair and table and the floor. After a few pleasantries, Vanderbilt asked Colie, "How do you feel?" "Fine," said Judge Colie. "Good," Vanderbilt replied, "I just had a call from New Jersey that I need to set down a case in the month of August and since you feel so well and have had a vacation, I would appreciate your taking it."[85] Judge Colie never forgave his wife for suggesting the visit.

It was with a curious mixture of admiration and resistance that the New Jersey bench and bar met Vanderbilt's reforms. Judge Harold R. Medina, chairman of the Section of Judicial Administration of the American Bar Association, told what happened in January 1951 when he was addressing the New Jersey State Bar Association:

It was one of the largest gatherings of judges and lawyers that I have ever seen. I have never been able to get over the habit of doing a certain amount of ad libbing; and in the middle of my speech I suddenly thought of one of my pet aversions in the administration of justice and I said, "By the way, there is another thing that I am against. As far as I am concerned this hurry, hurry business is out." I had intended to go on and say something about the courts not being sausage mills. But I did not get around to that as, to my utter amazement, everyone in the room jumped to his feet, the lawyers began throwing napkins in the air and raising a terrible hullabaloo. This was the reaction to Chief Justice Vanderbilt's reforms and the very effective methods he had been using to bring the administration of justice in the State of New Jersey up to date. It involved a lot of pressure and considerable mental anguish on the part of both lawyers and judges and my little remark brought them to their feet to let off steam. I looked down at the Chief Justice who was sitting beside me and was glad to see his face wreathed in a good-natured smile.[86]

No changes were made in the judicial establishment without the approval of a majority of the justices of the supreme court, yet it was the constitutional duty of the chief justice to put any policy decisions into operation. It was therefore Vanderbilt who bore the brunt of any reaction such decisions aroused. Each change was achieved at a very considerable cost in effort and time. "I used to hear of such a commodity as judicial leisure," Vanderbilt commented, "but I have not yet made its acquaintance during term time."[87]

By 1954 at age sixty-six, Vanderbilt had become conscious of the constant necessity to conserve his strength. "Regularly I get to the office at 8:00 A.M. and work here until 6:00 P.M., except Saturdays when I take off at noon. Unless I have someone coming in to see me from out of town I usually eat my lunch in chambers. This past week I have worked at home after dinner until 10:00 P.M. Sundays are no exception, although the pace on that day is not so hectic. I just cannot take on any greater load than I am carrying without danger of breaking down. . . . Very obviously I must make plans, first, to get all my work done during the day, second, reconstruct my evenings, and third, not only get plenty of sleep, but relieve myself from the wrangling pressure of rush jobs."[88]

Each Christmas he and Floss went to Jamaica for two weeks, each Easter to Spain or Italy—vacations that he called "my kind of life insurance against a physical relapse before the close of court at the end of June"[89]—and as usual spent their summers in Maine. But even on these vacations he always took a trunkload of work with him. Once in Rome for Easter, he telephoned Judge Alfred Clapp of the superior court when he learned that one of the members of Clapp's part of the appellate division was behind in two opinions. He said that if Clapp would write one, he would write the other if the briefs and records were mailed to him. The chief justice had no business doing work in the superior court and Judge Clapp told him this, promising to write one of the opinions and to call for reargument in the other case, which had to be decided on an issue which had not been argued.[90]

In the summer of 1955 he took on a job that cost him both his long vacation and an energy reserve that he would never regain. Later he would trace the roots of his weariness to these months when he had prepared a study on adult liberal education for a joint committee of the Ford Foundation and its subsidiary, the Fund for Adult Education, on the basis of which they were going to decide whether to continue the Fund for Adult Liberal Education or to revise its operations. Vanderbilt wrote to a Wesleyan fraternity brother:

Although I could not under our Constitution accept any payment for the task, I was very much interested in it from my experience of four years teaching when I was going through law school and one year thereafter. I said I would undertake it if I could have the assistance of two men who had worked with me in the Citizenship Clearing House. They traveled all over the country and then we collaborated from week to week and month to month on findings. . . . During July and August of 1955 I worked somewhere between 10 and 12 and 14 hours a day, but we did get the report done, I am very happy to say, to meet their deadline with an hour and a half to spare. . . . I came back in September last year without the slightest bit of reserve power, and I soon found that the only way I could cope with the situation was to go to bed between 9:00 and 9:30 every evening and spend every Saturday afternoon and occasionally an afternoon in the middle of the week in bed. . . . This summer will be the test as to whether or not I can pick up energy and charge my batteries so that I will enjoy life once more. Thus far I am making steady progress, but I am resolved to make it my first order of business for the whole summer to build up reserve. I just can't sit out on the lawn looking at Casco Bay and the presidential range of the White Mountains, but I can avoid pressure. I shall let you catechize me in the fall to see whether or not I am any good at all in keeping my own resolutions![91]

But with the rising tide of litigation, with the lists of cases growing despite the fact that each successive year the judges disposed of more cases, and with Justice Brennan gone, his seat unfilled, and Justice Oliphant suffering from eye trouble, Vanderbilt found himself "carrying the burden of the equivalent of two judges."[92] These circumstances eliminated any possibility of rebuilding his reserves of energy.

The more Vanderbilt realized his stamina was slipping, the more conscious he became of what lay ahead to be done. If he knew he was seriously affecting his health by continuing at his usual pace, the needs he perceived were too pressing and his pattern of living too set to stick to any fixed plan for relaxation. By July of 1958 his term as chief justice would be over when he became seventy, the retirement age for judges set forth in the 1947 Constitution. He would then go to the office that was being prepared for him at the Law Center and there complete the biography of Lord Mansfield he had been researching for twenty-five years, the history of the development of judicial administration in the United States he had begun in 1953 with the aid of the Carnegie Corporation, and the other writings and projects he had outlined on a dozen pages of foolscap paper.

To Dr. Royal A. Schaaf, his physician and personal friend, he wrote on January 9, 1957: "Floss and I reached home safely on Sunday after two weeks in Montego Bay. We had a very fine vacation there which enabled me to rejuvenate myself to a marked degree both physically and morally. I am resolved (my only resolution of the

New Year) not to think that I am responsible for the entire Supreme Court, but only for my own work, after having, of course, exhausted all efforts at 'peaceful persuasion.' . . . On my first two days of work this week, I find that I have accomplished twice as much as I could have in December and it is twice as good, proving the case, with me at least, for more frequent vacations."[93]

But less than a month later, the continual struggle to solidify the gains that had been achieved in the New Jersey courts against the opposition that occasionally flared again taxed his strength as the legislature and the governor began a campaign to take away from the supreme court all rule-making power in the field of evidence by granting the legislature the power to codify the laws of evidence.[94] "Unless I have suddenly become a poor guesser," Vanderbilt forecast, "I am going to have a continuation of the [*Winberry*] fight, this time out in the open, this coming term. Accordingly, I am taking every precaution to garner my strength so as to be ready for the fray."[95] At the same time, as the momentum created by the reorganization of the courts began to wear thin, some of his colleagues seemed to be finding it hard to "keep the faith; the bar, and I fear a considerable number of the judges resent very much my insistence that they keep up to date with their work. I don't want to take the battle to the people and particularly to the newspapers, but if I have to I know I will win."[96]

" . . . This has been a tough and most of the time a very lonely life," he wrote to Superior Court Judge Edward Gaulkin, one of his former law associates, in May of 1957 in a rare moment of despair when these problems were converging. "All too often I have felt like the proverbial voice crying in the wilderness. I still hope, optimistically, that the experiment has been worthwhile."[97]

A MORNING IN NEW JERSEY

The 1957 court term was a matter of meeting each crisis as it arose: making an unprecedented appearance before a legislative committee to protest the bill on the law of evidence, assuming the chairmanship of the Pretrial Conferences and Calendar Control Committee, which had been without a chairman since Justice Brennan's resignation, conducting the annual judicial conference in May, and revising and amending the rules of court thereafter. No matter how much was accomplished, there always seemed to be twice as much more to do. "As I get nearer and nearer to my 69th birthday," Vanderbilt wrote,

"I am prepared to concede that 65 years is a better retirement age for judges than 70, where they have substantial administrative responsibility in addition to judicial work. I must confess that this last year I had to push the old machine pretty hard."[98]

By June of 1957 he was winding up the work of the supreme court. "[W]e are in the home stretch of the last two weeks of our court year with all the 'horses' running at top speed in an effort to get, as usual, all of our cases disposed of before the end of the year."[99] All the while, however, he was looking ahead both to the summer, when he could rest, and to his retirement a year hence, when the problems of being chief justice would be lifted from his shoulders. On June 13 he wrote to a friend: "In July of next year I shall reach the retirement age and then I expect to return in the fall to the Law School. I am going to struggle to avoid getting tangled up in a multiplicity of activities (already my 'friends' are planning a career for me, including my taking over the management of the Republican party in this county, as I did for 30 years before I went on the bench, but they will find me very gun shy). On the contrary, I expect to devote myself to study and writing that may be of some assistance to the next generation of law students and to getting away from the hurly-burly of life that I have lived at the bar and in politics and the last ten years in judicial administration."[100]

Thursday evening, June 13, a testimonial dinner was to be given for Judge Frank L. Cleary of the superior court, who, having reached the age of seventy, was retiring. When asked who he would like to speak at the dinner, Cleary had replied, "Arthur—will he come?"[101]

Despite a week of humid New Jersey weather and the end-of-the-year rush to complete the work of the courts, Vanderbilt accepted for, as a lawyer, he had often argued before Judge Cleary, and Cleary had been one of the judges who had strongly supported the transition to the new court system through the early years of opposition. "I couldn't let him down, although the month is horribly crowded in the effort to dispose of everything ... before we rise on June 24th."[102] And Vanderbilt knew that after one more week of work, he could rest for the summer. "I will reach Maine late in the evening of June 24th."[103] "I can sit out on my front lawn and look across Casco Bay at the islands, and beyond on a very clear day we can see Mt. Washington and the entire Presidential Range eighty or ninety miles away. Unfortunately, if I am to stay there I have to do four or five hours dictating on a Soundscriber each day (all administrative work). But I can do it at what hours please, and I have a lot of time to read things for which there seems to be no chance at all during the court year, and also to visit with my children and their thirteen children."[104]

He was tired that night when called upon to speak at the Union County Bar Association dinner in honor of Judge Cleary, his voice so weak that at first no one could hear him; as he talked he gained strength and spoke for thirty minutes. Afterwards, Justice Jacobs and Judge Clapp drove him home.

On Friday, June 14, 1957, he left home to drive to the station as he had for forty-four years to reach his office well before the interruptions of the day began. But as he drove into the parking lot of the Short Hills station, he was struck by a sudden, tightening pain. Pulling on the emergency brake and holding his hand on the horn, he slumped over the wheel, unconscious.

Fellow early-morning commuters, hearing the horn and seeing him in his car, ran into the station to call the police, and within minutes two radio cars arrived. The policemen administered artificial respiration until an ambulance came and rushed him to Overlook Hospital in neighboring Summit.

Vanderbilt regained consciousness in the ambulance and struggled to free himself from an attendant. "Let me up. I have to get to the office."[105] But when he was admitted to the hospital shortly before eight o'clock, he was again comatose and was taken to a private room on the fifth floor.

There he was examined and attended by cardiac specialists. His condition was listed as "critical poor," and the physicians knew he had no chance to live.

That afternoon he joked with his nurse and chatted about being "discharged before long." Once he got to Maine, he would be fine. He would rest and read under the oaks and by the end of the summer be ready to start again as he always had.

On Saturday morning he asked for his secretary to come to the hospital. When she arrived, he dictated a draft of an opinion that would be due for the Thursday conference of the supreme court. Finishing it, he relapsed into a coma.

When television and radio stations and newspapers reported the news of his heart attack, calls and telegrams arrived from friends across New Jersey and the United States, from Canada, England, Italy, Spain, Libya, and Japan, asking about him and praying for his speedy recovery.

As the hours went by, his condition seemed to improve. He remained in an oxygen tent able to take only liquid nourishment, but he reported no pain. He talked and laughed with Floss, his children, and with Dr. Schaaf, who visited as a friend for a half hour Saturday night. But at 1:15 Sunday morning, June 16, 1957, he complained of dizziness, and a few minutes later his life was over.

By ten o'clock two days later, Christ Church in Short Hills began to fill with Wesleyan fraternity brothers, professors, and members of the Wesleyan board of trustees, former law associates, clerks, secretaries, clients, law school colleagues, including eighty-five-year-old Frank Sommer, former students, the Essex County Board of Chosen Freeholders, Essex assemblymen and senators, Clean Government leaders, political allies and adversaries, business associates, former members of the New Jersey Judicial Council, delegations from the American Bar Association and state bar associations, Law Center associates, delegates to the 1947 Constitutional Convention, New Jersey lawyers, judges from the New Jersey courts, the justices of the supreme court, chief justices and members of the bench and bar from across the country.

The main part of the church being closed because of construction work, the first to arrive crowded into the chapel. Soon more seats were set up in the church's Friendship Hall. When people continued to come, filling the corridors, a speaker system was arranged to carry the service to those outside.

At eleven o'clock the service began. A hymn was sung, Psalm 23 was read. The Reverend Herbert H. Cooper, the rector of the church and a friend of the family for twenty years, read a short tribute, "A Thanksgiving for a Good Life":

> Almighty God, who art the source of all Justice, Love, and Truth . . . We thank Thee for the inspiration given to us by Thy faithful servant Arthur and we entrust him to Thy never-failing care and keeping. . . . We pray for ourselves, O Lord, that we may continue the things he did so well, that we may keep the ground he has gained, that we may love those he loves so dearly, that we may rise to the high aspirations he holds for each of us and in that way show, in some small measure, our gratitude to Thee and to him for his having been among us. . . .
>
> May we in his memory, knowing that the time is short, dedicate ourselves anew to things right, and true, and good . . . in our Church, in our homes, in our courts, in our state and in our nation. May we follow his example, being inspired as he was by Thy beloved Son, our Savior, Jesus Christ. Amen.

The primary mission of the legal profession had always been to preserve individual freedom of thought and action to the fullest extent possible consistent with the equal rights of others and the public welfare. As the nature of freedom changed with the social and physical environment of the age, it had been largely the responsibility of lawyers at the bar, lawyers on the bench, and lawyers in the legislature to maintain the government and the law by adapting each to the changing times to promote a respect for the law and the growing concept of freedom. The mission of safeguarding and enlarging the sphere of human freedom under law by readjusting the law, without breaking the continuity of a legal system that had served English-speaking people for centuries, was never-ending.

Constancy and change. The ideas Vanderbilt advocated and the improvements he attained were not bold experiments; they were innovations based on historical precedent or existing practices altered and adapted to reflect the realities of the day and the outlook for the future, from the Clean Government movement patterned after Sommer's New Idea reform group, to the Law Center organized to embody the potential of the old English Inns of Court and the committees that had drafted the Federal Rules of Civil Procedure and the Federal Rules of Criminal Procedure, to the judicial establishment in New Jersey built on the theories of Roscoe Pound, the recommendations of Judge Parker, and the accumulated experience culled from the courts of England, the federal judiciary, and the most progressive judicial systems of other states. As important as were the reforms he achieved was a renewal through his work of the realization that a few men armed with a depth of conviction and an arsenal of facts could open a wedge through the bulwark of tradition, complacency, apathy, and opposition to bring about changes made necessary in the face of new conditions. Through studying, overhauling, simplifying, and modernizing, through a continual process of reappraisal and renewal, the great institutions of society could be preserved.

The reformer and idealist, Vanderbilt was not without a substantial amount of realism and aggressiveness necessary to achieve his goals. His work remained as blueprints for action. And the spirit of action reflected in his life to meet the challenges of change he had encountered in politics, in education, and in the law was the force that would be needed to build from the blueprints, a spirit captured in the words of Justice Holmes that he had inscribed at the entrance to the Law Center:

Law is the business to which my life is devoted, and I should show less than devotion if I did not do what in me lies to improve it, and, when I perceive what seems to be the ideal of its future, if I hesitated to point it out and to press toward it with all my heart.

Notes

PREFACE

[1]29 *A.B.A. Rep.* 395–417 (Part I, 1906). (Pound, who was dean of the Harvard Law School from 1916 to 1936, was a major intellectual force behind most of the law reform projects of the first half of the twentieth century.)

[2]Wigmore, "The Spark that Kindled the White Flame of Progress," 20 *J. Am. Jud. Soc'y* 176 (1937). (Wigmore, dean of the Northwestern University Law School from 1901 to 1929, was an active force in the American law reform movement.)

[3]*Ibid.*

[4]*Ibid.*

[5]*Ibid.*

[6]*Ibid.*

[7]Pound, "Arthur T. Vanderbilt: The Legal Educator," 6 *N.Y.U. Law Center Bull.* 3 (1957).

[8]Quoted in E. Gerhart, *America's Advocate: Robert H. Jackson* xiii (1956).

[9]Dewey, "Arthur T. Vanderbilt: The Political Leader," 6 *N.Y.U. Law Center Bull.* 5 (1957).

[10]Clapp, "In Memoriam: Arthur T. Vanderbilt," 12 *Rutgers L. Rev.* 1 (1957).

[11]Vanderbilt, *Minimum Standards of Judicial Administration* xix (1949).

[12]Vanderbilt, *The Challenge of Law Reform* 173 (1955).

CHAPTER I

[1]Two explanations have been advanced as to why the president of the United States attended this ceremony: (1) Shanklin, Sherman, and Root each had graduated from Hamilton College and had been friends since their college days. It is believed that, through the influence of Root and Sherman,

President Taft was persuaded to attend the installation, which was postponed until November to coincide with a tour he was making of New England. (2) It has also been suggested that while Shanklin was president of Upper Iowa University prior to coming to Wesleyan, he had stumped for Taft in the election campaign of 1908 and in return had received a promise from Taft to speak at the Wesleyan installation. (For these theories, I am indebted to Dr. Henry M. Wriston, Wesleyan class of 1911, who was the student press representative at the installation; to Dr. Victor L. Butterfield, former president of Wesleyan University; and to Professor Willard M. Wallace of Wesleyan.)

[2]ATV memorandum, Dec. 31, 1954, "Arthur T. Vanderbilt, 1888–1957— Political, Professional and Judicial Papers," Collection on Legal Change, Wesleyan University, Middletown, Conn., box 267. (Hereinafter, these Vanderbilt Papers will be cited as VP.)

[3]*Wesleyan Argus*, Nov. 18, 1909, at 4.

[4]James E. Stiles (ed.), *Seventy-Five Years of Gamma Phi: An Anniversary History of the Chapter of Delta Kappa Epsilon at Wesleyan University, Middletown, Connecticut* 227 (1942).

[5]*Ibid.*

[6]*Ibid.*

[7]"Mona Lisa," *The Oranges* (New Jersey), June 1, 1934.

[8]Stiles, 327.

[9]ATV to Dr. Harold A. Voorhis, Mar. 4, 1944, VP, box 378.

[10]His birth certificate indicates that his middle initial stood for no name. Whether or not it was a mistake, his name appeared once in a Newark High School publication, *The Ulula* (June, 1905, at 6), as Arthur Thornton Vanderbilt, and twice as such in the *Wesleyan Argus* (June 27, 1910, at 8 and June 29, 1910, at 8). In every other reference and in all signatures, his name appeared as Arthur T. Vanderbilt or Arthur T Vanderbilt. According to his wife, he considered T to be his full middle name.

[11]ATV to Jerome Richeimer, Aug. 6, 1938, VP, box 378.

[12]*Ibid.*

[13]ATV to Mrs. Raymond N. Crane, Feb. 8, 1952. I am indebted to Mrs. Crane, who was Vanderbilt's secretary from 1926 to 1941, for sharing this letter with me.

[14]"Pop Stearns Reminisces on 'My Boys,'" *Newark Sunday Call*, July 6, 1930, at 15.

[15]Scrapbook, VP, box 1.

[16]ATV to Wayland E. Stearns, Apr. 10, 1913, VP, box 4.

[17]ATV notation in his Wesleyan Scrapbook, VP, box 2.

[18]Jerome Spingarn, "Arthur T. Vanderbilt: Order in the Courtroom," 212 *Harper's* 61 (May 1956).

[19]ATV to William R. Vanderbilt, Nov. 1, 1939, VP, box 378.

[20]ATV to Harry W. Laidler, Feb. 10, 1950, VP, box 190.

[21]Vanderbilt in "Record of the Proceedings of the Seventy-Fifth Anniver-

sary Banquet, Breakfast and Business Meeting; Gamma Phi Chapter, Delta Kappa Epsilon Fraternity; Wesleyan University, Middletown, Conn., May 15–16, 1942," 53.

[22]ATV to Professor Samuel H. Brockunier, Feb. 12, 1945, VP, box 14.

[23]Stiles, 69.

[24]*Op. cit. supra* note 21.

[25]*Ibid.*

[26]George M. Dutcher, "Some Achievements of a Wesleyan Lawyer: Arthur T. Vanderbilt '10," *Wesleyan University Alumnus* 12 (October 1934).

[27]Vanderbilt, "The Citizenship Clearing House," in *The Citizen's Participation in Public Affairs* 159 (1947).

[28]ATV address at the Presentation of Portrait of Dean Frank H. Sommer, Apr. 24, 1950, 2, VP, box 263.

[29]*Ibid.*, 2–3.

[30]Walsh, Burnett, Reppy, "Biography of Frank Henry Sommer," 4 *N.Y.U.L. Rev.* 5–6 (1927). J. M. Blum, *Woodrow Wilson and the Politics of Morality* 43–45 (1956). See also James Kerney, *The Political Education of Woodrow Wilson* (1926).

[31]Bernstein, "The Crowded Years: Notes for a Biography of Arthur T. Vanderbilt," 6 *N.J.S.B.J.* 899 (1963).

[32]*Wesleyan Argus*, June 29, 1910, at 4.

CHAPTER II

[1]ATV address at the Presentation of Portrait of Dean Frank H. Sommer, Apr. 24, 1950, 2, VP, box 263.

[2]Remarks of Chief Justice Arthur T. Vanderbilt at the swearing-in exercises of the N.J. counsellors admitted Jan. 27, 1955, 9–10, VP, box 267.

[3]*Op. cit. supra* note 1.

[4]Shanklin to ATV, Aug. 24, 1911, VP, box 5.

[5]Arthur Moore to ATV, Oct. 1911, VP, box 5.

[6]Vanderbilt, *Men and Measures in the Law* 91 (1949). This particular phrase he used in connection with the study of consideration, but he expressed similar thoughts about his procedure classes: "Pleading was the beginning and the end of our course in procedure. . . . Many of the cases assigned for study, moreover, seemed remote from the realities of life; indeed, the only things that I remember with any distinctness from our study of demurrers, traverses, pleas in confession and avoidance, novel assignment and departure (the chief topics we studied) are that it was demurrable to plead that one threw a stone gently, but that it was not demurrable to plead that the events alleged occurred on the Island of Minorca, to wit, at London, in the parish of St. Mary le Bow in the ward of Cheap, provided one did it under a videlicet! All of this seemed to me then, and after thirty-four years of practice largely in the courts followed by some years on the bench still

seems to me, an utterly inadequate preparation for understanding what is going on in the courts today." Vanderbilt, *Cases and Materials on Modern Procedure and Judicial Administration* 5 (1952).

[7]Coleridge, "The Law in 1847 and the Law in 1889," 57 *Contemporary Review* 802 (1890).

[8]Coleridge, 7 *N.Y.B.A.R.* 71 (1884). For an excellent discussion of American procedural history, see *David Dudley Field Centenary Essays* (1949).

[9]R. Lum, *A Century In and Out of Court* 11–12 (1971).

[10]See "Report of the Special Committee to Investigate and Report a Method by Which the Administration of Justice May Be Improved," *N.J.S.B.J.* appendix 1, and 121–132, 132–142, 145–149 (1912).

[11]Vanderbilt, *The Challenge of Law Reform* 40 (1955).

[12]Alfred C. Clapp, to author, Jan. 28, 1972. Little information remains about Vanderbilt's law school career. There is no indication that his work was in any way exceptional. He did state that he ". . . learned law by taking courses under those I liked and not those I disliked." Among the former group were such professors as John W. Burgess, Munroe Smith, Frank J. Goodnow, John Bassett Moore, and Thomas Reed Powell. Vanderbilt, "Administrative Tribunals," 12 *Cincinnati L. Rev.* 3 (1938).

[13]Announcement card, VP, box 23.

[14]ATV to Willard G. Woelper, Apr. 1, 1957, VP, box 195.

[15]ATV address, Sixtieth Annual Dinner of the N.Y.U. Law Alumni Association, Feb. 10, 1948, VP, box 279.

[16]ATV address upon his retirement as County Counsel, Nov. 3, 1947, 9, VP, box 281 (hereinafter cited as "ATV: County Counsel").

[17]David W. Craig, "Chief Justice Vanderbilt," 39 *Pitt: A Quarterly of the University of Pittsburgh* 31 (1950).

[18]Lum, *A Century In and Out of Court* 32.

[19]Meador Wright, "Law, Politics, Pepsi-Cola and Vanderbilt," *The Oranges* (New Jersey) 19 October 1943.

[20]From the original draft of Vanderbilt, "From Where I Sit," 25 *Bar Examiner* 3 (1956), VP, box 267.

[21]1 F. J. Klein and J. S. Lee (eds.), *Selected Writings of Arthur T. Vanderbilt* 19–21 (1965).

[22]Isidore Hornstein, to author, Mar. 13, 1972.

[23]J. L. Bernstein, "Chief Justice Vanderbilt: Profile and Commentary," 3 *Reporter* 4 (February 1955).

[24]*Ibid.*

[25]*Ibid.*, 1.

[26]ATV to Judge Frederick W. Hall, July 21, 1954, VP, box 200.

[27]"ATV: County Counsel," 9.

[28]*Op. cit. supra* note 15.

[29]Williams, "Arthur T. Vanderbilt and Legal Education," 24 *N.Y.U.L.Q. Rev.* 4 (January 1949).

[30]"ATV: County Counsel," 9.

[31]Transcript of Addresses Delivered at the Cornerstone Laying Ceremo-

nies and the Cornerstone Celebration Dinner, 24 (Jan. 31, 1950), VP, box 263.

[32]Vanderbilt, "The Mission of a Law Center," 27 *N.Y.U.L. Rev.* 20 (1952).

[33]*Ibid.*, 22.

[34]Paraphrased from Jerome Spingarn, "Arthur T. Vanderbilt: Order in the Courtroom," 62, and George H. Williams to author, Oct. 14, 1971.

[35]T. H. Reed, *Twenty Years of Government in Essex County, New Jersey* 47 (1944).

[36]Report of J. Henry Bacheller and Jacob L. Newman, Commissioners, before Chief Justice William S. Gummere, June 14, 1919, VP, box 81.

[37]Shields to ATV, Feb. 18, 1919, VP, box 81.

[38]Eulogy on the Death of Edwin Ball Delivered by Arthur T. Vanderbilt, Apr. 25, 1929. Reprinted in "ATV: County Counsel," 3.

[39]"ATV: County Counsel," 12.

[40]*Newark Sunday Call*, September 1919, clipping, VP, box 81.

[41]"ATV: County Counsel," 10.

[42]*Newark Evening News*, Sept. 24, 1919, editorial.

CHAPTER III

[1]T. H. Reed, *Twenty Years of Government in Essex County, New Jersey* 66 (1944).

[2]*Ibid.*, 73.

[3]The house cost $40,000 without furnishings and between $45,000 and $50,000 furnished.

[4]*Newark Evening News*, Oct. 11, 1920.

[5]ATV to Mrs. Elizabeth A. Harris, Dec. 5, 1927, VP, box 81.

[6]"ATV: County Counsel," 13.

[7]Reed, 80.

[8]"ATV: County Counsel," 14.

[9]*Newark Evening News*, Nov. 3, 1920.

[10]Meador Wright, "Law, Politics, Pepsi-Cola and Vanderbilt," *The Oranges* (New Jersey) 37 (1943).

[11]*Op. cit. supra* note 5.

[12]*Ibid.*

[13]ATV to Judge Alexander Holtzoff, Oct. 18, 1954, VP, box 194.

[14]"ATV: County Counsel," 10.

[15]In 1922, Hudson County, population 690,730, employed six attorneys with aggregate salaries of $33,600. Nassau County, New York, population 303,053, employed four attorneys with aggregate salaries of $27,500. Westchester County, New York, population 520,947, had a legal department that cost annually over $50,000. See Reed, 96.

[16]"Platform of the New Jersey Republican Party: 1922" (issued by the New Jersey Republican State Committee), 8.

[17]1 *New Jersey Graphic* 3, 15 (Oct. 9, 1922).

[18]"Democratic Platform, 1922," 5, VP, box 81.

[19]Dayton D. McKean, *The Boss: The Hague Machine in Action* 48 (1940). John T. Cunningham, *New Jersey: America's Main Road* 283 (1966).

[20]Wright, 37.

[21]*Ibid.* I am indebted to Mrs. Jean Parrish of the Mobil Chemical Company of Richmond, Va., the company with which the Virginia-Carolina Chemical Company was merged in 1963, for a wealth of information about the early history of the company.

[22]From the original draft of "From Where I Sit," 5, VP, box 267.

[23]Isidore Hornstein to author, Mar. 13, 1972.

[24]George H. Williams, "Arthur T. Vanderbilt and Legal Education," 24 *N.Y.U.L.Q. Rev.* 6 (1949).

[25]Quoted in Vanderbilt, *John Cotton Dana: The Centennial Convocation* 17 (1957).

[26]*Ibid.*, 20.

[27]Mrs. Raymond N. Crane to author, May 21, 1974.

[28]*Op. cit. supra* note 23.

[29]Henry Young, Jr., to author, Jan. 26, 1972.

[30]ATV to Robert A. Vanderbilt, Oct. 2, 1938, VP, box 378.

[31]ATV to William R. Vanderbilt, Oct. 17, 1938, VP, box 378.

[32]ATV to Elizabeth A. Vanderbilt, Nov. 21, 1939, VP, box 378.

[33]ATV to his children, Sept. 13, 1954, VP, box 378.

[34]ATV to William R. Vanderbilt, Jan. 15, 1944, VP, box 378.

[35]Herold, "Profile of Justice Hall," 3 *N.J.S.B.J.* 372 (1960).

[36]Parker, "Memorial to Arthur T. Vanderbilt: Member of the Board of Governors, 1934–1937," 82 *A.B.A. Rep.* 203 (1957).

[37]"Unlawful Assembly in Paterson," 5 (Pamphlet published by the A.C.L.U., May 1925).

[38]Harry M. Wicks was the speaker whose condemnation of local officials had caused the chief of police to close the hall.

[39]*Op. cit. supra* note 37, 7–9.

[40]*Ibid.*, 5–6.

[41]*Ibid.*, 12.

[42]"Klan Votes on Strike," *N.Y. Times*, Oct. 22, 1924, at 9.

[43]State v. Butterworth, 104 N.J.L. 47 (1927).

[44]1 F. J. Klein and J. S. Lee (eds.), *Selected Writings of Arthur T. Vanderbilt* 34 (1965) (paraphrase).

[45]See generally, State v. Butterworth, Brief for Plaintiff-in-Error, in vol. 9 of Vanderbilt's briefs.

[46]State v. Butterworth, 104 N.J.L. 587, 588 (1928).

[47]II C. Reznikoff (ed.), *Louis Marshall: Champion of Liberty* 987 (1957).

[48]These quotes are from the A.C.L.U. pamphlet "The Victory in New Jersey" (June 1928), 3, and are taken from the *Newark Evening News, St. Louis Post-Dispatch*, and *New York Times*. For a valuable discussion of State v. Butterworth and, moreover, an excellent study of the growth of constitutional freedoms in this century, see P. L. Murphy, *The Meaning of*

Freedom of Speech: First Amendment Freedoms from Wilson to FDR (1972).

[49]"Public Fire Now Has 600 Agents," *Eastern Underwriter* 29 (Dec. 21, 1928).

[50]*Ibid.*

[51]ATV to Charles C. Lurich, Aug. 27, 1929, VP, box 81.

[52]Scrapbook, VP, box 1.

[53]A Senate investigation was conducted of the campaign expenses of Hamilton F. Kean, who was elected to the United States Senate from New Jersey in 1928. Salmon was summoned to appear before the Senate committee to testify. He decided at this time that he needed a vacation and so headed toward California on an unannounced automobile trip that took him more than a month. See Vic Hammerslag, "Salmon Had Knack of Being Missing When Sought," *Newark Star-Ledger*, Sept. 13, 1935.

[54]ATV statement from Washington, D. C., May 10, 1934, 1, VP, box 85.

[55]Wright, 30.

[56]ATV to Hendon Chubb, Dec. 26, 1934, VP, box 85.

[57]*Op. cit. supra* note 54. When Salmon died in 1938, it was found that he had left $299,000 in cash deposited in twenty-eight banks throughout New Jersey. "$299,000 Cash Left by Salmon," *Newark Evening News*, Aug. 8, 1938.

[58]Vic Hammerslag, "Jesse R. Salmon: Saint, Sinner, or What?" *Newark Star-Ledger*, Sept. 8, 1935.

[59]*Newark Evening News*, May 17, 1934.

[60]Wright, 40.

[61]*Op. cit. supra* note 54.

[62]"Hits Vanderbilt on Insurance," *Newark Evening News*, Oct. 10, 1934.

[63]*Op. cit. supra* note 54.

[64]ATV to Miss Jean Vanderbilt, Oct. 15, 1934, VP, box 378.

[65]ATV to Meador Wright, Dec. 1, 1933, VP, box 84.

[66]Newspaper clipping (source unknown), vol. 3 of Vanderbilt's American Bar scrapbooks, VP.

[67]*Op. cit. supra* note 65.

[68]ATV to Judge Alexander Holtzoff, Oct. 18, 1954, VP, box 196.

[69]*Newark Evening News*, May 10, 1934.

[70]Vanderbilt, "Standards for Citizenship," *Mechanical Engineering* 898 (November 1950).

[71]"ATV: County Counsel," 14.

[72]Dewey, "Arthur T. Vanderbilt: The Legal Educator," 6 *N.Y.U. Law Center Bull.* 5 (1957). For a complete economic profile of Essex County during these years, see Reed, 114–173.

[73]*Collier's* 13 (Oct. 10, 1938).

[74]See A. Steinberg, *The Bosses* 12–29 (1972).

[75]See generally, David Wittels, "What Is the Answer? Reporters Seek and Find Real Dictator," *New York Evening Post* (1938), undated clipping file, VP, box 96.

Reed, 175–176, presents the following comparisons of Essex and Hudson counties:

	1920		1935	
	Essex	Hudson	Essex	Hudson
Population	652,000	629,000	833,000	690,000
Tax levy	$4,850,000	4,863,000	$8,053,000	10,412,000
Levy per capita	7.44	7.73	9.66	15.07
Assessed valuation	$778,740,000	742,110,000	$1,709,487,000	1,239,802,000
Tax rate per $100	.62	.65	.47	.83

An attempt to corner Hague in court took place in New Jersey in the 1950's with the application of forty-nine Jersey City freeholders for a summary investigation into the municipal expenditures of Jersey City during Hague's administration, an application that included five hundred pages of affidavits and exhibits to support the charge of unlawful and corrupt expenditures. In In re Tiene, 13 N.J. 478 (1953), Chief Justice Vanderbilt for a unanimous court upheld the legality of the investigation against an array of technical arguments that had been brought against it. In Eggers v. Kenny, 15 N.J. 197 (1954), the decision of In re Hague, 105 N.J. Eq. 134, was overturned in holding that an investigating committee, the Board of Commissioners of Jersey City, seeking to disclose alleged violations of the criminal law by the municipal officers and employees of the city was, as a legislative body, a proper vehicle to conduct an inquiry even though the subject of inquiry could also be the proper concern of the courts and grand juries in the enforcement of the criminal laws. City of Jersey City v. Frank Hague, 18 N.J. 584 (1955), was an attempt by the city as a municipal corporation to recover from Hague money which he allegedly had extorted from city employees— to the extent of $15 million—as a condition to obtaining or retaining employment. Vanderbilt held that the city was a proper party plaintiff to recover from Hague and former city officials and remanded the case for further proceedings. Hague, however, died in 1956 before the case could be tried in the superior court, and the suit was never completed.

[76]Wittels, 6 (VP, box 96). In one district in the Jersey City election of 1933, no votes were cast for the opponent to Hague's organization candidate. Residents of that district filed affidavits with the superintendent of elections that they had voted for the candidate who was reported not to have received a single vote. An application was made to Chief Justice Brogan for an order to examine the ballot boxes. Brogan held that the superintendent of elections could not remove the seals from any ballot box or examine their contents and that, although the chief justice and associate justices of the supreme court had the authority to order a ballot box opened and its contents removed, satisfactory reasons for this special procedure had to be shown. Apparently, satisfactory reasons had not been shown in this particular case. Ferguson v. Brogan, 112 N.J.L. 471 (1934)

On another notable occasion in a Jersey City election, the books in the polling place showed that 500 people had cast ballots. Superintendent of

Elections John Ferguson reported that after 500 ballots had been counted, there were as many more ballots left in the box. Ferguson procured a court order to have the ballot box opened. But when Ferguson and his deputies started to examine the ballots in the presence of Thomas Brogan, then corporation counsel of Jersey City, Brogan stopped them. "The ruling," he said, "only permits you to open the box. It doesn't say anything about examining the ballots." Wittels, 8 (VP, box 96).

[77]It was Hague who had chosen Silzer as the Democratic candidate to oppose Runyon in the 1923 gubernatorial campaign. It is reported that Silzer was 34,000 votes behind Runyon when all votes were in except those of Hudson County. When Hague submitted Hudson's votes, Silzer was 46,000 votes ahead of his Republican opponent. Hague's fraudulent election practices were not then widely recognized, and there seems to be no indication that Runyon or Vanderbilt at that time attributed the Republican defeat to Hague's handiwork. Steinberg, 34.

[78]In 1954 after Hoffman died, a letter that he had written on his deathbed confessing that he had stolen over $300,000 of state funds during his one term as governor was made public. Spingarn, 62.

[79]Dayton D. McKean, *The Boss: The Hague Machine in Action* 78 (1940).

[80]*N.Y. Times*, letter to the editor (J.J.D.), undated clipping, VP, box 96.

[81]*Trenton State Gazette*, Sept. 14, 1927.

[82]Wittels, 3 (VP, box 96).

[83]McKean, 140.

[84]*Ibid.*, 139. I am indebted to Peter Artaserse; Alfred C. Clapp; Alfred E. Driscoll; Robert Winthrop Kean; Mrs. Abbie W. Magee; Anthony P. Miele; Joseph T. Sullivan; James R. Sutphen; Alexander P. Waugh; and Henry Young, Jr., for providing me with much useful information in understanding the Clean Government movement and Vanderbilt's role in it.

CHAPTER IV

[1]Roger Butterfield, "New Jersey Puts Its Judges to Work," 224 *Saturday Evening Post* 30 (May 17, 1952).

[2]I. S. Kull, *New Jersey: A History* 445 (1930).

[3]*New Jersey Statutes Annotated: Constitution of the State of New Jersey* 675 (1950). For a history of New Jersey's judicial system, see E. Q. Keasbey, *The Courts and Lawyers of New Jersey: 1661–1912* (1912).

[4]In 1803 the general assembly failed to reelect Justice Smith because of a change in the political control of the legislature when his fourth term expired. In 1832, Justice Drake incurred the wrath of the losers in a bitter controversy between rival factions of the Society of Friends, and the losers managed to elect enough members to the legislature in 1833 to bring about his defeat. Such incidents struck at the independence of a judge in deciding a case. See Vanderbilt, "Famous Firsts in Jersey Jurisprudence: An Acknowledgement of Indebtedness," 79 *N.J.L.J.* 249, 265 (July 12, July 19, 1956).

[5]"Report of the Judicial Council of New Jersey to the Senate and General Assembly of the State of New Jersey Pursuant to Joint Resolution No. 16 of the 155th Legislature," 37, VP, box 146.

[6]*Ibid.*

[7]Harrison, "New Jersey's New Court System," 2 *Rutgers L. Rev.* 67 (1948).

[8]Kull, 1144.

[9]ATV statement before Clean Government, May, 1937, 4, VP, box 92.

[10]Judges often simultaneously conducted their own law practices, a situation at which many citizens looked askance. With the court of errors and appeals composed of judges from other courts, the judges were placed in the undesirable position of reviewing their own and each other's decisions.

[11]J. Bebout, *The Making of the New Jersey Constitution* 11 (1945).

[12]Hartshorne, "Progress in New Jersey Judicial Administration," 3 *Rutgers L. Rev.* 162 (1949).

[13]For the historical background of the New Jersey judicial system, see Bilder, "An Historical Examination of the Court of Errors and Appeals," 65 *N.J.L.J.* 429 (1942); Bilder, "Restatement of the Case Against a Separate Court of Chancery," 66 *N.J.L.J.* 5 (1943); C. Erdman, Jr., *The New Jersey Constitution of 1776* (1929); Erdman, *The New Jersey Constitution: A Barrier to Government Efficiency and Economy* (1934); J. S. Erwin, *Law and Practice in the District Court of New Jersey* (1913); R. S. Field, *The Provisional Court of New Jersey with Sketches of the Bench and Bar* (1849); C. H. Hartshorne, *Courts and Procedure in England and New Jersey* (1905); F. B. Lee, *New Jersey as a Colony and State* (1902); McConnell, "A Brief History of the New Jersey Courts," 7 *West's New Jersey Digest* 349 (1954); H. C. Parke, *Courts and Lawyers of New Jersey* (1931); *Proceedings of the New Jersey State Constitutional Convention of 1844* (1942).

[14]*Report of the Judicial Council of New Jersey to the Governor* 5-6 (1930).

[15]Vanderbilt, "The Reorganization of the New Jersey Courts," 34 *Chicago B. Rev.* 161 (1953).

[16]ATV to George W. Davison, July 7, 1947, VP, box 18.

[17]*Op. cit. supra* note 15.

[18]L. R. Orfield, *Criminal Appeals in America* (1939); R. Pound, *Organization of Courts* (1940); R. Pound, *Appellate Procedure in Civil Cases* (1941); G. Warren, *Traffic Courts* (1942); E. Haynes, *The Selection and Tenure of Judges* (1944); L. R. Orfield, *Criminal Procedure from Arrest to Appeal* (1947); A. T. Vanderbilt, *Minimum Standards of Judicial Administration* (1949). For additional information about the National Conference of Judicial Councils, see Finch, "Work of the National Conference of Judicial Councils," *National Conference of Judicial Councils Handbook* 25-81 (1941); McClendon, "Judicial Council Movement," 25 *Mass. L.Q.* 11 (1940).

[19]Undated clippings from a number of national newspapers, vol. 1 of Vanderbilt's A.B.A. scrapbooks, VP.

[20]Vanderbilt, "Campaign to Modernize Judicial Administration," 22 *J. Am. Jud. Soc'y* 5 (1938).

[21]Vanderbilt, "The Bar and the Public," 62 *A.B.A.J.* 464 (1937).

⁴⁸McKean, 154.

⁴⁹*Ibid.*, 135.

⁵⁰*Ibid.*

⁵¹Thomas v. Casey, 121 N.J.L. 191, 192 (1938).

⁵²Thomas to Vanderbilt, Dec. 24, 1938, VP, display box. (Vanderbilt was handling the case at his own expense.)

⁵³ATV to Norman Thomas, Dec. 27, 1938, VP, display box.

⁵⁴Meador Wright, "Law, Politics, Pepsi-Cola and Vanderbilt," *The Oranges* (New Jersey) 43 (1943).

⁵⁵M. W. Martin, *Twelve Full Ounces* 88 (1964).

For an account of the litigation involved, see Charles G. Guth v. Loft, Inc., 23 Del. Ch. 255 (1939).

CHAPTER V

¹Clark, "Fundamental Changes Effected by the New Federal Rules," 15 *Tenn. L. Rev.* 551 (1939); F. James, Jr., *Civil Procedure* 8–21 (1965); R. W. Millar, *Civil Procedure of the Trial Court in Historical Perspective* 59–64 (1952); Mitchell, "Some of the Problems Confronting the Advisory Committee in Recent Months," 23 *A.B.A.J.* 966 (1937); "The New Federal Rules of Civil Procedure," 61 *A.B.A.R.* 423 (1936). Vanderbilt, *Cases and Materials on Modern Procedure and Judicial Administration* 12–21.

²T. Swisher, *Selected Papers of Homer Cummings* 225 (1939).

³The act also called for an annual judicial conference of each circuit at which the judges and representatives of the bar met for informal discussion of all matters relating to the administration of justice in the circuit.

⁴Parker, "The Federal Judiciary," 22 *Tulane L. Rev.* 575 (1948).

⁵53 Stat. 1223, 28 U.S.C. §444 (1940). Hughes, "Administrative Office of the United States Courts," 25 *Mass. L.Q.* 9 (1940); Medina, "Work of the Administrative Office of the United States Courts," 11 *F.R.D.* 353 (1951); Parker, "Integration of the Federal Judiciary," 56 *Harv. L. Rev.* 563 (1943); Shafroth, "New Machinery for Effective Administration of Federal Courts," 25 *A.B.A.J.* 738 (1938); Vanderbilt, "For Business Management of Federal Courts," 21 *J. Am. Jud. Soc'y* 195 (1938).

⁶Indeed, often the very existence of an agency remained quite well concealed. Wrote Vanderbilt:

> I had occasion in writing an article for the *Annual Survey of American Law* to attempt to list all of the administrative agencies of the Federal Government. I searched through the *United States Government Manual*, the *Congressional Directory* and the *Federal Register* and I thought I had discovered all of them. Then I looked out of my office window and saw a big building which had been commandeered by the O.D.B. Although it had been in existence for several years and was created by an act of Congress, the Office of Dependency Benefits is not listed at all in

the Federal directories and yet last year it served 6,000,000 soldiers and 11,500,000 of their dependents and drew 59,000,000 checks and expended $3,380,000,000. This superiority of the *Annual Survey of American Law* over the official reports is due solely to the circumstance of my being able to look out of my window and see the work of the O.D.B. going on a few hundred yards away. Truly we are governed by a government that nobody knows.

Vanderbilt, *The Doctrine of the Separation of Powers and Its Present-Day Significance* 71–72 (1953).

[7]*Report on Administrative Management in the Executive Branch of the Government* 39–40 (1937).

[8]60 Stat. 237 (1946), 5 U.S.C. §1001 (1946). For a legislative history, see House Report No. 1980, 79th Congress, 2d Sess., reprinted in *U.S. Code Congressional Service* 1195–1206 (1964). See also, "Additional Views and Recommendations of Messrs. McFarland, Stason and Vanderbilt," 27 *A.B.A.J.* 146 (1941); *Administrative Procedure in Government Agencies: Report of the Committee on Administrative Procedure* (reprinted by University Press of Virginia, 1968); K. C. Davis, *Administrative Law Text* 6–11 (1972); *The Federal Administrative Procedure Act and the Administrative Agencies* (1947); "The Federal Administrative Procedure Act Becomes Law," 32 *A.B.A.J.* 377 (1946); "Great Issues as to Administrative Procedure," 27 *A.B.A.J.* 95 (1941); C. McFarland and Vanderbilt, *Cases and Materials on Administrative Law* (1947); McGuire, "Administrative Procedure Reform Moves Forward," 27 *A.B.A.J.* 150 (1941); Schwartz, "The Administrative Procedure Act in Operation," 29 *N.Y.U.L. Rev.* 1173 (1954).

[9]Cummings, "The New Criminal Rules," 31 *A.B.A.J.* 236 (1945).

[10]Clark, Foreword to *Federal Rules of Criminal Procedure* at iv (N.Y.U. School of Law, 1946).

[11]Cummings, "The Third Great Adventure," 29 *A.B.A.J.* 654 (1943); Holtzoff, "Reform of Federal Criminal Procedure," 12 *Geo. Wash. L. Rev.* 119 (1944); Orfield, "The Federal Rules of Criminal Procedure," 26 *A.B.A.J.* 167 (1946); Vanderbilt, "New Rules of Federal Criminal Procedure," 29 *A.B.A.J.* 376 (1943).

[12]Uniform Code of Military Justice of 1950, 64 Stat. 108, 10 U.S.C. 80. For a legislative history, see *U.S. Code Congressional Service 1950*, 2222–2269. See also: "Association Aid Enlisted in Improving Army Courts-Martial," 32 *A.B.A.J.* 2551 (1946); "Improving Military Justice," 33 *A.B.A.J.* 45 (1947); "Military Justice: Changes Advised in Courts-Martial System," 13 *A.B.A.J.* 41 (1947).

[13]James E. Stiles (ed.), *Seventy-Five Years of Gamma Phi: An Anniversary History of the Chapter of Delta Kappa Epsilon at Wesleyan University, Middletown, Connecticut* 230 (1942). ATV to Jack B. Poor, May 17, 1957, VP, box 19. For additional information about the Gamma Phi renaissance, see E. Unlam, *Dynamo Jim Stiles: Pioneer of Progress* 223–235 (1959).

[14]*Record of the Proceedings of the Seventy-Fifth Anniversary Banquet,*

Breakfast and Business Meeting: Gamma Phi Chapter, Delta Kappa Epsilon Fraternity; Wesleyan University, Middletown, Conn. 53 (May 15–16, 1942).

[15]J. L. Bernstein, "Chief Justice Vanderbilt: Profile and Commentary," 3 *Reporter* 4 (1955).

[16]Vanderbilt, "Reorganization of the New Jersey Courts," 161.

[17]*Ibid.*

[18]A. Steinberg, *The Bosses* 63–64 (1972).

[19]Edison also immediately supported a plan to grant relief to the railroads from an overload of back taxes incurred during the Depression, a move which did not endear him to the mayor of Jersey City.

[20]Jack Alexander, "Ungovernable Governor," 265 *Saturday Evening Post* 8 (Jan. 23, 1943).

[21]IV *Proceedings of the New Jersey Constitutional Convention of 1947* 5 (1953).

[22]*Jersey Journal*, Nov. 25, 1941.

[23]*Newark Sunday Call*, May 3, 1942.

[24]Hague was also successful in helping to unite the New Jersey State Bar Association against the Hendrickson Constitution. "Led by a howling, hooting and extraordinarily large delegation of Hudson County lawyers, the Bar placed itself on record in opposition to the new constitution. Besides attacking the document for its 'radical' changes in the state's governmental system, the resolution hit hard at the nature and operations of the Hendrickson Commission. Asserting that seven men had usurped the right of the people to write their own constitution, the statement deplored the secrecy of their proceedings and the lack of any real public dialogue." R. J. Connors, *The Process of Constitutional Revision in New Jersey: 1940–1947* 46 (1970). This study, published by the National Municipal League, is an excellent, detailed history of the revision movement.

[25]Hague ran the mayor of Newark, Vincent J. Murphy, as the Democratic candidate for governor. Murphy failed to gain much support outside of Hudson County.

[26]The bill authorized the state of New Jersey to buy the machines and to pay for them out of general purpose funds which had been earmarked for the counties, like Hudson, that had refused to buy their own voting machines. Thereafter, with the use of the voting machines and the careful scrutiny of elections by the offices of the superintendent of elections and the commissioner of registration—offices which the Clean Government delegation had also sponsored—the number of votes cast in Hudson County in the gubernatorial elections decreased and the foundations of Mayor Hague's statewide power began slowly to crumble.

[27]ATV to Robert A. Vanderbilt, Nov. 24, 1943, VP, box 378.

[28]ATV to William R. Vanderbilt, Jan. 10, 1944, VP, box 378.

[29]ATV to Robert A. Vanderbilt, Jan. 31, 1944, VP, box 378.

[30]One of Mayor Hague's many statements on the subject was reprinted in the *Jersey Journal*, Oct. 5, 1943: "The proposal to throw New Jersey's constitution out the window and substitute a tricky new one with a court-

packing joker hidden away in it will be the most thoroughly defeated proposal ever submitted by a referendum to the people of New Jersey. The people will never consent to handing our courts over to a railroad lobby or to any plan which divests New Jersey's 500,000 fighting citizens of their rights to have a say in framing the basic law. . . ."

[31]The opposite side of this argument was that the problems of returning to a postwar society would be so great that it would be important to have a modern state government to facilitate the work.

[32]Connors, 102.

[33]*Ibid.*, 106.

[34]*N.Y. Times*, Nov. 8, 1944. Among the rumors spread by the Jersey City Teachers Association was that the new constitution would result in children going to school on Saturdays. Connors, 105.

[35]For an analysis of Hague's injection of religion into the campaign, see Connors, 101–108. It is estimated that over $300,000 was spent by Hague to block the new constitution, a figure five times greater than that expended by the proconstitution forces. Connors, 112.

[36]The remarks by Edge, Edison, and Vanderbilt are from the *Newark Evening News*, Nov. 3, 1944.

[37]For example, in March of 1943 he was retained to test the constitutionality of the Price Control Act and particularly an emergency court of appeals that was set up in Washington to summarily dispose of cries for redress from all over the country. Lockerty v. Phillips, 319 U.S. 182 (1943).

"Wendell Willkie had been retained in the matter but he dropped it like a hot potato when he discovered that it might be misunderstood by his farmer friends. The result is that I have had to work night and day in an effort to get the matter in shape. As a matter of fact, I got up one morning at 5, and another at 4, and the day of the argument at 3 in order to be thoroughly prepared." ATV to William R. Vanderbilt, Mar. 31, 1943, VP, box 378.

[38]Despite Vanderbilt's long friendship with Dewey, it was being rumored that he had more ambitious reasons for supporting Dewey's candidacy. His son-in-law Lemuel Bannister sent him a clipping from a California newspaper: "The rumored retirement of Chief Justice Harlan F. Stone will not come through at the end of the current Supreme Court term—certainly not until after the November elections. This may explain the help Dewey is receiving from Arthur T. Vanderbilt whose contacts are nationwide. Friends of Dewey report that Vanderbilt has been promised the Chief Justiceship, if and when."

On March 15, 1944, Vanderbilt replied to his son-in-law: " . . . I never heard of the chap or his column until his paragraph appeared, but friends of mine from all over the country have been sending it on to me—some congratulating me as if they were dealing with an event *in praesenti*, others being a bit more guarded in their comment, and some like yourself, uproariously amused. You can well imagine how an article like this will cause the fishy eye of the distinguished Chief Justice to become just a wee bit fishier as he looks at me with suspicion, thinking I am waiting his early mortal breakdown, on our occasional conferences on the work of the Criminal Law Rules."

"I can take what is said about me hereabouts—and at times it is plenty—with considerable equanimity and with the thought, probably utterly untrue to fact, that the public no longer believes it; but when one becomes the victim of national publicity, all he can do is to grit his teeth and cuss, which I have done every time the miserable clipping overtakes me." ATV to Lemuel Bannister, Mar. 15, 1944, VP, box 378.

[39]ATV to Robert A. Vanderbilt, Jan. 23, 1943, VP, box 378.

[40]ATV to Professor Alexander Thomson, Apr. 12, 1943, VP, box 13.

[41]For brief biographies of the deans from 1838 to 1943, see "Leadership and the Law School," address by Dean Vanderbilt, Fifty-Seventh Annual Dinner of the Alumni Association, Jan. 25, 1944. For a history of the School of Law, see L. Tompkins, "The School of Law," in *New York University, 1832–1932* 239 (T. F. Jones, ed., 1933). See also Reid, "Some Pages from the History of New York University School of Law," 36 *N.Y.S.B.J.* 13 (1964).

[42]See generally *New York University Self-Study: Final Report* 86–128 (1956).

[43]Vanderbilt, "Chief Problems Confronting the Bar and the Responsibilities of Our Law Schools with Respect Thereto," 8 *Am. L.S. Rev.* 1031 (1938).

[44]See Bell, "Legal Aid in New Jersey," 36 *A.B.A.J.* 355 (1950); Hartshorne, "Equal Justice for All: The Bar and the Indigent Criminal Defendant," 37 *A.B.A.J.* 104 (1951); "Legal Aid to Indigent Criminal Defendants in Philadelphia and New Jersey," 107 *U. Pa. L. Rev.* 812 (1959); Trebach, "The Indigent Defendant," 11 *Rutgers L. Rev.* 625 (1957); Vanderbilt, "An Experiment in the Trial of Indigent Criminal Cases," 32 *A.B.A.J.* 434 (1946).

[45] Vanderbilt, Preface to *Annual Survey of American Law* at i (1943).

[46]For a more detailed account of these innovations, see *Reports of the Dean*, N.Y.U. School of Law, 1943–1944, 1944–1945, 1945–1946, 1946–1947, 1947–1948. See also Williams, "Arthur T. Vanderbilt and Legal Education," 24 *N.Y.U.L.Q. Rev.* 1 (1949).

[47]ATV to Mrs. George Brainard, Mar. 13, 1944, VP, box 378.

[48]ATV to William R. Vanderbilt, May 14, 1945, VP, box 378.

[49]Vanderbilt, "The Idea of a Law Center," 23 *N.Y.U.L.Q. Rev.* 6–7 (1948). For further elaboration of Vanderbilt's concept of a law center, see "The Law School in a Changing Society: A Law Center," 32 *A.B.A.J.* 525 (1946); "Law School Study After the War," 20 *N.Y.U.L.Q. Rev.* 146 (1944); "The Mission of a Law Center," 27 *N.Y.U.L. Rev.* 20 (1952); "The Significance of the Legal Center," *Lawyer's Week* (Southwestern Legal Center) 59 (April 1951).

[50]"The Neglected Glory of Phi Beta Kappa," address by ATV, the Centennial Celebration of the Gamma of Connecticut, 1944.

[51]Named for two famous graduates of the School of Law, Elihu Root (1867) and Samuel J. Tilden (1841). See Gerhart, "The Root-Tilden Scholarships; A Unique Experiment in Legal Education," 37 *A.B.A.J.* (March 1951).

[52]Vanderbilt, Foreword to T. Reed, *Preparing College Men and Women for Politics* at v (1952).

[53]The Citizenship Clearing House became the National Center for Education in Politics in 1962. This organization expired in 1966 for lack of funding. For a history of the institution, see Hennessey, "Political Education and Political Science: The National Center for Education in Politics, 1947–1966," N.C.E.P. mimeographed report, 161 pages.

[54]See Elliott, "Judicial Administration's New Institute," 37 *J. Am. Jud. Soc'y* 38 (1953).

[55]ATV to Miss Evelyn M. Seufert, May 11, 1946, VP, box 36.

[56]*Bulletin of the New York University School of Law* 2 (November 1945).

[57]"As the acknowledged boss of Essex County, A.T. never asked me as his Congressman to vote any special way except once. That was a bill in the Ways and Means Committee, of which I was a member, to make taxable certain business earnings of subsidiaries of tax exempt corporations. New York University owned the Mueller Macaroni Company. A.T. asked me if we could not postpone the effects of that bill for one year, that he approved of the bill in theory, but that the University badly needed the full income from the Macaroni Company without taxes that year." Robert Winthrop Kean to author, Jan. 17, 1972.

In a special tax message to Congress in January of 1950, President Truman asked that the tax laws be strengthened to eliminate exceptions accorded to educational institutions that engaged in private business enterprises. The Mueller-New York University arrangement was cited as a classic case. "Tax-Exempt Status Is Denied to Concern That Aids N.Y.U.," *N.Y. Times,* May 28, 1950.

[58]ATV address, Opening Dinner of the New Building Fund Campaign of the N.Y.U. School of Law, June 6, 1946.

[59]ATV to Mrs. Jean Swartz, Jan. 7, 1947, VP, box 378.

[60]ATV address, Sixtieth Annual Dinner of the N.Y.U. Law Alumni Association, Feb. 10, 1948.

[61]Vanderbilt, "Reorganization of the New Jersey Courts," 161–162.

[62]Vanderbilt, "Brief For a Better Court System," *N.Y. Times Magazine* 67 (May 5, 1957).

[63]*Jersey Journal,* Nov. 4, 1946. Hague was only able to give Hansen a 69,729 vote plurality—a far cry from the landslides he produced for A. Harry Moore in the 1930's.

[64]Alfred E. Driscoll to author, Oct. 15, 1971.

[65]On Feb. 2, 1947, the *Newark Evening News* reported: "Unlike his predecessor, Governor Driscoll has no inclination to quarantine Hudson. He seems to want to bring it within the family of nations."

[66]"Statement by Arthur T. Vanderbilt before a Meeting of the Headquarter's Committee of the Clean Government Republican Committee on April 11, 1947," 4, VP, box 110.

[67]*Ibid.,* 2.

[68]*Op. cit. supra* note 64.

[69]*Op. cit. supra* note 66, 4.

[70]*Ibid.,* 5–6.

[71]ATV to Dean George A. Works, May 17, 1947, VP, box 37.

[72]ATV to Herbert Sims, July 7, 1947, VP, box 18.

[73]*Ibid.*

[74]*Op. cit. supra* note 60.

[75]ATV to Professor Bedford Thurman, Sept. 2, 1947, VP, box 18.

[76]ATV to Henry A. Ingraham, June 23, 1947, VP, box 18.

[77]*Op. cit. supra* note 72.

[78]Vic Hammerslag, "Vanderbilt Walks and Swims with Reporter at Maine Home to Disprove Rumored Illness," *Neward Star-Ledger* (undated clipping, July 1947), VP, box 110.

[79]*Ibid.*

[80]ATV to Mrs. Fannie Klein, August 1947, VP, box 37.

[81]ATV to Henry A. Ingraham, June 16, 1947, VP, box 18.

[82]*Op. cit. supra* note 66.

[83]*Ibid.*

[84]Alfred E. Driscoll to author, Apr. 24, 1974.

[85]*Newark Sunday Call,* Nov. 12, 1944.

[86]ATV to George W. Davison, July 7, 1947, VP, box 12.

[87]74 *N.J.L.J.* 293 (1947). Pound's complete blueprint for a modern court system is found in Pound, *Organization of Courts* (1940).

[88]The division of the superior court was actually only a formal vestige of the old system of separate law and equity courts because of the provisions in the judicial article, which stated that each division of the superior court "shall exercise the power and functions of the other" when justice requires and that "legal and equitable relief shall be granted in any cause." These provisions were later strengthened by a rule of the supreme court that provided that, if an action should chance to be instituted in a court which did not have jurisdiction over the subject matter, it should be transferred to the court having jurisdiction to be proceeded upon as if originally started there, and if on appeal it was determined that the court below lacked jurisdiction, the rule directed the appellate court to order the entry of judgment in the proper court. Litigants could now have all equitable and legal issues in a cause fully resolved in one court. With these provisions, the division of the superior court was only a sentimental reminder of the old division between law and equity, and proved a happy way of taking care of the yearnings for the former days which some members of the profession felt.

[89]Walker, *N.J.S.B.J.* (1912).

[90]In addition, opposition to the abolition of the court of chancery came from chancery judges who did not want to give up their powers as judges of a separate court and their patronage prerogatives; from a powerful clique of chancery lawyers who feared the end of their receivership bonanzas; and from those who felt that to demolish the court of chancery would be to make divorces readily obtainable in New Jersey.

[91]I *State of New Jersey Constitutional Convention of 1947: Convention Proceedings Record* 522, 525 (1949).

[92]For additional information about the Convention and for comparative

studies of the New Jersey court system before and after the adoption of the 1947 Constitution, see: H. Allen and C. Ransome, *Constitutional Revision in Theory and Practice* 158–161 (1962); Bebout, "Staging a Constitutional Convention," in W. B. Graves, *State Constitutional Revision* 67 (1960); Burling, "Functioning Under the 1947 Constitution of New Jersey," 23 *Temple L.Q.* 167 (1950); "Convention Committee Describes New Judicial System Adopted in New Jersey," 31 *J. Am. Jud. Soc'y* 138 (1948); English, "State Courts: New Jersey Reorganizes Its Judicial System," 34 *A.B.A.J.* 11 (1948); Harrison, "Judicial Reform in New Jersey," 22 *State Government* 232 (1949); Harrison, "New Jersey's New Court System," 2 *Rutgers L. Rev.* 60 (1948); *New Jersey Constitutional Convention of 1947* 5v (1949–1953); Paul, "Selling Judicial Reform," 36 *J. Am. Jud. Soc'y* 175 (1953); Rich, "Convention or Commission?" 37 *National Municipal Rev.* 133 (1948); Rich, "A New Constitution for New Jersey," 41 *Am. Pol. Sci. Rev.* (Dec. 1947); Stoffer, "Organization and Administration of the Courts," 4 *Rutgers L. Rev.* 1 (1949); Vanderbilt, "New Judicial System in New Jersey," 72 *N.Y.S.B.A. Rep.* 277 (1949); Woelper, "The Reorganization of the Judiciary in New Jersey," 1 *Sydney L. Rev.* 46 (1953).

[93]Harrison, "New Jersey's New Court System," 102.

[94]Medina, "Judges as Leaders in Improving the Administration of Justice," 36 *J. Am. Jud. Soc'y* 16 (1952).

[95]B. M. Rich, *The Government and Administration of New Jersey* 33 (1957).

[96]It was ironic that Hague's support of the constitution—which helped result in a Hudson County plurality of 131,358 in the November election—was his last showing of power in New Jersey politics. Under the consecutive administrations of three "disloyal" governors, Hague's patronage empire had receded back to Hudson County. When Hague supported General Eisenhower for the Democratic presidential nomination in 1948, Truman, upon winning the presidency, remembered Hague's attacks and siphoned away his federal patronage and power over Democratic national affairs. Hague had hoped to continue his puppet government by having his nephew elected to another four-year term as mayor of Jersey City in 1949. Public opinion about Hague, however, had shifted dramatically. As R. J. Connors analyzed in his study, *A Cycle of Power: The Career of Jersey City Mayor Frank Hague* 164–165 (1971):

In their service-connected travels, many Jersey Cityites learned that boss rule was considered outdated and disreputable by their fellow Americans. The city and the regime which they had been taught to regard with pride were scorned and ridiculed, largely because of national publicity emanating from the CIO affair, in which the mayor had shown his antagonism towards such basic liberties as freedom of speech and freedom of assembly. In the short range view of things, his battle with the CIO had been a Hague coup, solidifying city behind mayor because of its anti-Communist aspects. But in the long run the advantages to the regime of the CIO fight were dubious. When those in the armed services learned that "civil liberty" was not an ugly phrase, that freedom of speech was not a cloak to hide Communist subversion, they began to question the whole moral posture of Frank Hague. By war's end, "in every Jersey City street there were veterans of World War II who had been needled by their buddies about Hagueville and Haguetown. On every continent, this experience was repeated. Jersey City veterans in the lines, in the air, on the seas, men in military hospitals, in supply and service areas . . . had seen their city held up to ridicule. 'Why are we fighting a war for freedom here,' they had asked themselves, 'when we live under a dictatorship in our home town?' "

Hague, in the last years before his resignation, had become more and more an absentee mayor, ruling his city by telephone from his various vacation spots. With the specter of Hague's power a less immediate fear, for the first time the residents of Jersey City dared to express their displeasure with the city's slums, its uncollected garbage, its crumbling schools and decrepit streets and sewer systems, its bellicose police, and its outrageous taxes. Even within the inner circles of the Hague machine there was discontent over Hague's failure to retire his old lieutenants to make way for new workers, and a widespread feeling that only Irishmen received the monetary benefits of Hague-politics. His position had deteriorated so badly that in May of 1949 when he returned to his hometown, the Jersey City Horseshoe, to campaign for his nephew, he was jeered and pelted with rotten vegetables. Kenny's ticket won the slate by a landslide.

Hague in retirement continued the lavish lifestyle to which he had grown accustomed, marred only by occasional lawsuits. (See n. 75, chap. III.) On Jan. 1, 1956, at the age of seventy-nine, Frank Hague died in the Park Avenue apartment in New York City where he had spent the last years of his life.

[97]*Newark Evening News,* Nov. 2, 1947.

[98]Alfred E. Driscoll to author, Oct. 15, 1971.

[99]"Arthur T. Vanderbilt: Chief Justice of the New Jersey Supreme Court," 35 *A.B.A.J.* 791 (1949).

[100]Roger Butterfield, 3.

[101]ATV to Dean E. Blythe Stason, Dec. 1, 1947, VP, box 37.

[102]"New Jersey Goes to the Head of the Class," 31 *J. Am. Jud. Soc'y* 131 (1948).

[103]ATV to Bedford Thurman, Sept. 2, 1947, VP, box 18.

[104]ATV to Wilbert Snow, Jan. 21, 1948, VP, box 18.

[105]Vanderbilt, "The Idea of a Ministry of Justice Considered and Its Functions Distributed," 78 *N.Y.S.B.J.* 29 (1955).

[106]*Op. cit. supra* note 101.

[107]Vanderbilt's accomplishment of guiding the drafting of the Rules Governing the Courts of the State of New Jersey, and in general, of channeling the efforts of the bar and the public toward constitutional revision, was recognized in the summer of 1948 when President Robert C. Clothier of

Rutgers University conferred on him the honorary degree of Doctor of Laws, the fifteenth honorary degree he had received since 1938. Several weeks later in early September at the annual dinner of the American Bar Association held in Chicago, he was awarded the Bar Association's highest honor, the gold medal for "conspicuous service to the cause of American jurisprudence." The medal previously had been bestowed only fourteen times—to such men as Elihu Root, Professor Samuel Williston, Justice Oliver Wendell Holmes, Dean John H. Wigmore, Herbert Harley, Dean Roscoe Pound, Senator George Wharton Pepper, Chief Justice Hughes, Carl McFarland, and Judge John J. Parker. Presenting the medal, A.B.A. President Tappan Gregory summarized Vanderbilt's career and influence on American law:

> Lawyer, judge, educator, statesman, apostle of good government and the orderly administration of justice; a powerful, moving force for judicial and legislative reform; leader of the Bar of the nation during his thirty-five years of active general practice; Dean of the Law School of New York University; builder of a great Law Center; founder of a Clearing House to foster study and understanding of the duties of citizenship and to encourage participation in public affairs; energetic supporter of Judicial Councils and their work; tireless and farsighted artisan in constitutional revision when the need is apparent in the interest of good government; active participant, by appointment of the War Department, in reform of military justice; in the forefront among those selected by the Attorney General to collaborate with others in the creation of the Administrative Office of the United States Courts; head of the Advisory Committee appointed by the United States Supreme Court to draft rules of Criminal Procedure for the federal courts; architect of the new Judicial structure and Rules of Court in New Jersey; Chief Justice-Designate of that great State; and former president of the American Bar Association.
>
> In all these activities, in all these high offices, he has brought to bear the highest order of intellect and discharged his manifold duties with conscientious devotion, always inspired by those magnificent qualities of heart and mind which brought him to his present position of leadership and qualified him to render distinguished conspicuous service to his profession, to his fellow man, and to the cause of American jurisprudence. *Op. cit. supra* note 99.

[108]Vanderbilt, "New Rules of the Supreme Court in Appellate Procedure," 2 *Rutgers L. Rev.* 28 (1948).

[109]Vanderbilt, "New Rules of the Supreme Court on the Argument and Deciding of Appeals," 71 *N.J.L.J.* 2, 4 (Mar. 18, 1948).

CHAPTER VI

[1]Roger Butterfield, "New Jersey Puts Its Judges to Work," 224 *Saturday Evening Post* 144 (May 17, 1952).

[2]Vanderbilt, "Some Principles of Judicial Administration" (Alexander T. Morrison Lectureship Foundation, annual meeting of the State Bar of California), 18–19 (Oct. 5, 1950).

[3]*Op. cit. supra* note 1, 144.

[4]In an average court year, the justices each read 570 briefs of 12,160 pages or 3,698,000 words, approximately 280 pages a week, and in addition referred to about 300 appendixes supporting the briefs running to 40,500 pages or 12,150,000 words, about 1,020 pages a week. Arnold Martin, "Heart of Jersey's Court System," *Newark Sunday News Magazine* 6 (Apr. 25, 1954). The extent of their continual search to find measures to facilitate the judicial process was evidenced in Rule 1:3-9 of the New Jersey Rules specifying the size type for briefs: "Never smaller than small pica or 11 point type," and the type of paper on which the briefs were to be typed: "India eggshell, opaque and unglazed"—the formula that, after consultation with judges from many other jurisdictions, was found to reduce most of the eyestrain caused by light reflection.

[5]Vanderbilt, "Reorganization of the New Jersey Courts," 34 *Chicago B. Rev.* 165 (1953).

[6]Vanderbilt, "Our New Judicial Establishment: The Record of the First Year," 4 *Rutgers L. Rev.* 351 (1950).

See In re Greenberg, 15 N.J. 132 (1954), in which the New Jersey Supreme Court brought a disciplinary warning against an attorney who presented before the court his inferences from the facts as if they were the very facts themselves. Wrote Vanderbilt ". . . it is . . . obvious that the work of our appellate courts cannot go on satisfactorily if we cannot rely on the representations of counsel to us both as to the facts and as to the law." (135) "It necessarily follows that any future transgressions in this field must meet with severe disciplinary action, if the courts and the bar alike are to perform their duties to litigants and the public." (138)

[7]Vanderbilt, "Our New Judicial Establishment," 351.

[8]Parker to Vanderbilt, Nov. 7, 1947, VP, box 193.

[9]Address of Chief Justice Arthur T. Vanderbilt before the Advertising Club of New Jersey at the Essex House, Newark, N.J., 5–6 (May 2, 1951).

[10]*Op. cit. supra* note 1, 31.

[11]Vanderbilt, "Five Functions of the Lawyer," 40 *A.B.A.J.* 40 (1954).

[12]Jerome Spingarn, "Arthur T. Vanderbilt: Order in the Courtroom," 212 *Harper's* 64 (May 1956).

[13]Vanderbilt, *Improving the Administration of Justice* 121 (1957).

[14]*Op. cit. supra* note 11.

[15]Medina, "Judges as Leaders in Improving the Administration of Justice," 36 *J. Am. Jud. Soc'y* 16 (1952).

[16]*Op. cit. supra* note 11.

[17]Vanderbilt, "Record of the New Jersey Courts in the Fourth Year Under the New Constitution," 7 *Rutgers L. Rev.* 317 (1953). For a good discussion of New Jersey's pretrial procedures in action, see Ackerson, "Pretrial Conferences and Calendar Control: The Keys to Effective Work of the Trial

Courts," 4 *Rutgers L. Rev.* 381 (1950) and Brennan, "New Jersey Tackles Court Congestion," 40 *J. Am. Jud. Soc'y* 45 (1956).

After the cooperation of trial attorneys and judges had been won, another obstacle developed when the casualty companies began sending to the conferences young attorneys who knew little about the facts or law of the cases and had no authority to make admissions. The supreme court asked the companies to change their practice and to send each summons and complaint to trial counsel immediately after receipt so that counsel could come to the pretrial conference fully informed about the case and authorized to make the necessary admissions for the preparation of an adequate pretrial conference order. When the companies responded by telling the court that this would cost them more than $1,000,000 a year in increased legal fees, the court countered by asking how many millions of dollars they were saving by being able to take down their reserves against pending cases within six months instead of the traditional two to three years. When the matter was presented from that angle, the casualty companies agreed to cooperate because they were saving several times the million dollars involved in additional fees.

[18]Vanderbilt, "The Courts, the Public, and the Bar," 131 *N.J.L.J.* 33 (1954).

[19]Vanderbilt, "The New Rules of the Supreme Court on the Argument and Deciding of Appeals," 71 *N.J.L.J.* 4 (Mar. 18, 1948).

[20]*Op. cit. supra* note 6, 351–352.

[21]*Annual Survey of American Law* 838 (1955).

[22]Spingarn's notes for "Arthur T. Vanderbilt: Order in the Courtroom," VP, box 371.

[23]ATV address, "The Essentials of a Sound Judicial System," Northwestern University Law School, Jan. 13, 1953. Wrote Vanderbilt in Milk Drivers v. Shore Dairies, Inc., 8 N.J. 32, 38 (1951): "The design of our rules of court is to facilitate business and advance justice, to make practice just and simple, and to prevent unreasonable delay and expense, and it is the duty of all judges to see that these salutary objectives are not perverted." The supreme court made repeatedly clear that a litigant would never be allowed to lose on procedural grounds or through a mistake of remedy. Thus the most important rule of court was Rule 1:7–9, a catch-all to ensure that the rules themselves did not become a source of litigation: "The rules of court shall be considered as general rules for the government of the court and the conducting of causes; and as the design of them is to facilitate business and advance justice, they may be relaxed or dispensed with by the court in any cases where it should be manifest to the court that a strict adherence to them will work surprise or injustice." In comparison, the legislative rules governing the old court system did not have this flexibility.

[24]A central function of the judicial conference was to submit to scrutiny proposed court rules to locate their technical difficulties. In much the same way that the rule-making process had progressed in 1948, these proposed rules were then submitted to the supreme court for the review, acceptance, or rejection of the seven justices. In the first two years under the new

constitution, to refine and perfect the rules that had originally been drafted, fifty-one new rules or amendments to rules governing practice and procedure were adopted by the supreme court. At the end of five years, a complete revision of the rules was promulgated.

[25]*Op. cit. supra* note 9, 2.

[26]*Op. cit. supra* note 1, 144.

. . . I was shocked about ten days ago [Vanderbilt reported in 1949 to a meeting of the New Jersey Institute for Practicing Lawyers] to read in one of the newspapers published in one of the large cities of this state, that the new rules have slowed down the work of the criminal courts. No longer was it possible to swear in all the witnesses in 30 cases at one time, at the opening of court at 10 o'clock, and no longer was it possible to call on the witnesses in these 30 cases, being heard in the criminal court without a jury, to testify from where they sat in the courtroom, and no longer was it possible to send a man to the County Penitentiary, or, perchance, State's Prison, without a stenographic record being taken.

Imagine it! They regarded these new rules, enforcing due process of law according to a well established tradition, as an innovation. It reminded me of a notice published at a western university. The notice read: "It is a tradition of this University that bicycles shall not be ridden on the walks of the campus. P.S.: This tradition will start next Monday." What we are trying to do in some of the counties is to restore what has always been regarded as the only sound method of procedure, but has been so long in the discard that a change is regarded as an innovation.

Vanderbilt, Introduction in *The New Practice* 12–13 (M. Schnitzer, ed., 1949).

[27]Vanderbilt, *The Challenge of Law Reform* 93 (1955).

[28]*Op. cit. supra* note 1, 143.

[29]Vanderbilt's disclosure of the breakdown in traffic law enforcement and his revelation that 95 percent of the American people received their only experience in court in traffic courts, led to the formation of the National Committee on Traffic Law Enforcement by the American Bar Association. Its main activity was sponsoring a nationwide traffic safety educational program.

[30]ATV to Anthony P. Savarese, Jan. 19, 1949, VP, box 195.

[31]*Op. cit. supra* note 2, 8–9.

[32]Vanderbilt, "Impasses in Justice," 267 *Wash. U.L.Q.* 299 (1956). See also Katcher, "Traffic Court Program in New Jersey," 8 *N.J.S.B.J.* 1207 (1964); Vanderbilt, "Traffic Law Enforcement and the Sixteen Resolutions of the Chief Justices and the Governors" (printed by the Institute of Judicial Administration, 1953).

[33]Vanderbilt, "The Use and Abuse of Dissenting Opinions," Chicago Conference of Chief Justices, 1 (August 1950).

[34]*Op. cit. supra* note 9, 4–5.

[35]Vanderbilt, "Response to Award of Gold Medal of the New Jersey State Bar Association at the 52 Annual Dinner of the Association," 52 *N.J.S.B.A.J.* 194 (1950).

[36]ATV to Professor Warren A. Seavey, Apr. 28, 1952, VP, box 179.

[37]*Ibid.*, 2. "Many of our dissenting opinions," Vanderbilt commented, "have come from a rear guard action attempting to go back to the good old days. . . . They were, in a sense, like the peculiar bird that had the acquired habit of flying backward because it didn't like to go any place except where it had been." *Op. cit supra* note 33, 1–2.

[38]The legislature subsequently overruled the decision of the majority. *N.J.S.* 3A:3-16.

[39]In Lionshead Lake, Inc. v. Wayne Township, 10 N.J. 165, 173 (1953), Vanderbilt held that an ordinance fixing a minimum living-floor space was reasonable and valid: "We may take notice without formal proof that there are minimums in housing below which one may not go without risk of impairing the health of those who dwell therein. One does not need extensive experience in matrimonial causes to become aware of the adverse effect of overcrowding on the well-being of our most important institution, the home."

Fred v. Old Tappan, 10 N.J. 515, 523 (1952), held that an ordinance that no one should excavate or remove soil for sale or use, except in connection with construction on premises, without obtaining permission from the mayor or city council, was a valid exercise of the police power. " . . .it took nature 1,000 years to produce a single inch of [top] soil. It appears, moreover, that top soil is the best and most fertile of soils and has water absorbing and retaining qualities not to be found in the lower strata of soil. In the light of the evidence before us we are inclined to the view that the prohibition against removing the top six inches of soil is not arbitrary and unreasonable."

Fischer v. Bedminster, 11 N.J. 194, 204, 205 (1952), held that a township zoning ordinance which restricted construction of residences in a strictly rural area upon a plot of less than five acres was not unreasonable *per se:* "As much foresight is now required to preserve the countryside for its best use as has been needed to save what could be salvaged of our cities. . . . It must, of course, be borne in mind that an ordinance which is reasonable today may at some future time by reason of changed conditions prove to be unreasonable. If so, it may then be set aside."

[40]S. 58 introduced Aug. 23, 1948.

[41]71 *N.J.L.J.* 389 (1948).

[42]N.J. Laws 1950, ch. 171.

[43]63 *A.B.A.Rep.* 523 (1938). Two classic statements on the subject are Pound, "The Rule-Making Power of the Courts," 12 *A.B.A.J.* 599 (1926); and Wigmore, "All Legislative Rules for Judiciary Procedure Are Void Constitutionally," 23 *Ill. L.J.* 276 (1928). See also Hyde, "From Common Law Rules to Rules of Court," 22 *Wash. U.L.Q.* 187 (1937); Vanderbilt, *Minimum Standards of Judicial Administration* 91–145.

[44]*N.J. Constitutional Convention of 1947*, Report of the Committee on the Judiciary, 5, 17 (Aug. 26, 1947).

[45]1 *Constitutional Convention*, 146–147.

[46]4 *Constitutional Convention*, 729. Interestingly enough, it seems as if the "subject to law" phrase might have been retained by the Committee on the Judiciary because of the influence of the chairman, Frank H. Sommer. Wrote Vanderbilt:

> I must not pass by the 1912 Practice Act without mentioning two more matters of present day significance. The draftsmen of the act, particularly Mr. Charles Hartshorne and Dean Frank H. Sommer, both of whom were then serving as bar examiners, knew well the Supreme Court—or perhaps I had better say, the Chief Justice—with whom they were dealing, for while giving the Court the broadest of rule-making powers they annexed to the Act a complete set of rules which were to be deemed rules of court and which were to supersede conflicting statutory and common law regulations theretofore existing until new rules were made by the Court. By this simple device they took good care that the spirit of the Practice Act would not be sabotaged either by the failure to adopt rules of court or by the adoption of reactionary measures. They were willing to have the rules which accompanied their Act stand comparison with any rules which the Court itself might promulgate, but such comparison never became necessary. The Court never abrogated their rules and for the most part they still stand. That they had sound ground for their fears, however, is demonstrated by the fact that the provisions of the rules relating to the very matter that we are going to learn about this afternoon—the settlement of issues before trial—were frustrated by the simple failure of the Supreme Court of that day to designate a commissioner in each county to carry out the provisions of the rules with respect to preliminary references. A burnt child dreads the fire even when he has reached the age of threescore and ten, and perhaps that is why the grant of rule-making power in the new Constitution as to practice and procedure is "subject to law." Be that as it may, if I have any understanding of the intentions of seven men, I can say with confidence that that particular phrase of the Judicial Article will never need to be invoked.

Vanderbilt, "The New Rules of the Supreme Court on Appellate Procedure," 8.

[47]Winberry v. Salisbury, 247–248.

[48]*Ibid.*, at 248.

[49]*Ibid.*, at 264, 265.

[50]*Ibid.*, at 266, 267.

[51]S. Concurrent Res. No. 10.

[52]ATV to Dean Roscoe Pound, Dec. 26, 1951, VP, box 179.

[53]*Ibid.*

[54]Pound, "Procedure Under Rules of Court in New Jersey," 66 *Harv. L. Rev.* 44–45 (1952).

[55]A full discussion of Winberry v. Salisbury appears in Kaplan and Greene, "The Legislature's Relation to Judicial Rule-Making: An Appraisal of *Winberry v. Salisbury,*" 65 *Harv. L. Rev.* 234 (1951); Pound, "Procedure Under Rules of Court in New Jersey"; and Warach, "The Rule-Making Power: Subject to Law?" 5 *Rutgers L. Rev.* 376 (1951). Law review notes concerning the decision include: 31 *Boston U.L. Rev.* 97 (1951); 36 *Iowa L. Rev.* 569 (1951); 25 *N.Y.U.L. Rev.* 903 (1950); 24 *Temple L.Q.* 477 (1951); 99 *U. Pa. L. Rev.* 418 (1950). Other discussions include: Kearns, "Rule-Making in New Jersey: Denial of a Republican Form of Government?" 41 *A.B.A.J.* 435 (1955); Levin and Amsterdam, "Legislative Control over Judicial Rule-Making: A Problem in Constitutional Revision," 107 *U. Pa. L. Rev.* 1 (1958); Hall, "Judicial Rule-Making Is Alive But Ailing," 55 *A.B.A.J.* 637 (1969).

[56]Vanderbilt remained actively involved with some of the affairs of the School of Law during his years as chief justice by serving as chairman of the Citizenship Clearing House, president of the Institute of Judicial Administration, president of the Law Center Foundation, and a member of the Council of New York University.

[57]Address by Dr. Harry W. Chase, Cornerstone Laying Ceremonies and the Cornerstone Celebration Dinner, Jan. 31, 1950.

[58]*Los Angeles Times,* Sept. 4, 1953.

[59]J. D. Weaver, *Warren: The Man, The Court, The Era,* 190 (1967).

[60]Dwight D. Eisenhower, *The White House Years: Mandate for Change,* 228–229 (1963).

[61]Weaver, 183.

[62]*Nation,* Aug. 15, 1953.

[63]Associate Justice William O. Douglas knew of Nixon's and Knowland's pressure on Eisenhower ("Earl Warren's Way: 'Is It Fair?'" *Time* 66–67 (July 22, 1974)). Another high Republican politician reported the same story to me, but wished to remain anonymous. See also, H. J. Abraham, *Justices and Presidents* 237 (1974).

Eisenhower later remarked that Warren's appointment was "the biggest damnfool mistake I ever made." *Time* 67 (July 22, 1974).

[64]Weaver, 193. In each of his appointments after Warren, Eisenhower insisted that his nominees have had some judicial experience. H. J. Abraham, *The Judicial Process,* 57 (1968).

[65]For an account of the political maneuverings behind the Warren appointment, see Raymond Moley to ATV, Oct. 26, 1953, VP, box 255.

[66]In a diary-type record Vanderbilt kept during his years as dean, he entered on May 15, 1946: "Sam Kaufman telephoned me that he had not been able to sleep he was so excited at the news he had heard in Washington yesterday. Three different Senators had told him that Chief Justice Hughes had proposed my name to the President. Poor Chief Justice. It seems that the President had sent for the former Chief Justice who said that no member of the Court would do, because of their internal conflicts. It must be an outsider, and it must be one who has the confidence of the Bar; only in this way could the Court hope to regain any part of its prestige. Sam asked me

what I thought should be done about the matter, and I said absolutely nothing. After a long pause, he agreed that I was right. I told him I would still prefer to be dean of the Law School. I don't think he believes me." VP, box 378.

[67]ATV to Douglas McKay, Oct. 14, 1953, VP, box 255.

[68]*Ibid.*

[69]ATV to George K. Batt, Oct. 25, 1953, VP, box 255.

[70]ATV to Raymond Moley, Oct. 27, 1953, VP, box 255.

[71]ATV to Judge Alexander Holtzoff, Oct. 18, 1954, VP, box 255.

[72]ATV to Harry Haines, Oct. 16, 1954, VP, box 255.

[73]"The President's initial choice had been [New Jersey's] able Chief Justice, Arthur T. Vanderbilt, who had achieved an outstanding national reputation as head of the then recently reorganized New Jersey court system." H. J. Abraham, *The Judicial Process*, 71 (1968).

[74]Eisenhower, 230.

[75]ATV to W. Gordon Murphy, Aug. 8, 1947, VP, box 18.

[76]ATV memo, Dec. 31, 1954, 1–2, VP, box 267.

[77]During these years he also wrote many articles and several books, including *Men and Measures in the Law* (1949); *Minimum Standards of Judicial Administration* (1949); *Cases and Other Materials on Modern Procedure and Judicial Administration* (1952); *The Doctrine of the Separation of Powers and Its Present-Day Significance* (1953); *The Challenge of Law Reform* (1955); *Judges and Jurors* (1956); and *Two Decades of Improving the Administration of Justice* (1957).

"Believe it or not," Vanderbilt wrote in August of 1956, "two years from now I will retire under a provision which I had written into the New Jersey Constitution. . . . I am planning to establish myself in a comfortable room at the Law Center of New York University and see if I can still do some writing. When my friends ask me why I write so many articles I tell them it is because I do not want to lose whatever power I have. They think it is funny, but it is very real. I know any number of men who have intended to 'write' when they retire, but they quickly find out that the power is one which atrophies if it has not been used regularly." ATV to Professor A. McKinley Terhune, Aug. 1, 1956, VP, box 378.

Also during his term as chief justice, Vanderbilt helped establish two more organizations to further ensure a continuing improvement in the quality of American justice. Realizing that there was no exchange of information among judges of the appellate courts in various states, he encouraged the Section of Judicial Administration of the American Bar Association to found in 1949 the Conference of Chief Justices. The highest judicial officers of the forty-eight states met each year for four days prior to the annual meeting of the American Bar Association to exchange ideas and to discuss common problems. These conferences were designed to help the chief justices understand appellate practices in other states and so to evaluate and improve practices in their own state. An example of one of their first projects was a nationwide survey that presented a detailed picture of traffic law enforcement in the forty-eight states and led to the adoption by the Conference of sixteen resolutions to improve traffic law enforcement. These resolutions were then recommended by the chief justices to the bar associations and legislatures of their own states.

The second organization was started in the summer of 1956, an annual three week session for appellate judges under the auspices of the Institute of Judicial Administration at the Law Center. In attendance at this program were judges of the courts of last resort from a number of states and judges from the federal courts of appeal. For three weeks, this group studied, with the aid of instructors from their own group and outside experts, the recent developments and trends in the more important fields of law with which their courts dealt and the basic problems in the operation of appellate courts. The purpose of the seminar was to prepare lawyers recently appointed to the bench for their judicial work and to refresh more experienced judges.

Both the Conference of Chief Justices and the Seminar for Appellate Judges marked the first time that judges had sat down to study systematically the problems of their profession in an effort to better equip themselves to perform the duties of the high offices they held.

For a discussion of these organizations, see "Conference of Chief Justices," 33 *J. Am. Jud. Soc'y* 70 (1949); Dethmers, "Ten Years of Progress: The Conference of Chief Justices," 45 *A.B.A.J.* 47 (1959); Hartshorne "Conference of Chief Justices," 36 *J. Am. Jud. Soc'y* 51 (1952); "Seminar for Appellate Judges Conducted at N.Y.U. Law School," 40 *J. Am. Jud. Soc'y* 80 (1956).

[78]ATV to Chester Barnard, Jan. 8, 1957, VP, box 194.

[79]From a transcript of ATV address at a luncheon of the National Conference of Bar Examiners, "From Where I Sit," 1 (1956), VP, box 267.

[80]Justice William J. Brennan, Jr., to author, Jan. 28, 1972.

[81]*Op. cit. supra* note 76, 6.

[82]Brennan, "After Eight Years: New Jersey Judicial Reform," 43 *A.B.A.J.* 499 (1957).

[83]Professor Willard Heckel to author, Jan. 25, 1972.

[84]"Announcement of Change in Court Schedule," VP, box 225.

[85]Alexander P. Waugh to author, Apr. 5, 1974.

Despite these types of pressures and a crusty public exterior, a less visible part of Vanderbilt's personality was his real concern for the people who worked with him. For example, when he learned that one of the county court judges was in the hospital, he sent the following note:

Dear Dick:

It was not until yesterday that I learned of your illness. I have just heard that you are planning to go home tomorrow and coming back to work next Monday. I don't blame you for wanting to get home at the earliest possible moment, but let me caution you against attempting to return to work next Monday—you had better take considerable more time to recuperate—and above all, let me urge you not to attempt to attend the meeting of the

Assignment Judges next Monday evening. I will ask Mr. McConnell [the Administrative Director] to prepare a memorandum of our conclusions at an early date and let you have a copy of it in lieu of your attending the group meeting.

ATV to Judge Richard J. Hughes, Jan. 12, 1955, VP, box 200.

[86]*Op. cit. supra* note 15, 22–23. On the occasion of the 57th Annual Dinner of the New Jersey State Bar Association in 1955, a similar reaction is evident in an ode to Chief Justice Vanderbilt sung to the tune of "You're a Grand Old Flag:"

> You're a grand old Judge
> You're a high level Judge
> And forever a Judge you will be;
> Though you've oft been flayed,
> Our courts you've made,
> A model of judiciary;
> Jersey Justice sure
> For the rich and the poor,
> And our ulcers we owe to thee,
> Should old acquaintance be forgot,
> Take your hat off to A
> Take your hat off to A
> Take your hat off to ATV.

N.J.L.J. (May 19, 1955).

[87]ATV to Dr. W. Homer Turner, June 6, 1955, VP, box 196.

[88]*Op. cit. supra* note 76, 39.

[89]ATV to Col. Charles L. Decker, May 2, 1956, VP, box 196.

[90]Alfred C. Clapp to author, Jan. 28, 1972.

[91]ATV to James E. Stiles, July 23, 1956, VP, box 195.

[92]ATV to James E. Stiles, Nov. 30, 1956, VP, box 195.

[93]ATV to Dr. Royal A. Schaaf, Jan. 9, 1957, VP, box 196.

[94]Levin and Amsterdam, "Legislative Control over Judicial Rule-Making: A Problem in Constitutional Revision," 107 *U. Pa. L. Rev.* 1, note 93 (1958), briefly presents the history of the controversy:

> Judge Learned Hand has been quoted as asserting that rule-making power with respect to evidence "has been a very contentious subject." . . . The New Jersey experience bears this out. In 1954 a committee was appointed to report to the supreme court with respect to revision in this area. They did so in 1955. . . . In September, 1955, an editorial in *N.J.L.J.*, recognizing the problem posed in the light of the *Winberry* decision, attempted to offer a constructive suggestion. After noting that "this is not the occasion for a philosophical discourse on the distinctions between 'substance' and 'procedure,'" went on to urge that it "would be best to have the Legislature enact the Code as an entirety, and then have the Supreme Court adopt it as a whole." . . . A legislative commission appointed thereafter

recommended a significantly different set of provisions than that of the supreme court committee. It urged that the legislature retain responsibility for the Evidence"Rules,"and invited the supreme court to recommend amendments to the legislature when such became necessary.

A compromise was later arrived at after Vanderbilt's death. The legislature established a Rules of Court Commission under the guidance of a United States District Court judge. Through this commission, the legislature could work in cooperation with the supreme court in making changes in practice and procedures that could be interpreted as being within the province of either the supreme court or the legislature. *N.J.S.A.* 2A:84-33.

[95]ATV to James E. Stiles, Feb. 2, 1957, VP, box 196.

[96]ATV to James E. Stiles, Apr. 23, 1957, VP, box 196.

[97]ATV to Judge Edward Gaulkin, May 27, 1957, VP, box 200.

[98]ATV to Herbert L. Simms, May 15, 1957, VP, box 196.

[99]ATV to Professor Bernard J. Rubenstein, June 1, 1957, VP, box 196.

[100]ATV to Dr. W. Homer Turner, June 13, 1957, VP, box 196.

[101]ATV to Earl C. Berger, May 29, 1957, VP, box 196.

[102]*Ibid.*

Once, in 1954, the Union County assignment judge reported to Vanderbilt that it had become necessary to renovate Judge Cleary's courtroom and that, to accommodate this work, he had requested Judge Cleary to suspend court hearings for the day the construction work would take place. Judge Cleary was reluctant about losing the time and so the assignment judge sought approval from the chief justice for the course of action he had requested. Wrote Vanderbilt: "If any other judge but Frank [Cleary] were to be so reluctant over losing a day of trial work for such a meritorious reason I should be inclined to think that my leg was being pulled a bit gently, but with Frank's devotion to duty I am sure that he is absolutely sincere in his attitude."

ATV to Judge Richard J. Hughes, Feb. 5, 1954, VP, box 198.

[103]ATV to William Purintan, June 12, 1957, VP, box 196.

[104]ATV to Professor A. McKinley Terhune, June 1, 1957, VP, box 196.

[105]*Op. cit. supra* note 90.

A Note on Sources

For the reader who wishes to pursue an idea or incident introduced in this book, notes have been included that will lead to the most relevant primary or secondary sources. A bibliography of Vanderbilt's writings is included in 1 F. J. Klein and J. S. Lee (eds.), *Selected Writings of Arthur T. Vanderbilt* 213–223 (1965), and a table of his judicial opinions, classified by subject, is included in 2, 265–271. In addition, Professor Klein's bibliography, *Judicial Administration and the Legal Profession* (1963), is an invaluable guide to the scattered writings in the field of judicial administration. Copies of all Vanderbilt's court briefs, volumes 1–98, are bound and shelved in the law firm of Vanderbilt and Siegel, 155 South Livingston Avenue, Livingston, New Jersey. His awards, testimonials, citations, and honorary degrees are hung in the faculty lounge at the Law Center of New York University. Of uppermost value in preparing this book were his papers, which are a part of the Collection on Legal Change at Wesleyan University, Middletown, Connecticut. Contained in 377 record storage boxes occupying 400 linear feet, these papers cover the entire span of Vanderbilt's life. They include an extensive correspondence which, while fragmentary from 1906 to 1930, is complete thereafter; scrapbooks of his high school and college years; course notes from Wesleyan University and Columbia University Law School; teaching notes from New York University School of Law; scrapbooks and clipping files of the history of the Essex County Republican League and Clean Government from 1919 to 1948; scrapbooks of his year as president of the American Bar Association; documents and transcripts from the many organizations, councils, committees, conferences, and institutions in which he was active; copies of his addresses, articles, and books; notes and rough drafts of his writings; drafts of judicial opinions; appointment books; work schedules; Dictaphone recordings; fragments of diaries; photographs; and clipping files and miscellaneous files covering the activities which engaged his interest throughout his life. Documents listed as being in box 378 are still in my possession and will be deposited in the Collection on Legal Change.

Index